JOURNEY

into

WHOLENESS

A Strategy to Partner With God's
Heart to Walk Into Wholeness

Rev. Dr. Carolyn R. Allen

JOURNEY INTO WHOLENESS

PUBLISHED BY

Rev. Dr. Carolyn R. Allen, 1025 Vance Ave., Fort Wayne, IN 46805

SCRIPTURE SOURCES

Unless otherwise noted, scripture references are from The Holy Bible, New American Standard Bible, (NY: Cambridge University Press, 2013).

The Holy Bible, New Living Translation, (Carol Stream, IL: Tyndale House Publishers, Inc., 1996, 2004, 2007, 2013, 2015).

The Holy Bible, The Message, (Carol Stream, IL: Tyndale House Publishers, Inc., © Eugene H. Peterson, 2002. UBP NavPress).

The Holy Bible, English Standard Version, (Wheaton, IL: Good News Publishers, © 2001 by Crossway Bibles).

The Holy Bible, Amplified Bible, (Grand Rapids, MI: Zondervan, © 1954, 1958, 1962, 1964, 1965, 1987 by the Lockman Foundation. ARR. UBP. www.Lockman.org).

ISBN: 978-1-48359-475-0 (print)
ISBN: 978-1-48359-476-7 (eBook)

"Lord Jesus I long to be perfectly whole,
I want You forever to live in my soul,
Break down every idol, cast out every foe,
Now wash me and I shall be whiter than snow."

CONTENTS

I. FOUNDATIONS

II. MINISTRY

III. APPLICATION

DEDICATION

I dedicate this book to Ron, my husband, best friend and partner in ministry. Ron has often described himself as a "book widow" as I have taken time to write. He has faithfully and kindly cooked meals, been my "in-house" theologian, and spent evenings alone while I have worked. Thank you Ron for your continual words of encouragement and belief in me. You always believe for more from me than I can for myself. You have been calling forth my best for almost 50 years. Thank you. I love you forever!

ACKNOWLEDGMENTS

I'm shouting out a huge "Thank you" to Pastor Dave Frincke. You encouraged this project and lightened my pastoral responsibilities at Heartland Church to give me time to write. It wouldn't have happened without your support, patience and insights.

Heartland Church has at its core the culture and spiritual atmosphere for creativity and gifts to grow and prosper. Heartland wants everyone to play to his or her strengths and be who God says they are. This posture has encouraged my heart so much and released the creativity the Holy Spirit has placed within me. Thank you for the safe atmosphere to experiment and grow. I know the prayer warriors have been on duty as I have labored on this project. You are a huge part of this work. The wonderful staff helped me guard my time and sent me home more than once saying, "Go home and write!" Thank you to my beloved Heartland family!

Heather Burgette, thank you for your work in editing this manuscript. You have been kind and gentle as you have corrected and made suggestions that have helped make this book what it is.

Dr. Mark Virkler, your generosity in giving permission to use your article in this book is overwhelming. May God return favor that you have released to your own life and work.

Linda Roeder, your kind words of encouragement, suggestions and prayers have helped keep me stay on course. I value our friendship.

Lora Thrasher, thank you for taking time to read the manuscript and give me helpful insights for how to present concepts. You asked some hard questions that helped clarify my thoughts. You challenged me to think deeper and broader.

People who have had a major influence on my thinking and spiritual growth as it relates to healing the whole person that are reflected in this book are Ron Allen, Neil Anderson, Richard Foster, Francis Frangipane, Jack Frost, Chip Judd, Chester & Betsy Kylstra, Dr. Caroline Leaf, Joyce Meyer, John & Paula Sandford, David Seamands, Mark Virkler, Dallas Willard, and John Wimber.

ENDORSEMENTS

"I've had the privilege of being with Carolyn in ministry situations where she used the tools found in this book to help people find healing and freedom from wounds of the soul. One of my greatest joys as a Pastor is seeing people healed and transformed by the power of the Holy Spirit. *Journey Into Wholeness* is full of practical tools for anyone who wants to partner with the Holy Spirit in His transformational work. Carolyn's teachings have been instrumental in my own spiritual journey and have equipped many at Heartland, including myself, to be more effective in ministry.

I will be recommending this book to pastors, ministry teams, counselors and those who are involved in pastoral care ministry. If you have a desire to grow in personal healing, you will find *Journey Into Wholeness* to be an incredibly rich resource."

Rev. Dave Frincke
Senior Pastor, Heartland Church, Fort Wayne, Indiana

"Journey Into Wholeness is a book born out of my wife, Carolyn's almost 50 years of experience partnering with me in pastoral ministry. Over the years as she has worked through her own challenges and struggles, Carolyn has consistently pursued help and training to understand and successfully cope with wounds and hurts that have undermined her ability to live life to the fullest as a woman of Christian faith. As years went by and she experienced

breakthrough, it became widely recognized that she was a person of compassion and real help for others who were struggling toward wholeness. I highly recommend her tome as a practical, Biblical, and healthy way to look at life and make redemptive choices."

Rev. Dr. Canon Ronald Allen
Founding Pastor, Heartland Church, Fort Wayne, Indiana

"*Journey Into Wholeness* is the powerful testimony of how one church has created SoulCare, a pastoral care service, to bring healing to the hearts of those they are called to minister to. *Journey Into Wholeness* begins by teaching people how to hear the voice of the Wonderful Counselor so they can experience true heart transformation through the power of the Holy Spirit. People experience release from generational curses, deliverance from demons and deep forgiveness in conjunction with several other spiritual protocols. You will see that this is far more effective than psychology, religious legalism or personal self-effort. This is the kind of ministry people are hungry for, and that the church is called to provide. THIS WORKS! Enjoy this teaching testimonial, as Carolyn Allen shares their story of how pastoral care has been fleshed out in their church, Heartland Church, in Fort Wayne, Indiana."

Dr. Mark Virkler
President, Christian Leadership University

"If you long for transformation, and want wisdom and insight into the power of Jesus' healing words, you have found the right book. This is the first book I am giving to people who want their church to grow in the healing ministry!"

Rev. Canon William Beasley
Greenhouse Movement, Anglican Church of North America

PREFACE

Journey Into Wholeness describes how Heartland Church of Fort Wayne, Indiana demonstrates pastoral care, a ministry called SoulCare. Providing ministry that is available through a local church for the community is dear to my heart. I am a minister's daughter, I am a minister's wife, and I am a minister. Church life and work is what I have known and been a part of all my life. I love local expressions of the Body of Christ.

Worship and healing are two of the building blocks of Heartland Church's DNA. The third building block is everyone gets to "play" in all we do as a community. We all participate in growing together, healing together, worshipping together, and doing Kingdom of God works together.

This book addresses Heartland's foundations of practices and principles for taking care of the soul – our inner wellbeing. Ministry to the soul affects physical healing as well. We endeavor to minister to the whole person as we grow in our understanding of God's provision for us in Jesus Christ.

The power of worship in our lives cannot be overlooked. It permeates everything we do at Heartland. Worship affects our whole being: body, soul and spirit. It is so important that it deserves attention of its own. That task is for another time. Another book on this glorious subject will follow soon.

The Westminster Confession of Faith (1646) says "The chief end of man is to glorify God and to enjoy Him forever." One of the ways Scripture highlights this is in Matthew 22:37: "You shall love the Lord your God with all your heart, with all your soul, and with all your mind."

To know God is to love Him. To love Him is to worship Him. He is the only One worthy of all our adoration, worship and praise. All things come from Him.

He is the Source of all life. "For from Him and through Him and to Him are *all* things. To Him be the glory forever. Amen." (Romans 11:36)

"By Him all things were created, both in the heavens and on earth, visible and invisible, whether thrones or dominions or rulers or authorities – all things have been created through Him and for Him." (Colossians 1:16)

Every minister develops a theology for pastoral care based on how they view God, which affects how they view others and themselves. This book is descriptive of some of those principles that are foundational to and descriptive of our practices. Increasingly we realize the impact that principles and practices have as we walk out the mission of the Church: to make disciples of Jesus Christ. (Matthew 28:18-20)

A revelation of the Father's heart in our journey of following Jesus is always progressive. Therefore we expect in the seasons to come, as the Lord tarries, we will grow even more in our understanding of the Father's love for us and how we can apply that reality to our daily lives.

There is always a dynamic in pastoral care of making sure we have the log taken out of our own eye before we address someone else's issues. (Matthew 7:1-5) The reality is we don't get the log totally removed from our own eye. We all find ourselves in need so approaching the ministry of pastoral care with humility is an important mindset. We are all on this journey together and are honored and privileged when we are invited into someone's life for care and ministry. We take these opportunities seriously and treat them as a sacred trust.

One of my life Bible passages describes my assignment and passion so clearly:

> "We proclaim Him, admonishing every man and teaching every man with all wisdom, so that we may *present every man complete in Christ.* For this purpose also I labor, striving according to His power, which mightily works within me." (Colossians 1:28-29)

The Message translation says verse 29 so well: "That's what I'm working so hard at day after day, year after year, doing my best *with the energy God so generously gives me.*" It is comforting to know God supplies the power for my assignment and passion.

To that I say Amen and joyously continue my work to present every person in my realm of influence complete in Christ.

The three sections of this book move the reader from foundational concepts through practical ministry to personal application.

Part One presents foundational biblical principles from which we endeavor to minister. Principles covered are kingdom of God truths that affect how we view God, others and ourselves.

Part Two presents SoulCare, an approach that ministers to the whole person – body, soul and spirit. We endeavor to present those in our realm of influence "complete in Christ." We work out our salvation with the understanding that salvation is "being saved out from under the devil's power and restored into the wholeness of God's order and wellbeing by the power of the Spirit."

As we minister, we take into consideration specific areas that affect our daily lives: generational patterns and curses, word curses, vows, bitter root judgments, soul ties, ungodly thought patterns, life's hurts, and demonic interference. Examples for prayers are presented that will launch you into a conversation with the Lord Jesus to release freedom.

Part Three presents some tools I have developed to help people apply truth to daily living. The intentional work does not end with a ministry session. It marks the beginning of a journey to develop new habits of thinking. New thought patterns will initiate new feelings and behavior. There is Scripture and science to back this up!

Achieving wholeness and completeness is a walk in the Spirit, a process that needs ongoing attention. This is the journey God invites us to take with Him.

PART 1

FOUNDATIONS

CHAPTER 1

PASTORAL CARE FOUNDATIONS

Journey Into Wholeness describes how Heartland Church of Fort Wayne, Indiana demonstrates pastoral care, a ministry called SoulCare. We partner with the Holy Spirit to bring God's intended wholeness to all areas of our lives. Wholeness – salvation, healing and deliverance – is what Jesus provided for us on the Cross. SoulCare takes us on a journey with Jesus into a lifestyle of learning how to live in the wholeness He has already given to us.

SoulCare is the result of a life-long pursuit of Scriptural understanding and application, both personally and corporately to the Body of Christ. We embrace the best legacies of pioneers in the field of ministering to the whole person. We continue to yield to God's infinite ability to reveal more understanding in and through us. With the foundation of Scripture and blending our experience and study of several streams and models in the Church, SoulCare emerges as a unique and practical expression of ministry.

We have learned to rely on the Holy Spirit for answers to our questions about life challenges. We pause, ask and listen for counsel from the most Wonderful Counselor anyone could ever have. This dynamic teaches the person seeking help how to use tools that will guide them for the rest of their life. In addition to asking key questions, we consider spiritual roots that affect current challenges in our lives. The result is ever increasing wholeness in Christ.

After working with people in pastoral care for almost 50 years, I have learned that helping people connect to Jesus is the most important thing I can ever do with and for them. We all have struggles that at times become overwhelming and we get stuck. We have probably all had an experience where someone has said something like this to us:

"You'll be all right. Just get over it and go on."

"Just put it behind you and forget it."

"You know what the Bible says…why aren't you doing that?"

We try and try and try to do the "right" thing. Yet we never get different results. We get discouraged and want to give up. We want to do better in becoming more like Jesus, but like the Apostle Paul, we cry out "Why do I keep doing the things I don't want to do?" (Romans 7:15-20)

For many years I struggled internally, longing to be made whole. I was tired of being broken and fractured. I would hear and sing the old hymn "Lord Jesus I Long to Be Perfectly Whole," weeping and desiring for that reality in my life. How to get there, I did not know, but it was my heart's cry many years before I began to experience rest and peace in my soul. How thankful I am that I have found and continue to find rest for my soul in Jesus. (Matthew 11:29)

Here are the words to the hymn – maybe it's your heart's cry, too:

"Lord Jesus I long to be perfectly whole,
I want You forever to live in my soul,
Break down every idol, cast out every foe,
Now wash me and I shall be whiter than snow.

Lord Jesus, look down from Your throne in the skies,
And help me to make a complete sacrifice,
I give you myself, and whatever I know,
Now wash me and I shall be whiter than snow.

Lord Jesus, for this I most humbly entreat,
I wait, blessed Lord, at Your crucified feet,
By faith, for my cleansing I see Your blood flow,

Now wash me and I shall be whiter than snow.

Lord Jesus, You see that I patiently wait,
Come now, and within me a new heart create,
To those who have sought You, You never said "No,"
Now wash me and I shall be whiter than snow." [1]

Dallas Willard is quoted as saying our soul is the "essence of our being." When we neglect our soul life, we neglect the most important part of our being. Because our inner life is unseen, it is easy to neglect. But eventually it cries out loud enough that we must give attention to its health and well-being. Genesis 2:7 says that "God formed man of dust from the ground, and breathed into his nostrils the breath of life; and man become a living soul." Willard says, "what is running your life at any given moment is your soul. It isn't external circumstances, thoughts, intentions or feelings – but your soul. The soul is that aspect of your whole being that correlates, integrates, and enlivens everything going on in the various dimensions of the self." [2]

We need to take care of the soul – it needs transformation that can only come about with the revelation and help of the Holy Spirit. John Ortberg quotes Dallas Willard in "Soul Keeping" as saying, "The most important thing in your life is not what you do; it's who you become. You are an unceasing spiritual being with an eternal destiny in God's great universe." [3] Knowing God and becoming who God says we are is our desired destination as we move forward on our journey into wholeness. Intimacy with God enables us to look at all areas of our lives that have influenced and formed our soul, wounds and all, to the present time.

CHANGE YOUR THOUGHTS…
CHANGE YOUR LIFE

I have learned that a big part of the dilemma we face on this journey is how we have developed habit patterns of thought that are not God's thoughts. We develop a worldview based on our experiences that have not been taken through the filter of the cross of Jesus Christ. Then we develop unhealthy emotional responses and behavioral patterns that in no way reflect the Fruit of the Spirit. We often think if we just do it 'right' one more time, it will take hold and we will be changed. No. What changes us is the scriptural admonition to be "transformed by the renewing of the mind." (Romans 12:2) We don't get changed by "doing" differently; we are changed by "thinking" differently.

> ## We don't get changed by "doing" differently; we are changed by "thinking" differently.

Mark 1:15 says it this way "The time is fulfilled, and the kingdom of God is at hand; repent and *believe* in the gospel." Mark doesn't say repent and '*do*', but repent and *believe*. As a new creation we have the mind of Christ. (1 Corinthians 2:16) We want to learn how to think like Jesus. Believing the Gospel, the good news of Jesus Christ, and habituating ourselves in the truth, will then produce a healthy emotional life and godly Spirit-led behavior.

An important concept foundational to pastoral care is the truth that we have a God-given gift, the *power of choice.* We get to choose what we think, how we feel, how we behave, and to whom we will submit our life. Most of us give no thought to this powerful ability and how it affects our present and future. Everyone gets to choose. The difference between bondage and freedom lies in helping people realize the importance of choosing their thoughts. This reality addresses the victim mentality and helps people see they are free to choose their responses to life events rather than just accepting that those events define them and their future. If we don't learn to take responsibility for our own choices, we will never be free. God created us with a free will. If we don't embrace that, we will always blame others for our problems. One of the biggest hindrances to freedom for someone who struggles with a victim mentality is the failure to take responsibility for their choices.

When I begin to help someone who is "stuck" and asking for help, one of the first questions I ask the Lord as I pray for them is *"Who do you say this person is and what do you want me to know about them?"* God wants us to learn how to recognize one another in the spirit (2 Corinthians 5:16). When we can see people how God sees them in our interactions with them, we can begin to say: "You are not that (an old man that thinks and behaves that way), but you are this (a new man that thinks and behaves this way). In our time together we are going to focus on who you are in Christ and as you are being transformed we will tear down old habit patterns of thinking that are stopping you from walking in newness of life. You are a Saint learning how to be a Saint."

Most likely the person who has come for help is discouraged and feels defeated because they have tried to "do" better without results. They might be telling themselves they are a failure, a bad person. They may be saying that they will never get better or they *must* be doing something wrong or they would be healed. Hearing someone tell them who they are in Christ and begin to call it into reality can be a source of hope. We all need to hear what Jesus thinks about us. It's always good and always for our wellbeing.

Another area of our lives that is neglected and is foundational in pastoral care is incomplete forgiveness. Helping people get clean in their relationship with God, others, and themselves is crucial for walking in newness of life. We will discuss forgiveness in detail because this issue is so important in caring for our souls. When not attended to, it can hinder walking in healing and freedom.

Many in the wider Body of Christ have influenced our approach of caring for a person's body, soul and spirit. We have learned from the Scriptures, teachings at conferences, books, relationships with others who minister in similar areas of healing, and our own interaction with people and the Holy Spirit. Focusing on specific areas of our lives that affect thoughts, feelings and behavior has produced good fruit. This has moved us forward on our journey into wholeness.

TESTIMONIALS

Here are some of the statements from people who have benefited from our approach to ministry.

"This ministry gives you tools you need to recognize ungodly thought patterns and the strongholds that are keeping you from God's best for your life."

"This ministry is like going through a cluttered house straightening up and throwing some things out that don't belong and aren't needed."

"This is spiritual cleaning."

"This ministry is a way to be free of hindrances and oppressions by removing any legal ground Satan uses against us. It begins by forgiving."

"This ministry creates a safe and loving environment to deal with painful hurts from the past."

"This is a ministry model that leads you to freedom from the things in your life you can't seem to get past."

"This ministry is a way to help believers get set free."

"This ministry is being set free and growing into the person God created me to be."

"This ministry is revealing and freeing."

"This ministry has taught me the importance of forgiveness and has helped me heal relationships and memories that I thought were forever broken. I now walk in confidence knowing whose child I am."

"I have learned how to listen to God, to wait on Him and to accept His love for me."

"This ministry has shown me how to pray for myself and my family and how to equip us to defeat the strongholds passed down from generations."

"It is incredible to see the Holy Spirit direct the ministry time."

"Jesus does not give up on any of us. He has made provision for us to be free of lies, habits, hindrances and oppression."

"I came not knowing what to expect and walked away with hope, forgiveness and faith."

"I employ the Word of God to bring my thoughts under control of and in agreement with what God says."

"I was anxious when I came, but felt so safe."

These are just a sample of testimonies from people who are now experiencing freedom as a result of ministry focused on the whole person. It works!

All of the material and questions presented in this manual will be of benefit for personal use as well as when helping others. My heart for this book is that the reader will personally receive, embrace and apply truth to areas of need in their own life. Then, the reader will be able to give away what the Father so generously has given to them – healing for a broken soul.

> ## "You teach what you know... you impart who you are."

"You teach what you know... you impart who you are." [4] I can teach someone the facts, but what they need for their own transformation is to see the life of Christ lived through me. We learn by seeing life modeled. The disciples learned how to be like Christ by being with Him and watching Him model Kingdom-of-God life.

John Wimber was a wise spiritual father to many. He taught and modeled this discipleship loop: 1. I do it. 2. I do it while others watch. 3. Others do it while I watch them. 4. I leave them doing it and I do it with someone else. [5]

Knowledge is good, but actually applying what we learn is necessary for a changed life. Our journey into wholeness is a process that always includes application of truth. The Bible calls this wisdom – knowing what to do with biblical truth. My desire is that what you learn will be applied in daily life to deepen your relationship with God and others and yourself, learning to love like God loves. (John 17:23)

Scattered throughout the material are questions to ask of yourself or the Holy Spirit in order to gain insight that will lead to freedom. The questions are designed to help us recognize root issues we can then take responsibility for, and lead us to Jesus for His perspective and solution. These questions will be in italics and be preceded by the instruction to " Pause, Ask and Listen (*PAL*)".

QUESTION-CENTERED MINISTRY

I have come to appreciate this model of question-centered ministry. Other models adopt a direct approach, telling the person seeking help what they should think and/or do. Asking questions requires the person to participate in their healing. Jesus modeled asking questions for us in many ways through the Gospels when ministering to people. One of my favorite stories when Jesus asked a question is in John 5, where He asked a man who had been ill 38 years, "Do you want to get well?" Seriously?? You would think so. The reality is sometimes we make friends with our illness or dysfunctional behavior and feel comfortable with it. If we were to get well, we might lose our identity with the illness and not know who we are or how to act. We get afraid of the unknown or what it might take to get well and hold back, staying stuck. Questions have a way of getting us to the heart of the matter.

> ## Questions have a way of getting us to the heart of the matter.

It is not only important to ask the right questions, but to ask the right Person the right questions. Ask the Holy Spirit your questions. Partner with the person requesting help to form questions that will connect them with the wisdom of God for their particular issue.

No doubt you will notice some of the questions are repeated, some with the same thought but different wording. This is intentional. Some questions are so important they apply to many issues being addressed in our lives. I also know that while a question presented in one form will connect with one person, a question formed just a bit differently will connect the same thought to another.

QUESTIONS ARE POWERFUL

Question-centered ministry can be powerful with the understanding that questions are directed to God so we can hear His answer. Listening to the responses to questions can give insight for the direction of follow-up questions. The goal is getting to the root issue while keeping the focus of the dialogue with Jesus.

Questions lead to Holy Spirit led discovery, not rational analyzing.

Questions lead to true wisdom, not man's ideas.

Questions lead to intimacy and deeper knowledge in relationships.

Questions asked of the Lord lead to a deeper knowledge of His character and develop a confidence in the person of their relationship with God.

Questions can reveal a teachable spirit, which is necessary when change is required for transformation.

Questions can help discern that one is taking responsibility for their own life. It requires participation.

Questions will call forth humility – "I am willing to consider I could be wrong. I will inquire of the Lord to search my heart."

Questions can have the power to change an attitude of "I'm right – think like I think," to "I'm willing to entertain another possible perception."

Questions can lead to reflection that results in peace when the voice of the Lord is heard and embraced.

Questions help convert the problem-oriented focus to a Godly solution-oriented focus.

TIPS ON QUESTION-ORIENTED PASTORAL CARE

Ask questions that lead people to Jesus for the answer.

Ask a question and then listen. You may need to be silent for a few minutes for the person to process the information…wait for it because it will be worth it. The person is learning how to ask the right question and listen to the Holy Spirit for an answer.

Ask open-ended questions – ones that will require more than a one-word answer.

Ask present-future oriented questions. This will enable the person to focus on the moment and where God wants to take them.

Ask questions that give opportunity for a God-focused response, instead of asking questions that condemn and judge others or self.

For example:

THIS	NOT THIS
PAL: "Holy Spirit, what are you working into my life right now?	"What's wrong with me?"
"What do you want in this situation?"	
PAL: "Holy Spirit, what solution do you have for this situation?"	"Whose fault is this?"
	"Who did this?"
PAL: "Holy Spirit, would you help me describe exactly what happened in this situation?"	"Why is this person so stupid, selfish, bitter, hateful, angry, blind?"
"What do you want me to learn?"	
"What do you want me to see and understand?"	
"Is there another way to look at this situation or person?"	
"What is going on in their life right now that I need to know about?"	

PAL: "Holy Spirit, will you help me lay down my right to be right?"

"How can I prove I'm right?"

"What do you want to say to me about my heart and my participation in what has just taken place?"

PAL: "Holy Spirit, what are your possibilities in this situation with this person?"

"Why even bother? This always happens and it will never change."

Some of my team members often ask "How do you know what question to ask?" There really is no formula. As I continually process what is happening in the ministry session I ask two questions: *PAL: "Holy Spirit what is the focus of the challenge right now? Holy Spirit, what question will enable this person to connect with you on this issue so they can experience your healing?"*

Ministering with the view that God desires wholeness involves many aspects. While right questions can be beneficial and powerful, the context of the dialogue must be Christ-centered. Jesus is the Word that sets us free. We will consider the foundational teachings of *The Power of Forgiveness, The Power of the Cross, The Power of Choice, The Power of Perspective, The Power of God Speaking,* and *The Power of Christ in Me.* We will also discuss *The Power of Hearing God Speak,* as it is crucial to our approach of ministering to the whole person.

You may be thinking this approach to ministry sounds really involved and time consuming. It is an intentional look at what has been sabotaging an experience of freedom in Christ. Yes, it is involved. Yes it requires a time commitment on the person receiving help and the team who commits to praying, planning and being present for ministry. Our spiritual lives are at stake…it is worth the time and effort. It is a part of discipleship mandated by Jesus and a fulfillment of Isaiah 61 to impart hope to the broken-hearted.

Working with people can be frustrating, discouraging and exhausting. We always must remember that God is in charge. God does His part, I do my part, and hopefully the person seeking help does his/her part. Here is some of the best advice a mentor on pastoral care ever gave me that I continually keep in mind:

**I am not the answer to any person's need.
I cannot fix anyone's problem.
I am not anyone's power source.**

Once we get those truths established in our thinking we get in touch with what Jesus asks us to do…be someone in their life that will direct them to Jesus and facilitate healing in the power of the Holy Spirit. It is a delight to partner with God to care for souls. Don't give up!

"We proclaim Jesus Christ, admonishing every man and teaching every man with all wisdom, so that we may present every man complete in Christ. For this purpose also I labor, striving according to His power, which mightily works within me."
(Colossians 1:28-29)

This Scripture helps me keep on track. I am hopeful for a fruitful return on the investment I make in people in His power, wisdom and anointing.

Would you consider joining me on a journey into wholeness for yourself and others? Let's help everyone we can along the way.

The Spirit of the Sovereign Lord is upon me,
for the Lord has anointed me
to bring good news to the poor.
He has sent me to comfort the brokenhearted
and to proclaim that captives will be released
and prisoners will be freed.
He has sent me to tell those who mourn
that the time of the Lord's favor has come,
and with it, the day of God's anger against their enemies.
To all who mourn in Israel,
he will give a crown of beauty for ashes,
a joyous blessing instead of mourning,
festive praise instead of despair.
In their righteousness, they will be like great oaks
that the Lord has planted for his own glory.
They will rebuild the ancient ruins,
repairing cities destroyed long ago.
They will revive them,
though they have been deserted for many generations.

Isaiah 61:1-4 (NLT)

CHAPTER 2

THE POWER OF GOD SPEAKING

"Pursue love, yet desire earnestly spiritual gifts, especially that you
may prophesy. For one who speaks in a tongue does not speak to
men but to God; for no one understands, but in his spirit he speaks
mysteries. But one who prophesies speaks to men for edification and
exhortation and consolation. 1 Corinthians 14:1-3

"Darlin', would you come join me up here
for a minute?" drawled the postmaster from Throckmorton, Texas. He was
looking right at me. I shook my head no and slid underneath my husband's
shoulder. I was terrified. There was no way I was going up front. I didn't have
a clue what was happening.

Have you ever noticed that God can sometimes be sneaky to set up
experiences He wants us to have? That's how I found myself at a Baptist
church on the north side of Houston. A friend had invited us to go hear a
"great Bible teacher." I love hearing the Word taught, so I said we would go.

We listened to a great teaching. When the speaker said he was going
to transition into personal prophetic ministry, I was surprised. I looked
at my watch to find he had taught for an hour and half. I had not been
exposed to a teaching gift such as this man had.

I wondered, "What is personal prophetic ministry?" We were sitting on the front row because that's where our friend took us. I was nervous, not knowing what to expect. That's when the teacher looked at me and gave me that invitation, "Darlin', would you come join me up here for a minute?"

When I declined his invitation he gently said, "That's okay. I can come to you." His eyes engaged with mine as he walked over to me. "The Lord shows me that you have a problem with anger. But that's okay. He understands and is here to help you. He loves you." The room was so quiet you could have heard a pin drop to the floor. It was difficult to breathe. I stayed stuck under Ron's arm in order to feel safe, but strangely enough I was not embarrassed. The teacher's demeanor was quiet and gentle. As he looked into my eyes I felt warm inside. I also felt a genuine love touch me in the depth of my being. He said some other things the Lord told him about me. One was that the Lord would use me in the healing ministry.

That was my introduction to prophecy, God speaking a personal word to me through someone else. It sparked an interest and a desire to learn more. I am forever grateful it wasn't a bony finger pointing at me as the messenger shouted all my sins in an angry voice. Scolding only produces defensiveness. Instead, I knew it was a message from the Father's heart to me and I was loved. I was being called to something more.

Scolding only produces defensiveness.

Not only was the message right on, but the manner in which it was delivered was Christ-like. It opened my heart to healing. Love took away embarrassment and shame. I could receive help for what was hindering my walk with Jesus. I didn't have to pretend anymore.

As I pondered that initial introduction to personal prophecy, I desired to be that kind of messenger for others. I wanted to be able to see what was in a person's heart from God's perspective. I wanted to speak words of comfort and correction with gentleness and compassion.

Based on my experience and the desires it stirred, I define personal prophetic ministry as *hearing, seeing, or sensing the heart of the Father for a person or situation and communicating it in a manner it can best be received.*

Jesus always expressed the Fruit of the Spirit in His interactions with people. That's His character and nature. He always expressed the heart of the Father. That is our goal as well.

PURPOSES FOR PROPHECY

In 1 Corinthians 14:1-3, the apostle Paul lists three purposes for prophecy: edification, exhortation and consolation.

Edification is an architectural term that has to do with building one's structure, dwelling place or edifice. It has to do with building, establishing, instructing and improving. It is about our foundation and our covering. The foundation from which we live life needs to be strengthened as a result of a prophetic word.

Sometimes our foundations are faulty based on perceptions that don't agree with God. We believe lies about God, others and ourselves. Prophetic ministry can expose those lies. It can help establish healthy thought patterns based on God's truth.

Faulty foundations will eventually crumble. Read this story in Matthew 7:24-27 (NLT) where Jesus talks about two kinds of foundations.

"Anyone who listens to my teaching and follows it is wise, like a person who builds a house on solid rock. Though the rain comes in torrents and the floodwaters rise and the winds beat against that house, it won't collapse because it is built on bedrock. But anyone who hears my teaching and doesn't obey it is foolish, like a person who builds a house on sand. When the rains and floods come and the winds beat against that house, it will collapse with a mighty crash."

Listening to and applying the words of Jesus makes the difference between a wise and foolish man. The house built on a faulty foundation was washed away when storms came. The house built on a solid foundation stood firm.

Edification through a prophetic word is about making sure our foundation, our structure and our covering are in proper alignment. Any error embraced at any time must be corrected for the end product to be solid and useful.

QUESTIONS ABOUT EDIFICATION TO *PAL* WHEN PREPARING TO DELIVER A PROPHETIC WORD

"Holy Spirit, how do you see this person before me right now? What is their true identity in you? How do you want me to address the issues that are broken rather than healed?"

"Holy Spirit, is what I'm about to share going to strengthen this person's foundational understanding about your character? Is there a misunderstanding of who you are that needs to be addressed?"

"Holy Spirit, is there something you want to strengthen or correct concerning their identity in Christ?"

"Holy Spirit, is this person in a safe place to work through the changes you want to do?"

As a messenger from God, you may readily see the negative expressions of attitude and behavior of the person. You may discern prophetically some issues that are not godly. It's easy to see what is wrong. One of my prophetic mentors used to say; "You don't have permission to kill someone with your words unless you have the power and authority to raise them from the dead." Seeing what needs help is only a piece of the picture. A messenger from God will deliver it in a manner it can be received. It builds (edifies), not tears down.

> "You don't have permission to kill someone with your words unless you have the power and authority to raise them from the dead."

Exhortation used to sound like a harsh word to me. When I heard it I always thought I was about to be scolded. Fear and anxiety would arise if someone said; "I have a word of exhortation for you."

Exhortation is translated as "comfort" several times in Scripture. The word is "*paraklesia.*" [6]

Paraklesia means to comfort, console, to entreat, to invite, to call to one's side, beg, instruct and teach, to call near, to invoke, to be of good comfort, or to give desire to. Wow. How did we ever get the idea that exhorting was to tell someone all their faults in a demeaning manner? That is not the heart of the Father.

It is interesting to note that one of the names of the Holy Spirit is *parakletos.* [7] (John 14:26) The Holy Spirit is one who is summoned, called to one's side, to one's aid. It is one who pleads another's cause before a judge, a counsel for defense or legal assistance. A *parakletos* is one who intercedes. This describes the role of the Holy Spirit.

> Prophecy is a gift of the Holy Spirit so it will be received and delivered in the Fruit of the Holy Spirit.

Prophecy is a gift of the Holy Spirit so it will be received and delivered in the Fruit of the Holy Spirit.

When we embrace the understanding that we are to see one another in the Spirit, not with the natural eye, we are seeing them for who they are becoming. (2 Corinthians 5:16-17) Each person needs to know how Jesus sees him or her. A prophetic word is a perfect avenue for this to be revealed and or confirmed. There is always a gap between how we think and behave in the present, and who we are becoming in Christ. This "gap" is where the intercessor is positioned for prayer and exhortation. This is where the intercessor calls forth what is to come with faith. Faith is calling into existence those things that we cannot see with the natural eye. (Hebrews 11:1)

Exhortation is an invitation to something more that God has for us. There is something better than what we have been experiencing. Exhortation calls us to that something better with comfort, compassion, encouragement, teaching, prodding, and begging.

Yes, begging. When we see someone on the wrong track, we can join the Father's heart and with compassion keep asking him or her to please consider truth. We plead and invite them to come to the source that will empower them to walk in newness of life. Instead of saying, "Stop sinning or you will go to hell," invite them by saying, "Look dear one, you have the DNA of Jesus Christ in you and you are gentle, not angry. You are kind, not mean. You are steadfast, not wavering. You have divine help to be this…come…be this." How wonderful to have an invitation rather than a scolding!

Exhortation is positive, not negative. Love believes the best. A prophetic messenger has the privilege to invite people to the best.

QUESTIONS ABOUT EXHORTATION TO *PAL* WHEN PREPARING TO DELIVER A PROPHETIC WORD

"Holy Spirit, is there anything in my heart that will hinder this person hearing your word of invitation to something better?"

"Holy Spirit, is what I'm about to share going to call forth what you want to establish in their life?

"Holy Spirit, how can I positively call forth what You see and want to invite this person to?"

Some personality types and behaviors cause us to judge and withdraw our approval. It is difficult to prophesy the heart of the Father when we are judgmental. Judgment hinders our ability to see in the Spirit. We begin to look at the natural, focusing on what is wrong rather than what God says is right about them.

A messenger from God learns to extract the precious from the vile. Jeremiah 15:19, "…if you extract the precious from the worthless you will become my spokesman." Something precious is valuable, prized, rare and glorious. Can we look at the unlovely as precious? God does.

PAL: Holy Spirit, would you fill my heart with your love for this person? I desire to be used to draw them closer to You."

Consolation means to comfort. The Greek word is *paramythia*. [8] It means an address, whether made for the purpose of persuading, or of arousing and stimulating, or of calming and consoling. It is speaking closely to anyone.

A word picture might be a mom holding her child when they are wounded in order to make it all better. Consolation imparts a great degree of tenderness.

When we are speaking a word of consolation we are speaking "with" someone, not "at" them. The messenger is skilled in empathy. Empathy is the ability to perceive another's feelings correctly and respond appropriately.

QUESTIONS ABOUT CONSOLATION TO *PAL* WHEN PREPARING TO DELIVER A PROPHETIC WORD

PAL: "Holy Spirit, is what I am about to share going to draw this person close to you so they can be comforted? Can I speak with a sense of nearness that will heal their heart?"

As you minister prophetically, be on the alert for people who are lonely, rejected and abandoned. Don't always look for the people who seem to get the attention of the visiting prophet. Look for the ones Jesus is looking for.

Be aware that you may have a message for someone, but it may not be God's timing to communicate that word. *PAL: "Holy Spirit, I am sensing this for this person. Is now the time to speak it, or do you want me to wait?"* Always be sure you have God's permission to share. You may have seen God's heart in order to intercede.

The prophetic gift, more than any other, is a bonus gift from God. That's why 1 Corinthians 14:1 says to *earnestly desire* it. A message from the Father's heart can open up a stubborn, hurting, unhealed heart in a moment. It paves the way for truth to be established. It paints a picture of how God sees the person so they can have a destination in life. It helps people make a decision to pay the price of renewing the mind to agree with God.

Prophecy is a gift used to reveal the love of the Father. God loves to speak to us.

> Prophecy is a gift used to reveal the love of the Father. God loves to speak to us.

CHAPTER 3

THE POWER OF HEARING GOD SPEAK

"My sheep hear My voice, and I know them, and they follow Me."
John 10:27

HEARING GOD SPEAK IS A FUNDAMENTAL SKILL
for SoulCare ministry sessions. Some people freak out and say they can't hear
His voice, but when you begin dialoguing with them and explain different
ways people hear God speak to them, they begin to relax and enter in with
anticipation for what God will say to them personally along the journey.

Some helpful questions to ask are:

"How do you best connect with God?"

"Do you tend to hear him speak to you in your thoughts, see
pictures or words, or sense His presence?"

"When do you feel the closest to God?"

"Do you connect to God through nature? Music? Reading the

Scriptures?"

These questions help people realize there are many ways to hear God speak and connect to Him. It is freeing to realize they don't have to hear in the same way as someone else.

By the time the prayer sessions are concluded, the person has grown in their ability to connect with God, believing deep in their heart that God *does* speak to them and they *can* hear. It is a beautiful thing to watch develop!

It is an incredible reality to know that God talks to His children. Hearing His voice releases power for us to grow in confidence as we obey Him, taking steps of faith to live the life He died to provide for us.

We are privileged as Christians to have a God who loves to speak to His followers. He desires a personal relationship with each one of His children and loves to carry on a dialogue with us. He wants us to know Him. "This is eternal life – that they may *know* God." (John 17:3) John 10:27 says, "My sheep hear My voice."

Sometimes we are too busy and don't take time to be quiet to hear His voice. Some people don't know God wants to talk to them. Some have been hearing His voice and haven't recognized it. When I teach and do training on hearing God speak to us, I ask people to sing a familiar song like "Happy Birthday" or "Jesus Loves Me" in their head – not audibly. When they are done I ask if they "heard" the tune and the words in their head. The answer is yes. I explain that is how God's voice sounds to us. We hear it in our mind, just not audibly. It seems to help bridge the gap from the mystical to the practical.

The Lord revealed four simple keys to Mark Virkler based on Habakkuk 2:1-2. These principles unlocked Mark's heart to hear the voice of his Shepherd and his hope is it will do the same for all who try them. No one can teach on this subject better than he can.

The following is an excerpt from an article written by Dr. Mark Virkler. It is included with permission. You can access the full article in Appendix A.

"*HOW TO HEAR GOD'S VOICE*" (Dr. Mark Virkler) [9]

The first key to hearing God's voice is to go to a quiet place and still our own thoughts and emotions. (Habakkuk 2:1) Psalm 46:10 encourages us to be still, let go, cease striving, and know that He is God. In Psalm 37:7 we are called to "be still before the Lord and wait patiently for Him." There is a deep inner knowing in our spirits that each of us can experience when we quiet our flesh and our minds. Practicing the art of biblical meditation helps silence the outer noise and distractions clamoring for our attention.

The second key to hearing God's voice is: **As you pray, fix the eyes of your heart upon Jesus, seeing in the Spirit the dreams and visions of Almighty God.** Habakkuk was actually looking for vision as he prayed. He opened the eyes of his heart, and looked into the spirit world to see what God wanted to show him.

God has always spoken through dreams and visions, and He specifically said that they would come to those upon whom the Holy Spirit is poured out (Acts 2:1-4, 17).

Being a logical, rational person, observable facts that could be verified by my physical senses were the foundations of my life, including my spiritual life. I had never thought of opening the eyes of my heart and looking for vision. However, I have come to believe that this is exactly what God wants me to do. He gave me eyes in my heart to see in the spirit the vision and movement of Almighty God. There is an active spirit world all around us, full of angels, demons, the Holy Spirit, the omnipresent Father, and His omnipresent Son, Jesus. The only reasons for me not to see this reality are unbelief or lack of knowledge.

In his sermon in Acts 2:25, Peter refers to King David's statement: "I saw the Lord always in my presence; for He is at my right hand, so that I will not be shaken." The original psalm makes it clear that this was a decision of David's, not a constant supernatural visitation: "I have set (literally, I have placed) the Lord continually before me; because He is at my right hand, I will not be shaken" (Psalm 16:8). Because David knew that the Lord was always with him, he determined in his spirit to *see* that truth with the eyes of his heart as he went through life, knowing that this would keep his faith strong.

In order to see, we must look. Daniel saw a vision in his mind and said, "I was looking...I kept looking...I kept looking" (Daniel 7:2, 9, 13). As I pray, I look for Jesus, and I watch as He speaks to me, doing and saying the things that are on His heart. Many Christians will find that if they will only look, they will see. Jesus is Emmanuel, God with us (Matthew 1:23). It is as simple as that. You can see Christ present with you because Christ *is* present with you. In fact, the vision may come so easily that you will be tempted to reject it, thinking that it is just you. But if you persist in recording these visions, your doubt will soon be overcome by faith as you recognize that the content of them could only be birthed in Almighty God.

Jesus demonstrated the ability of living out of constant contact with God, declaring that He did nothing on His own initiative, but only what He saw the Father doing, and heard the Father saying (John 5:19,20,30). What an incredible way to live!

Is it possible for us to live out of divine initiative as Jesus did? Yes! We must simply fix our eyes upon Jesus. The veil has been torn, giving access into the immediate presence of God, and He calls us to draw near (Luke 23:45; Hebrews 10:19-22). "I pray that the eyes of your heart will be enlightened...."

The third key to hearing God's voice is recognizing that God's voice in your heart often sounds like a flow of spontaneous thoughts. Therefore, when I want to hear from God, I tune to chance-encounter or spontaneous thoughts.

Like Habakkuk, I was coming to know the sound of God speaking to me (Habakkuk 2:2). Elijah described it as a still, small voice (I Kings 19:12). I had previously listened for an inner audible voice, and God does speak that way at times. However, I have found that usually, God's voice comes as spontaneous thoughts, visions, feelings, or impressions.

For example, haven't you been driving down the road and had a thought come to you to pray for a certain person? Didn't you believe it was God telling you to pray? What did God's voice sound like? Was it an audible voice, or was it a spontaneous thought that lit upon your mind?

Experience indicates that we perceive spirit-level communication as spontaneous thoughts, impressions and visions, and Scripture confirms this in many ways. For example, one definition of *paga*, a Hebrew word for intercession, is "a chance encounter or an accidental intersecting." When God lays people on our hearts, He does it through *paga*, a chance-encounter thought "accidentally" intersecting our minds.

The fourth key, two-way journaling or the writing out of your prayers and God's answers, brings great freedom in hearing God's voice. God told Habakkuk to record the vision (Habakkuk 2:2). This was not an isolated command. The Scriptures record many examples of individual's prayers and God's replies, such as the Psalms, many of the prophets, and Revelation. I have found that obeying this final principle amplified my confidence in my ability to hear God's voice so that I could finally make living out of His initiatives a way of life.

I have found two-way journaling to be a fabulous catalyst for clearly discerning God's inner, spontaneous flow, because as I journal I am able to write in faith for long periods of time, simply believing it is God. I know that what I believe I have received from God must be tested. However, testing involves doubt and doubt blocks divine communication, so I do not want to test while I am trying to receive. (See James 1:5-8.) With journaling, I can receive in faith, knowing that when the flow has ended I can test and examine it carefully.

The four simple keys that the Lord showed me from Habakkuk have been used by people of all ages, from four to a hundred and four, from every continent, culture and denomination, to break through into intimate two-way conversations with their loving Father and dearest Friend. Omitting any one of the keys will prevent you from receiving all He wants to say to you. The order of the keys is not important, just that you *use them all*. Embracing all four, by faith, can change your life. Simply quiet yourself down, tune to spontaneity, look for vision, and journal. He is waiting to meet you there.

You will be amazed when you journal! Doubt may hinder you at first, but throw it off, reminding yourself that it is a biblical concept, and that God is present, speaking to His children. Relax. When we cease our labors and enter His rest, God is free to flow (Hebrews 4:10).

Why not try it for yourself, right now? Sit back comfortably, take out your pen and paper, and smile. Turn your attention toward the Lord in praise and worship, seeking His face. Many people have found the music and visionary prayer called "A Stroll Along the Sea of Galilee" helpful in getting them started. You can listen to it and download it free at www.CWGMinistries.org/Galilee.

After you write your question to Him, become still, fixing your gaze on Jesus. You will suddenly have a very good thought. Don't doubt it; simply write it down. Later, as you read your journaling, you, too, will be blessed to discover that you are indeed dialoguing with God. If you wonder if it is really the Lord speaking to you, share it with your spouse or a friend. Their input will encourage your faith and strengthen your commitment to spend time getting to know the Lover of your soul more intimately than you ever dreamed possible.

IS IT REALLY GOD?

Five ways to be sure what you're hearing is from Him:
1. Test the origin. (1 John 4:1)

2. Compare it to biblical principles.

3. Compare it to the names and character of God as revealed in the Bible.

4. Test the Fruit. (Matthew 7:15-20)

5. Share it with your spiritual counselors. (Proverbs 11:14)

A couple of excellent questions to start your dialogue with God are simple: *"I love you Lord. What do you want to talk about this morning?"* Or start with a passage from the Gospels and *PAL: "Holy Spirit, what do you want to say to me about this passage? What does this mean for me today?"*

A helpful summary to remember Dr. Virkler's four keys is:

Stop, Look, Listen, and Write.

For a deeper study and to grow in your ability to hear God's voice visit his website www.cwgministries.org. The book *"4 Keys to Hearing God's Voice"* is available there with many other helpful resources.

CHAPTER 4

THE POWER OF FORGIVENESS

"Be kind to one another, tender-hearted, forgiving each other, just as
God in Christ also has forgiven you." Ephesians 4:32

OUR FIRST IN-DEPTH TEACHING IS ABOUT FOR-
giveness, because it is the basis for freedom in our lives. John Arnott says forgiveness is a "key to blessing." [10] Who doesn't want freedom and blessing? It
permeates every level of ministry in this approach to wholeness. It is a key activation in the process to freedom because the Cross of Jesus Christ is central to
the life of one who follows Christ. The cross is all about Jesus' sacrifice for us,
in that He died so our sins can be forgiven and we can become new creations.

FORGIVENESS DEFINED

There are two words in particular that are translated as forgive, forgave and
forgiveness in the New Testament that relate to our discussion about forgiveness. The Greek word "*aphiemi*" means primarily "to send forth, send away, to
remit or forgive." [11] It has to do with "sending away" debts, sins and trespasses.
It means to completely cancel the debt, to remit the punishment due to sinful

conduct, the removal of the cause of the offense. It means to let it go and give it up. When the conditions of repentance and confession are met, there is no limitation to the reach of Christ's forgiveness. [12] This word is used in the passages in Matthew we often turn to when we are thinking about forgiveness. (Matthew 6:12-14, Matthew 18:21-35; also Mark 11:25-26)

The other Greek word is "*charizomai*," which means, "to bestow a favor unconditionally." [13] This word is used when referring to an act of forgiveness whether divine or human. It means to show one's self as gracious, kind and benevolent. Paul frequently uses this word as he does in Ephesians 4:32 and Colossians 3:13. He is exhorting us to graciously be restored to one another by granting a pardon and forgiving one another, just as God in Christ has forgiven us.

Forgiveness as *Merriam-Webster.com* defines it:

To cancel a debt:

To grant relief from payment

To go before and give release to

To pardon, excuse an offense, without extracting a penalty

To give up resentment against an offender

To choose not to hurt those who have hurt you

To let go, disregard, let it be [14]

My working definition: *Forgiveness is an intentional decision I make, with the empowerment of the indwelling Holy Spirit, to lay down my desire and requirement for any payment from or punishment for my offender. It is a choice I make to pardon a debt owed to me, including the consequences I am currently living out as a result of the offense.*

Forgiveness releases healing. When we forgive we find ourselves in a place to be forgiven by God. When we forgive we break a bondage that keeps us tied to the person we are holding something against. There are times the offense is so great that it is difficult to forgive and release others from the debt we think they owe us. That's why forgiveness is foundational to all ministry areas targeted in SoulCare.

We must exercise the spiritual fruit of patience with each other as we learn how to walk through the process of forgiveness. We can't allow ourselves the rationalizations we've made to keep us from actually living out the reality of forgiveness as Jesus taught it. He said to forgive one another as He has forgiven us, and to maintain a lifestyle of forgiving others. (Ephesians 4:32, Matthew 18) This is an impossible standard to reach without the help of the Holy Spirit indwelling us.

> *The level of freedom experienced while extending forgiveness is directly related to the depth of my understanding of the debt I think is owed to me, and my willingness to cancel that debt.*

The level of freedom experienced while extending forgiveness is directly related to the depth of my understanding of the debt I think is owed to me, and my willingness to cancel that debt.

It is the nature of the "old" man to find ways to get out of taking responsibility for things said and done. We are very creative to come up with excuses why we should not have to forgive fully from the heart. We want to get by with saying the words, "I forgive you," and then put a condition on the forgiveness.

Some of the rationalizations we employ in order to protect ourselves from totally forgiving:

I forgive you but I don't have to like you.

I forgive you but I don't trust you.

I forgive you but I don't want to be your friend and spend time with you. I will keep you at arm's length so you won't have a chance to hurt me again.

I forgive you and can be nice to you as long as I don't have to spend any time with you or see you.

I forgive you but I will avoid you.

While we need to be real with our thoughts and feelings, we must be careful that our hearts continue to pursue forgiveness with the character and attitude of Christ.

I think the teaching of the church in general (religious cultures) has actually inoculated us from being real with forgiveness. It is not so much that the teaching content has been wrong; it has been incomplete. Too many rationalizations allow us to keep protecting our heart from hurt and our desire to see the other person "pay" for what they have done. We cloak our unforgiveness with religious platitudes and psychological excuses. When we say "I forgive you, but…" we can suspect there will be another layer of forgiveness to work through.

RECONCILIATION, RESTORATION, RESTITUTION

There are at least three possible outcomes as a result of the act of forgiveness: Reconciliation, Restoration (which includes Rebuilding Trust and Reciprocity), and Restitution.

When forgiveness is first given and received the relationship is reconciled. You have decided to come back together and into some degree of relationship. You choose to change your perception about what caused the separation and renew your friendship. (Matthew 5:24)

Depending on each person's decisions and responses, the relationship may move to restoration. In this stage you experience the opportunity to rebuild trust and enjoy your relationship with a deepened level of intimacy. You continue to diligently work to mend what has been broken.

"Finally, brothers, rejoice. Aim for *restoration*, comfort one another, agree with one another, live in peace; and the God of love and peace will be with you." (2 Corinthians 13:11 ESV)

Rebuilding trust is a difficult assignment when it has been broken. Trust is based on a person's character. When I experience broken trust in a relationship I am learning to PAL: "*What was/is this relationship based on?*" If the relationship is based on what I need from it (significance, friends, relationship) then when trust is ruptured, the relationship will crumble.

If a relationship is based on anything except God's love, when trouble comes, separation and distrust will occur.

When we try to re-establish trust, we must begin with forgiveness. Our capacity to trust must be healed and restored.

God doesn't ask us to forgive anyone he isn't willing to forgive, and He doesn't ask us to forgive anyone any more than he has forgiven us. (Colossians 3:12-14) How much has He forgiven us? He has removed our sins from us as far as the east is from the west. (Psalm 103:12)

Rebuilding trust involves facing fear: fears of rejection, of being hurt again, of betrayal, of abandonment – you fill in the blank. What is hidden keeps us bound to the work of the Enemy and to the person we are seeking to be set free from. Secrets and lies are devastating. Our thoughts turn to "Will this happen again?" Fear of being re-wounded paralyzes us. When we are established in the fact that God is trustworthy we will be able to run to Him for safe keeping in the middle of our pain and get His perspective. His perspective can change everything.

PAL: "Holy Spirit what do you want to say to me about _____ right now? I have been thinking this _____ about them. Is it okay with you that I think that? Do you have something else you want me to think about them?"

Rebuilding trust takes time. There are no deadlines other than our own. Just begin the process and let God lead.

PAL: "Holy Spirit what do you want this relationship to look like right now? What initiatives do you want me to take?"

Rebuilding trust requires truth. We must learn how to speak the truth in love. Speaking the truth in love is accomplished only as we are immersed in the nature and character of Jesus because He *Is* Love. One aspect of the Fruit of the Spirit is love. Truth is not just a set of facts – it is a person, Jesus Christ. We learn to speak only what Jesus would speak in a situation to those who are in our lives to help transform our character to look like Jesus. I refer to these people in my life as grace growers.

If we endeavor to rebuild trust before we are healed of the pain of betrayal we will most likely wound others with our words. Even when the words are true they can wound. We must have the heart of the Father to learn how to speak truth in love.

PAL: "Holy Spirit, what would you like to say to me about this person's trustworthiness? How can I learn to speak the truth with a design for restoration and not harm?" "What do you want this relationship to look like in this season? How much involvement do you want me to have with _____ right now?"

Sometimes I am stopped in my tracks when I ask myself this question: *"How trustworthy am I for other people?"* Ouch!

I included a short questionnaire in Appendix B that can help as you are evaluating your maturation in Christ, and as you evaluate relationships you are in or are considering investing in.

We may experience an occasion when one person does not want to be reconciled or restored to relationship even when we ask for forgiveness or extend it. There must be reciprocity for relationship to exist. According to *Merriam-Webster Dictionary*, reciprocity is the practice of exchanging things with others for mutual benefit. It is a relationship in which two people agree to do something similar for each other, allowing each other to have the same rights.

In the case of abuse when it is not safe to be in relationship with a person, one still has the ability to forgive, but restoration and reciprocity are not likely to take place. I do not advise people to go back to an abusive relationship when they are in danger. A *PAL* for the person to ask, as they might experience guilt over this, thinking they are to forgive and forget, is *"Holy Spirit, what do you want this relationship to look like right now? What boundaries do you want in place for me with this person at this time?"* The Lord very well may say there will be no relationship and the boundaries are no contact whatsoever. This has happened as I have worked with people and it shocks the person because they are sure they are "suppose" to forgive and just go through whatever they had to in order to be a good Christian. The Holy Spirit is the best Counselor ever! We need to ask Him and listen!

If there is no reciprocity does it mean you don't need to forgive or that your heart cannot be healed if this happens? The requirement for forgiveness stands – it is God's command. Other people's responses do not get to determine your obedience to God. Other people's responses do not get to determine God's ability to heal your heart even when the possibility for reconciliation and restoration seem impossible.

Other people's responses do not get to determine God's ability to heal your heart.

Unfortunately, doing the right thing does not guarantee the outcome you desire. But the sacrifice of obedience and the transformation of your thought process to agree with God about the person and the situation can heal your wounded heart.

Another person's negative response to your request for reconciliation and restoration will hinder relationship, but it does not determine your ability to obey God and to move ahead in your journey with Christ with a healed heart.

Restitution rarely happens. If I break or damage something that belongs to someone else I can ask and receive forgiveness and be reconciled and restored with no limitations. If I am able I should pay for the damage and make it right. If I back into someone's mailbox and break it I should take responsibility for it and either fix it or buy a new one. If I am the cause of a wreck in which someone loses a limb, I cannot replace that limb. However, at the direction of the Holy Spirit I may be able to help in some way that expresses the genuineness of my repentance and request for forgiveness. *PAL: "Holy Spirit, what consequences have my actions and or words caused for this person? Is there something you would like me to do on behalf of this person?"* Sometimes consequences (for ourselves and others) are thought patterns that lead to habit patterns of behavior. We can ask forgiveness for those as well, when we become aware of them. Either the Holy Spirit or the other person will need to inform us of those consequences.

Many times we hear that forgiveness is a choice, an act of our will. We just forgive and all will be well. We are told we need to forgive if we want to be a good Christian, so just do it and hope the feelings will follow later. Then you wonder why your emotions and heart are still not settled when you bump up against the person who offended you and/or sinned against you.

Forgiveness is not just an exercise that affects our hearts on the surface. It goes to the deepest places in our hearts. Scripture has a lot to say about forgiveness.

GOD REQUIRES FORGIVENESS

God requires forgiveness. It is a non-negotiable. "Be kind to one another, tender-hearted, forgiving each other, just as God in Christ also has forgiven you." (Ephesians 4:32) Forgiveness does not depend on my feelings, the fairness of the situation, or who was right or wrong. We are to forgive.

God requires us to forgive if we have been offended. "Whenever you stand praying, if you have anything against anyone, forgive him [drop the issue, let it go], so that your Father who is in heaven will also forgive you your transgressions *and* wrongdoings [against Him and others. "But if you do not forgive, neither will your Father in heaven forgive your transgressions." (Mark 11:25,26 AMP)

God requires us to forgive if someone is offended with us. We are to leave our offering at the altar when we become aware someone has something against us and go to him to be reconciled. (Matthew 5:23,24)

There are consequences when we make a choice to not forgive. We will not be forgiven. "If you forgive others for their transgressions, your heavenly Father will also forgive you. But if you do not forgive others, then your Father will not forgive your transgressions." (Matthew 6:14-15)

When we don't forgive we will be given over to the tormentors. This places us outside of God's protection. (Matthew 18:34)

God wants as much forgiveness as is necessary for unbroken relationship. "How often shall my brother sin against me and I forgive him? Up to seven times?" Jesus said, "I do not say to you, up to seven times, but up to seventy times seven." (Matthew 18:21-22) In other words, until forgiveness isn't needed anymore.

You can make a decision in advance to not take up offense. "Great peace have they who love your law: and nothing shall offend them." (Psalm 119:165 KJV)

Keeping our minds and hearts saturated with God's Word and our wills surrendered enables us to live in a posture of forgiveness before the offenses are even committed. Most mornings I make this declaration: "Whatever happens today I will not take up offense." Predetermined responses are very helpful so we don't get caught off guard.

> "Whatever happens today
> I will not take up offense."

God never asks me to forgive more than He has already forgiven me. "… just as the Lord forgave you, so also should you." (Colossians 3:13)

God wants us to forgive from the heart. The parable in Matthew 18 tells us how to forgive from our hearts. It takes God's grace to do this. Sometimes we start with the decision (our will) to forgive, but He wants us to learn how to follow through and be genuine from the heart. (Matthew 18:35)

Forgiving from the heart begins with recognizing and acknowledging we have unresolved offenses. We need to have a desperate desire to be free. Walking in freedom is a daily discipline. (Matthew 6)

It is helpful to acknowledge that when someone sins against us, they have stolen something from us. I cannot forgive or cancel a debt when I don't know what it is. To determine what we think they owe us PAL: *"Holy Spirit, what are the consequences in my life right now that are a result of what they said or did to me?"*

When someone steals from me, I have been violated and betrayed. A normal reaction is anger and perhaps fear or abandonment. The point is that I must realize what has been taken from me. Otherwise I minimize the effect of it on my soul and take in woundedness that if not healed could lead to unforgiveness, ungodly thoughts, hidden wounds in the heart and an opportunity for demonic influence.

If we look at what *was* and what *could* have been, we can see what was taken from us. We need to forgive that person. As a result of childhood abuse I lost my innocence, a carefree childhood, a sense of security, a sense of being protected, loved and cared for, and the ability to trust. Losing the ability to trust affected my relationship with people in authority –my mom, dad, pastors, men, bosses, and husband. Ron fits most of those categories for me (husband, pastor, man, boss), so we have had a lot to work through. Our first years of marriage were rough, as we had no realization of the abuse. The abuse was so traumatic for me I repressed it until my mid-thirties.

FORGIVENESS IS COSTLY

Forgiveness is costly. It cost Jesus His life. It will cost me pride, control and the desire for revenge. Sometimes it costs me my sense of fairness.

If someone takes $20 out of my billfold and later comes back to tell me they took it, spent it and have no way to pay me back, could I forgive them? I will probably have grace to say,

"That's okay. I cancel your debt of $20. You don't have to pay me back."

Maybe later they come and say, "Oh by the way I took your Visa card, too. Here it is. Will you forgive me for taking your Visa card?"

"Okay. I forgive you."

Then I get my Visa bill and it is maxed out. Now I am responsible for that person's $10,000 spending spree. I am left with a consequence to live out. How am I going to take care of this mess? I am angry. I already forgave them for taking my Visa card. I didn't "know" what they had stolen from me until later. Now there is another level of forgiveness to extend. Is it fair? Should I have to pay for this? Will I do it? Or will I stay angry and demand justice?

Recognizing all the consequences I was living as a result of the abuse didn't happen all at once. As I realized a consequence I would forgive and receive healing. God continued to speak truth to my heart.

When we demand justice from or for someone else that is what we will get in return. The law of sowing and reaping is in play. However I judge someone else is the standard from which I will be judged.

When someone sins against you *PAL: "In what way has this offence/sin against me affected my life?" "What consequence(s) am I living out right now as a result of this sin against me?"*

The answers to these questions will tell you what it will cost you to forgive. *Will* you pay this price? Consider also the consequence of your decision. Do you want *mercy* or do you want *justice* for yourself?

A consequence if you decide not to forgive is that the Father can't forgive you. That separates you from intimacy with Him. Would you rather pay the price of broken relationship with God or the price of letting go and forgiving the wrong done to you? Letting go releases freedom.

Forgiveness is progressive in nature.

Forgiveness is progressive in nature. We make an initial decision to forgive. We continue to walk in forgiveness as we become aware of consequences and other details of the event that took place. Forgiveness is like a lot of kingdom principles that involve past, present and future truth.

We did forgive, we are forgiving and we will continue to forgive the person for a specific sin against us. We have been forgiven, we are being forgiven and we will be forgiven. We have been saved, we are being saved, and we will be saved.

Forgiveness becomes possible as we see the offender from God's perspective. In the Matthew 18:25 parable, we see the person was not able to pay the debt. Why? It is sometimes hard to forgive when we don't understand the debt. In Matthew 18 the person wasn't able to pay because they didn't have anything in the bank to pay with.

Perhaps in our situation the other person had a love deficit, a parenting skill deficit. They did to us what was done to them.

My father grew up during the Depression. His family lost everything. His father died and my father had to quit high school to work and support their family. A poverty mentality, "We'll never have enough" permeated his thinking and affected my whole family. He never recovered from the consequences of that experience.

My mother's father left her family when she was five years old. He had affairs and gambled the family finances. Her mother had to scrimp for everything, food included. She was cold and harsh, not nurturing at all. There was little love in the love bank. There were many self-protective habits of thinking and behaving put into place that left future generations vulnerable. There was an inability to "pay" because there was a deficit in their love bank account.

We all have an Enemy that wants to rob, kill and destroy us. Remember, our parents and everyone else had an Enemy from the day they were born too. We are not blaming our parents for anything. We are just trying to understand so ungodly patterns can be broken. We have a loving Father that wants to heal us. He has overcome the Enemy that wants to destroy us. We have the power to choose a path that will lead us into the future God has for us.

People who live with inner pain will be explosive. They will lash out at us to stop us from hurting them.

We all live and react out of the emotional health we have experienced.

We all live and react out of the emotional health we have experienced.

Some of our reactions and responses are positive, some are negative. Every person who has ever hurt us, sinned against us, or offended us has first been hurt. When we begin to see others as God sees them and understand how the Enemy has wounded them, we can begin to forgive from the heart and we release ourselves from offenses, hurts and wounds. A great question to *PAL* when you are struggling to forgive a person is *"Lord, how do you want me to think about this person right now?"*

You have probably heard this said and it is good to remember it:

Hurting people hurt people.

Healed people can help heal people.

Hurting people hurt people. Healed people can help heal people.

This is an important truth to remember and declare: I *can* forgive because of the nature of the person of Jesus Christ who lives in me. God *is* love. For what He requires of me, He first equips me as a gift. He has given Himself as a sacrifice for me and made possible an exchanged life. "I have been crucified with Christ; and it is no longer I who live, but Christ lives in me; and the life which I now live in the flesh I live by faith in the Son of God, who loved me and gave Himself up for me." (Galatians 2:20)

Since He dwells in me and I in Him (1 John 3:24, 4:13,16; 1 Corinthians 3:16), all the Fruit of the Spirit is available to me all the time. The key is to *let Him* live His life in and through me. I am equipped with everything necessary for life and godliness. "...His divine power has granted to us everything pertaining to life and godliness, through the true knowledge of Him who called us by His own glory and excellence." (2 Peter 1:3)

After I have forgiven others I can come to God with faith and confidence asking Him to forgive me, believing He will do it because His conditions have been met. *This part of forgiveness is called repentance.*

> *Repentance means to change the way you think which will result in a new way of feeling and behaving.*

Repentance means to change the way you think which will result in a new way of feeling and behaving. Repentance is marked by a radical change in the direction of a life. When we repent God promises two things: Forgiveness and cleansing. "If we confess our sins, He is faithful and righteous to forgive us our sins and to cleanse us from all unrighteousness." (1 John 1:9)

Scripture admonishes us to "bear fruit in keeping with repentance." (Matthew 3:8)

Repentance is not:

Having a good cry.

Having a show of emotions.

Just being sorry for the hurt we've done.

Coming and saying "I'm sorry about that…I won't do it again."

> *Repentance requires action.*

Repentance requires action. Read this passage from 2 Corinthians 7:7-13 from The Message:

"I know I distressed you greatly with my letter. Although I felt awful at the time, I don't feel at all bad now that I see how it turned out. The letter upset you, but only for a while. Now I'm glad—not that you were upset, but that you were jarred into turning things around. You let the distress bring you to God, not drive you from him. The result was all gain, no loss. Distress that drives us to God does that. It turns us around. It gets us back in the way of salvation.

We never regret that kind of pain. But those who let distress drive them away from God are full of regrets, and end up on a deathbed of regrets. And now, isn't it wonderful all the ways in which this distress has goaded you closer to God? You're more alive, more concerned, more sensitive, more reverent, more human, more passionate, more responsible. Looked at from any angle, you've come out of this with purity of heart. And that is what I was hoping for in the first place when I wrote the letter. My primary concern was not for the one who did the wrong or even the one wronged, but for you—that you would realize and act upon the deep, deep ties between us before God. That's what happened—and we felt just great."

GODLY SORROW VS WORLDLY SORROW

Godly sorrow leads to true repentance. Worldly sorrow leads to death. Remorse is of the natural man; repentance is of the spiritual man.

Remorse or worldly sorrow is of the flesh. It says, "I'm sorry I got caught. I'm sorry I blew it." It doesn't lead to the Cross and changed behavior. Worldly sorrow is concerned with self, pride, reputation and being right. It leads to self-hatred and self-condemnation. Worldly sorrow justifies behavior and blames others, God or circumstances.

Repentance or godly sorrow causes us to see the hurt we have inflicted upon others. Godly sorrow allows us to know we have grieved the Holy Spirit by our actions. It is more concerned with other's needs than our own. Repentance means we lay down our pride and the need to be right. We begin to hate hurtful habitual patterns. True repentance leads us to do whatever we can to heal the heart of the one we hurt.

Godly sorrow changes behavior, because it changes the way we think. *For repentance to be complete, behavior has to change.* I am ready for repentance when I start to think there is something not right in *me.* I stop looking to blame others for my situation. I must own my own sin. No one creates or causes sin in me. Others are used in my life to reveal what is already in my heart.

RESISTING THE WORK OF FORGIVENESS

At times we resist asking for forgiveness. When we live in habitual sin or believe that our sin is too great to be forgiven we are not ready for the work of forgiveness. Sometimes we think we don't deserve to be forgiven, putting ourselves in the place of God.

It is difficult to work with the mindset that one doesn't deserve to be forgiven. The person either thinks what they have done is too bad or that they are a flawed, unworthy person. That is an ungodly stronghold that must be demolished and replaced. The truth is we are forgiven, chosen, redeemed, loved, adopted, sealed, blessed, and accepted – among other such beautiful, wonderful blessings. (Ephesians 1)

Trauma, tragedy, difficult circumstances and unanswered prayer can cause our faces and hearts to be turned away from God. Trust is broken and separation takes place. When you are disappointed with God it is hard to repent because you usually blame God for the pain in your life. You cannot ignore this reality in your life. This is usually connected to a Life's Hurt that is not yet healed. One cannot forgive God, because He doesn't need our forgiveness. He does *not* sin. But one can confess their anger and disappointment towards Him and ask forgiveness for embracing a faulty view of Him and living their life based on it.

"I am He who blots out your transgressions for My own sake and remember your sins no more." (Isaiah 43:25) Forgiveness is His idea. It has always been His heart to forgive us, even when we were still sinners. (Romans 5:8)

Sometimes we still hold ourselves accountable for some "horrible" sin in our past. We have asked over and over again for forgiveness and God has forgiven. When forgiveness has been received we must apply the truth in our life. That often includes forgiving ourselves.

The command to "love your neighbor as yourself" (Matthew 22:39) is taught but not applied in most of our circumstances. We try to hold ourselves accountable and put ourselves on guilt trips even after we know God has forgiven us. Sometimes I talk about letting ourselves "off the hook." We keep blaming and accusing ourselves. It is time to change how we think about ourselves. When God says we are forgiven, we need to agree with Him. He sees us as holy and blameless, as new creations, as saints. (Ephesians 1:4, 2 Corinthians 5:17) Who are we to disagree with Him?

It is important to note that learning to love yourself is not self-love, but humility. A humble mindset is one that agrees with God. God wants me to agree with Him and see myself like He sees me. If God says I am a pastor and I try to achieve significance by being an accountant I am basically full of pride. I think know better than God. If I agree with Him to be a pastor, then I will be the best pastor I can possibly be with His help.

> Working through forgiveness that will have lasting results requires a revelation of the Father's love for us.

Working through forgiveness that will have lasting results requires a revelation of the Father's love for us.

How many of us believe in the incredible Goodness of God? Do we really believe that God is *for* us?

That revelation is so radical. He is so committed to us He *gave* His only Son to be a ransom for us. (John 3:16, 1 Timothy 2:6)

This truth has been a difficult one for me to embrace and receive: "The Father loves me as much as He loves His Son, Jesus." Oh my! This is a paraphrase of John 17:23.

My unhealed emotions wouldn't let me embrace and receive this biblical truth. Why? My thoughts told me I was not worthy to be loved. I had to decide to let my theology be dictated by my emotions, or choose to hear God speak the truth and embrace it. There were places in me still believing God couldn't love me.

Most of us live out of our emotions. Most ungodly thought patterns are rooted in wounded emotions. Unhealed life's hurts are fertile ground for ungodly thought patterns to take root.

It is effective to say out loud, *"Because I have asked and received forgiveness from you Father, I choose to forgive myself for_____. I will not be beating myself up about this anymore. I am going to agree with you Father! I am loved, redeemed, forgiven, chosen, accepted and blessed."*

RESISTANCE TO FORGIVING OTHERS

If we do not know the Scriptures, we will not understand the importance of forgiveness. Sometimes we think we have to "feel" forgiving before we can forgive. These ungodly thoughts hinder our ability to forgive: "This is just too much to forgive. I can never do it. They don't deserve it."

When we think and say it is too hard to forgive someone, we are disagreeing with God. *We can forgive because of the nature of the person of Jesus Christ who lives in us. God is love. Forgiveness is possible because of His supernatural indwelling presence that empowers us. He commands it of us. He has equipped us to fulfill His commands.*

Fear is always a factor that can stop us from extending forgiveness for an offense or hurt. We might think it is unfair for the offender to get off the hook and not pay for their sin. Fear of being taken advantage of is a hindrance. Fear of being out of control keeps a self-protective defense in place. Fear of being vulnerable is scary.

WHEN FORGIVENESS IS NEEDED

Some *PAL* questions and thoughts to consider knowing if forgiveness is needed:

I lose my peace when I think of _____ because I think they owe me _____.

Ask this question: What did they steal from me?

Think of the way things are (or were) and how they could be (or could have been) different. This will be a clue as to what they "stole" from you.

How has what they said/did affected my life? What have been the consequences for me?

The person I would like least to bless is _____. (OUCH!!)

When I think about forgiving someone who has hurt me, my biggest fear is _____.

WHAT FORGIVENESS IS NOT [15]

Sometimes it is helpful to explore what something is "not" in order to realize the full impact of what it "is." Following are some thoughts about what forgiveness is not and what it is.

Forgiveness is *not* forgetting. God has the ability to forget the sin, we don't. When we forgive, the memory of the offense remains, but the pain, anger, and bitterness leave and we forget the person owes us a debt.

Forgiveness is *not* just a decision. Forgiveness *begins* with a decision to forgive. It then continues with a commitment to resist temptations to revisit the offense and entertain anger and resentment. Forgiveness is a process that requires examination of the heart. The act must be genuine. Forgiveness always flows from a heart of love that is demonstrated in relationship.

Forgiveness is *not* approval of what someone did to you.

Forgiveness is *not* excusing or justifying what they did to you.

Forgiveness is *not* denying or being blind to what they did.

Forgiveness is *not* rationalizing the offense, saying, "It wasn't that bad."

Forgiveness is *not* pretending we are not hurt. This is dishonest.

Forgiveness does *not* necessarily result in instantaneous healing. Sometimes our heart still hurts after we have forgiven. When the offense has been forgiven, then the healing can begin. Forgiveness just begins the process.

If the offense follows a generational pattern, the person needs the generational sins and curses broken and the mind needs to be renewed. It is easy to believe lies about God, others and ourselves. If the lies are attached to a wound, healing comes when the Lord comes to comfort and speak words of life. Most likely there will be demonic interference that needs to be addressed. Legal grounds for the demons to be present need to be taken back through activating the power of the Cross.

PAL: When I think about the list of things forgiveness is NOT, the one(s) I sometimes embrace in my life is (are) _____.

WHAT FORGIVENESS IS [16]

Forgiveness is being aware of what someone has done and being willing to cancel his or her debt to us.

Forgiveness chooses to keep no record of wrong. (1 Corinthians 13:5 NLT)

Forgiveness refuses to punish the offender.

Forgiveness makes a choice not to gossip about what the offender did to you. (This is not the same as reporting criminal behavior.)

Forgiveness is merciful. It decides to give a gift the offender does not deserve. It gives them what they need.

Forgiveness flows from the heart, not just a mental decision.

Forgiveness is letting go of bitterness so it cannot take root in the heart.

Forgiveness is choosing to believe God's goodness and not blame Him for what happened.

Forgiveness includes forgiving yourself.

Forgiveness is a process.

Forgiveness is relational. It is about maintaining connection.

Another helpful exercise in your journey of forgiveness as it relates to what forgiveness *is*:

PAL: "When I think about what forgiveness IS, how am I practicing (or not practicing) these principles?"

Pray a prayer asking God to help you be real with Him and others when you have been hurt and have taken up an offense.

I found this exercise helpful in my journey learning about forgiveness:

Identify scriptures that teach about forgiveness and craft some personal prayers that will help you on your journey as you forgive. I have included a list of scriptures for your use in APPENDIX B.

EXAMPLES

Lord, as hard as this may be for me to comprehend or rationalize, Your Word is clear: if I forgive others when they sin against me, You, my heavenly Father will also forgive me. (Matthew 6:14)

Father God, if I do not forgive others their sins, You will not forgive my sins. (Matthew 6:15)

To make this even more personal, you could *PAL* something like this:

Lord, as hard as this may be for me to embrace right now, Your Word is very clear: If I forgive _____(a specific name) for sinning against me by _____ (be specific about what sin they committed against you), then You will also forgive me. I need your forgiveness. Thank you so much for that promise. I **recognize** my need to forgive and right now I choose to **forgive** _____(name) for _____(say what they did to you). I am willing to also forgive them for these **consequences** that have affected my life as a result of their actions/words: _____ (Name specific consequences. *PAL: "Holy Spirit what consequences am I now living that are a result of what _____said or did to me?"*)

If I have **judged** them in any way, I **repent** and ask you to forgive me, Father. (*PAL: "Lord have I judged _____ in any way? How have I judged them?"*) Lord, would you please **forgive me**? (Pause and Listen for His answer to you. We know He will forgive, because He has promised to, but when our heart hears His answer the healing goes deep.)

*PAL: "Lord, are there any ungodly thought patterns I have adopted and lived my life based on as a result of what _____ said/did to me? I **repent** for living under these lies. Would you please forgive me?*

Thank you Father for your forgiveness! (*PAL: "Lord, what is the gift you have produced in my life through this situation I am to focus on? What is the Fruit of the Spirit you are developing?"*)

Because you have forgiven me, I choose to **forgive myself** for allowing my life to be guided by _____ (fear, resentment, bitterness, grudged, anger, hatred, lies).

Thank you for the gift of forgiveness. With your help, I will continue to walk out the grace you have given me to walk in newness of life.

I pray this in the Name of Jesus. Amen.

Forgiveness flows between God, others, and us. It is a dynamic in which we work from the past to the present as we go through ministry to the whole person.

If people are deceased, confess the sin to God. We can no longer release them from their sin. We can however, appropriate (put into practice) the power of the Cross in order to release ourselves from the consequence of their sin. If the ancestor is living we confess and forgive (release, cancel the debt, and pardon) them. The living can be released from the sin. Then we repent of any way we have entered into our ancestors' sins. *PAL: "Lord how have I entered into my ancestor's sin(s) in my thinking, feeling and/or behavior?"*

APPROPRIATION

Appropriation is an important concept to embrace as we move through the process of SoulCare. It has to do with our posture of receiving and applying what God offers to us.

Merriam-Webster Dictionary defines the word appropriate as "taking exclusive possession of, to own." [17] God wants us to receive, own and apply the provisions, the realities and the victories of the Cross. When we operate from this understanding we believe, receive, own, and apply or put into practice what He has provided for us through giving Himself and shedding His blood on the Cross. We need to appropriate forgiveness – from God, for and from others, and for ourselves.

HAVE I REALLY FORGIVEN?

You know forgiveness is being expressed from the heart when love flows again from your heart toward the person who has hurt or offended you. You have no expectation of any retribution. Less and less you find yourself thinking thoughts like "I forgive them but I don't have to like them. I forgive them but I don't have to spend time with them. I forgive them but I don't have to be around them. I forgive them but I don't trust them. I forgive them but I will hold them at arm's length."

We might even say forgiveness is at work...when we have forgiven like Jesus forgave us...totally completely, unconditionally, embracing one another even when we know the risk of being betrayed and hurt again. We know forgiveness is working in our heart when we can think of the offense without anger and hurt and pain being stirred in our emotions. All that we feel is a desire to love and accept and bless, when we love them like Jesus loves us.

We know forgiveness is doing its work "when you can see the gift God has produced in your life through the situation. The hurt has been healed." [18] I have become a compassionate counselor/minister as I have allowed God to heal the hurts from abuse and betrayal. As I allowed God to heal my heart, He developed the Fruit of the Spirit. God uses every experience we have when we yield it to Him for His redemption and healing. (Romans 8:28-30, Galatians 5:23)

These thoughts are not to put you on a guilt trip or to make you question finished business. It's rather a reality check to see if you have forgiven from the heart, not just by a decision of your will. As Paul encouraged the Galatians, let's begin and end in the Spirit (not the flesh).

You can see that forgiveness plays a huge part in our journey into wholeness. Often when someone comes to my office, they say at the beginning of ministry time..."I know, I know...you are going to ask me if there is anyone I need to forgive." I just smile and say "That's probably a good place to start.

Let's ask Jesus that question and see what He says to you." *PAL "Jesus, is there anyone you want me to forgive so I can move forward in my journey to being made whole?"*

"Therefore, as God's chosen people, holy and dearly loved, clothe your-selves with compassion, kindness, humility, gentleness and patience. Bear with each other and forgive whatever grievances you may have against one another. *Forgive as the Lord forgave you.* And over all these virtues put on *love,* which binds them all together in perfect unity." (Colossians 3:12-14)

If you find yourself in a position that love is still not flowing from your heart, *PAL* again: *"What did they steal from me? What will it cost me to let go of that and let love flow toward them?"*

Our end goal is to look like Jesus in character and conduct.

"God is at work in my present circumstances to remove the wrong and impart the right, indwelling and empowering me so I can choose a willing heart towards Him as He forms the character and conduct of Jesus in me, so that the world may know the Father's love." Pastor Ron Allen

PRAYER FOR FORGIVENESS

Lord, as hard as this may be for me to embrace right now, Your Word is very clear: If I forgive _____ *(a specific name)* for sinning against me by _____ *(be specific about what sin they committed against you),* then You will also forgive me. I need your forgiveness. Thank you so much for that promise. I **recognize** my need to forgive and right now I choose to **forgive** _____ *(name)* for _____ *(say what they did to you).* I am willing to also forgive them for these **consequences** that have affected my life as a result of their actions/words: _____ *(Name specific consequences. PAL: "Holy Spirit what consequences am I now living that are a result of what _____ said or did to me?")*

If I have **judged** them in any way, I **repent** and ask you to forgive me, Father. (PAL: *"Lord have I judged* _____ *in any way? How have I judged them?"*) Lord, would you please **forgive me**? (Pause and Listen for His answer to you. We know He will forgive, because He has promised to, but when our heart hears His answer the healing goes deep.)

PAL: *"Lord, are there any ungodly thought patterns I have adopted and lived my life based on as a result of what* _____ *said/did to me? I* **repent** *for living under these lies. Would you please forgive me?*

Thank you Father for your forgiveness! (PAL: *What would you like for me to think about* _____*(person/situation) instead of how I have been thinking? What gift have you given me as a result of this person/situation? I want to be grateful, repent and change.*)

Because you have forgiven me, I choose to **forgive myself** for allowing my life to be guided by _____ (fear, resentment, bitterness, grudged, anger, hatred, lies).

Thank you for the gift of forgiveness. With your help, I will continue to walk out the grace you have given me to walk in newness of life.

I pray this in the Name of Jesus. Amen.

CHAPTER 5

THE POWER OF THE CROSS

"The word of the cross is foolishness to those who are perishing, but to us who are being saved it is the power of God."
1 Corinthians 1:18

ALL OF THE MINISTRY AREAS IN SOULCARE ARE possible because of what Jesus did for us when He gave His life on the cross. His shed blood makes the exchanged life possible.

At Heartland Church we purposefully position a large cross in the center of our space for community gatherings. The message of the Cross is central to our understanding and practice of the Gospel of Jesus Christ. We also participate in an act of ongoing thanksgiving every week at the Communion Table. We are intentionally habituating ourselves in the truth of God's grace for us.

The message of the Cross is multifaceted. What Jesus did for us includes forgiveness, justification, reconciliation and freedom from the old sin nature. We have been given an opportunity for a BIG EXCHANGE. Several years ago, during one of my ministry sessions the Lord asked me to begin wearing a cross necklace to help remind myself of all the things He did for me on the cross. I didn't have any cross necklaces at that time as I really was not fond of them. But as I obeyed and used the visual reminder to reinforce the truths of the provisions of the cross, I now miss having it on if I wear another piece of jewelry. I have several cross necklaces that are all beautiful. They all speak to me of the wonders of the incredible gift Jesus gave when He willingly gave His life on the cross.

Let's never forget. These provisions are what we remember when we partake of the bread and cup at the Communion Table.

PROVISIONS OF THE CROSS

Forgiveness

> "*If* we confess our sins, He is faithful and just to
> forgive us our sins, and to cleanse us from all unrigh-
> teousness." (1 John 1:9)

Forgiveness is central to everything that takes place in the process that continually makes us like Jesus. We need to receive God's forgiveness, forgive others and forgive ourselves. Not only does God require repentance from our own sins, we must forgive others. When we don't forgive others, God can't forgive us.

The Big Exchange

Jesus took our place – he paid the penalty for our sin. Let that soak in! What an incredible gift – let's receive it and put the provision into practice in our daily lives!

> "He Himself bore our sins in His body on the cross, so
> that we might die to sin and live to righteousness."
> (1 Peter 2:24)

> "He personally carried our sins in his body on the
> cross so that we can be dead to sin and live for what is
> right."
> (1 Peter 2:24 NLT)

This means we get to exchange weariness for rest, worry and anxiousness for peace, doubt and fear for trust, hopelessness for hope, helplessness for the power of God, hate, resentment and bitterness for love, sadness and depression for joy, impatience for patience, instability for faithfulness, self-indulgence for self-control, harshness for gentleness, self-centeredness for Jesus-centeredness, addictions for freedom, my will for God's will, anger for faith, sinner mentality for saint mentality, old sin nature for new creation.

This is a deal we don't want to miss out on!!

Justification

When we believe and receive Jesus Christ we are given a right standing before God. We are declared blameless before Him. We are free from the guilt of sin.

> "God demonstrates His own love toward us in that
> while we were yet sinners, Christ died for us. Much
> more then, having now been justified by His blood,
> we shall be saved from the wrath of God through
> Him." (Romans 5:8-9)

Righteousness

Through the cross of Jesus Christ we have been made acceptable to God. It's all because of His gracious lovingkindness.

> "He made Him who knew no sin to be sin on our
> behalf, so that we might become the righteousness of
> God in Him."
> (2 Corinthians 5:21)

Reconciliation

The Cross put us into a right relationship with God. We can be at peace in our relationship with God.

> "It was the Father's good pleasure for all the fullness
> to dwell in Jesus and through Him to reconcile all

things to Himself, having made peace through the blood of His cross." (Colossians 1:19-20)

"Now all these things are from God, who reconciled us to Himself through Christ and gave us the ministry of reconciliation, namely, that God was in Christ reconciling the world to Himself, not counting their trespasses against them, and He has committed to us the word of reconciliation." (2 Corinthians 5:18-19)

Freedom from Sin Nature

"If we have become united with Him in the likeness of His death, certainly we shall also be in the likeness of His resurrection, knowing this, that our old self was crucified with Him, in order that our body of sin might be done away with, so that we would no longer be slaves to sin: for he who has died is freed from sin...Consider yourselves to be dead to sin, but alive to God in Christ Jesus." (Romans 6:5-7, 11)

"For this reason the Father loves Me, because I lay down My life so that I may take it again. No one has taken it away from Me, but I lay it down on My own initiative. I have authority to lay it down, and I have authority to take it up again." (John 10:17-18)

If you don't believe in the work that Jesus did on the cross for you there is nothing you can do about your sinful nature and fallen state. That's why we joyfully take seriously the provisions of the cross – we believe them, receive them and apply their truths to all the ministry areas targeted in SoulCare.

Exploring each of the targeted areas (*Unforgiveness, Generational Patterns and Curses, Ungodly Thought Patterns, Healing Life's Hurts, Demonic Interference*) with the help of the Holy Spirit helps us clean up and grow up. Many find freedom from being "stuck" as they engage with and embrace God's healing work through this process.

CHAPTER 6

THE POWER OF PERSPECTIVE

"…to all who are beloved of God (in Rome), called as saints: Grace to you and peace from God our Father and the Lord Jesus Christ."
Romans 1:7

"I have been crucified with Christ; and it is no longer I who live, but Christ lives in me; and the life which I now live in the flesh I live by faith in the Son of God, who loved me and gave Himself up for me."
Galatians 2:20

HOW WE THINK ABOUT OURSELVES AND OTHER people when we approach pastoral care is really important. We will either have compassion and patience or we will be merciless, impatient and judgmental. We will either see others and ourselves from Jesus' viewpoint or we will see them as they are acting in the flesh and judge them. Do we see ourselves as a saint or a sinner?

Judging never healed anyone.

Judging never healed anyone. In fact it works in opposition to healing because most usually when we are judged our first reaction is to get defensive. When that happens it becomes difficult to gain God`s perspective because we have moved from living in the Spirit to living in the flesh. God didn't send His Son to condemn the world, but that the world through Him would be saved. (John 3:16-17) Remember, salvation means to be saved *out from under the Devil's power and restored into the wholeness of God's order and well being by the power of God's Spirit.* In a real sense, Jesus came to rescue us from the work of the Devil.

A few years ago I had a major shift in my thinking about my relationship with Jesus and it greatly affected how I view people coming for pastoral care.

I grew up in a very religious, legalistic culture. I would go to the altar over and over again asking forgiveness when I had sinned. I would feel "clean" until I messed up again. Then I would think I needed to start over again with God. Sound familiar to anyone? A reoccurring thought I had was "I'm just a terrible sinner and I always will be. There is something wrong with me that I keep messing up. Why do I keep doing what I don't want to do?" (Romans 7:18-19) I would feel defeated and helpless most of the time. I felt caught in a trap, knowing there was more but didn't know how to get there. Jesus said you will know the truth and the truth will set you free. (John 8:32) What truth was I missing? I certainly wasn't experiencing freedom in some areas of my life.

Reading Romans didn't help much because I didn't understand it. But I could identify with Paul in his wrestling with moving out of the old man's way of thinking into the new, and his frustration with his behavior. If I am indeed a new creation, why do I keep doing what is wrong (sinning)? (1 Corinthians 5:17; Romans 7:18-19) How do I get out of this dilemma?

So I kept pressing in and asking the Holy Spirit to teach me, being willing to be challenged in my thinking and to lay down the perceptions that were not godly. In some teachable moments the Holy Spirit began to open my ability to see things from His perspective rather than the religious, legalistic way that was taught and modeled for me. I had a paradigm shift. It was like getting a new prescription for my glasses, getting new lenses and being able to see things in focus.

There has been a continual controversy over this issue in the history of the church: When a person becomes a believer, are they considered to be a saint, or still a sinner? I thought, "Well if I sin I must be a sinner. I should call myself a sinner." So I thought like a sinner. "There is no hope for lasting change. This is who I am so no wonder I act this way; this is my identity." My core identity remained "I am a sinner."

I went through the scriptures and marked every place believers were called "saints" and was amazed. Could this be true? Does God see me as a saint? If I am a saint, why do I continually feel disqualified and think I will never measure up? I knew the way I had been thinking wasn't working for me and I needed a change. For Romans 12:2 to be true for me (be transformed by the renewing of your *mind*) I had to change my thought patterns. If you want your life to change, to be more like Jesus, you will need to change the way you think.

Change your thoughts … Change your life!

Allowing the Word of God to reshape what you think to be true about God, others and yourself is a transforming, healing process. When we see life's hurtful experiences through a filter that doesn't include God's perspective (His Word), we develop ungodly thought patterns. Adopting a sinner mentality as my core identity hindered me from embracing God's grace to be the saint He says I am.

This change has been a process for me. I moved from "I'm just a sinner" to "I'm a sinner saved by grace" (which is true) to "I'm a saint *learning* how to be a saint." It totally transformed areas of my thinking, which in turn affected my feelings and my behavior.

I realized that I didn't really know my identity in Christ even after being a Christian for almost all of my life. Learning what it means to have an exchanged life is continuing to set me free! "I have been crucified with Christ. It is no longer I who live, but Christ who lives in me. And the life I now live in the flesh I live by faith in the Son of God who loved me and gave himself for me." (Galatians 2:20)

The Epistles began to make sense in new ways as I read and re-read them. Some will point out that Paul referred to himself as the foremost of sinners, which he did in 1 Timothy 1:15. This reference was made in the context of his life before he experienced the touch of Jesus that opened his eyes to who Jesus was and eventually to Paul's true identity. (Acts 9) Remember Paul thought he was doing what he should to be a good Jew, killing Christians – men, women and children. Can you imagine the guilt and shame Paul had to work through when he realized what he had done?

In both 1 Timothy 1 and 1 Corinthians 15 Paul refers to this former life, the life of a sinner. He quickly adds "But by the *grace* of God I *am* what I am, and His *grace* to me was not without effect." (1 Corinthians 15:10) Paul embraced an understanding that he had a NEW identity and the old life of Paul (the life of a legalistic murderer) no longer could identify him. He began to live his life as determined by his new identity *IN* Christ. Studying through the Epistles noting the phrase "in Christ" will revolutionize the way you think – and that will affect your behavior. I highlighted every "in Christ" reference and habituated myself in them daily. This change in my thought patterns was both an initial revelation to me, as well as an ongoing process of repetition and rehearsal to establish this new way of thinking. New thinking led to new feelings that led to new behaviors. I was finally having the breakthrough I'd been seeking all those years.

The phrase "by the grace of God" caught my attention and I looked up the word *grace* to make sure I understood it. I had always heard the definition of grace to be "unmerited favor". While it is that, the studies from *Oxford Dictionary of the Christian Church, Thayer's Lexicon* and *Zodhiates Word Study Dictionary* add a needed understanding that helps us as believers learn how to live the exchanged life. These are some of the phrases from these sources that helped me form a working definition of grace that has changed my life. My added notes for emphasis are in italics.

"Grace of God" from the *Oxford Dictionary of the Christian Church:* [19]

63

- "The supernatural assistance of God bestowed upon a rational being with a view to his sanctification." (*Sanctification is the process in which my mind, will and emotions are brought into an understanding of holiness and righteousness with God. This work has been done IN Christ, and is now being worked out and walked out as we learn how to walk in the Spirit. Philippians 2:13*)

- "Sovereign divine favor shown towards man."

- "Divine energy (*dunamis power!*) working in the soul." (*Note – the soul, our mind, will and emotions, is the area of our being that needs transformation after our spirits have been made brand new in accepting Jesus as Lord and Savior.*)

Thayer's Greek-English Lexicon of the New Testament: [20]

- G5485 – Charis – translated grace. "Of the merciful kindness by which God, exerting his holy influence upon souls, turns them to Christ, keeps, strengthens, increases them in Christian faith, knowledge, affection and kindles them to the exercise of the Christian virtues." (*Note how the influence on our souls by God through the gift of grace keeps turning our attention to the character of Jesus present within us to transform us. The Fruit of the Spirit is being formed because of His divine influence and power. Kindness is emphasized throughout the definition – not judgment. God didn't send Jesus into the world to condemn the world, but that the world would be saved through Him. John 3:16-17*)

- "Grace sets you up for a spiritual condition as of one *governed* by the *power* of *divine grace*. Grace is the aggregate of the extremely diverse powers and gifts granted to Christians."

- *Zodhiates Word Study Dictionary* [21]

- "The divine influence upon the heart and its reflection in the life."

Can you see the depth of the meaning of grace that God has given as a gift is so much more than what most of us have been taught?

The concept of grace we embrace enables us to see one another in the Spirit and empowers us to embrace the truth of who Christ is in us and who we are in Him. How we understand grace has the power to launch us into a Holy Spirit-empowered ability to walk in the Spirit.

> Certainly grace is not a license to sin. It *is* a gift to be embraced and applied to our daily life as we realize the divine influence that is available at all times and dwelling within us.

Certainly grace is not a license to sin. It *is* a gift to be embraced and applied to our daily life as we realize the divine influence that is available at all times and dwelling within us. As we cooperate and yield to this grace, we become like Jesus in character and conduct.

The working definition from which I operate in light of this word study is this: *Grace is God's divine supernatural power that indwells us and empowers us to walk in newness of life.* This is Philippians 2:13 in action – "*it is God who is at work in you,* both to will and to work for His good pleasure."

This is THE BIG EXCHANGE! His life for my old one! Christ now lives in me. I have died and my life is now hidden WITH Christ IN God! (Colossians 3:3). Wow!

To top it off, I have God's supernatural DNA, His divine nature, living in me, empowering me with everything I need to live a godly life. (2 Peter 1:3-4)

I am identified *with* Christ:

in His death (Romans 6:3,6; Galatians 2:20; Colossians 3:1-3),

in His burial (Romans 6:4),

in His resurrection (Romans 6:5, 8, 11),

in His life (Romans 5:10,11),

in His power (Ephesians 1:19, 20)

in His inheritance (Romans 8:16, 17; Ephesians 1:11, 12)

When I was born again my spirit was made new and God saw me as holy and blameless, as a brand new person. (Ephesians 1:4) This does not mean I am sinless. There is only one who is sinless – Jesus Christ. (Hebrews 4:15; 2 Corinthians 5:21; 1 John 3:5; 1 Peter 2:22) Sin *can* continue to dwell in my body and make its appeal. (Romans 6:7, 14) I have the *Power to Choose*, the option of saying no to that appeal based on God's divine supernatural power that indwells me and empowers me to walk in newness of life! I sin in direct relationship to old mindsets that have not been destroyed and renewed according to the mind of Christ. While my spirit was made brand-new, my soul needs transformation. That's why the Scripture instructs us to be transformed by the renewing of our minds. (Romans 12:2)

The *power* of sin was broken at the Cross of Jesus Christ. The power of the cross has provided a way for me to choose to be who I am *in* Christ, and to set my will to choose truth. The Holy Spirit leads us into all truth (John 16:13) and that is what sets us free from all the old man ways of thinking. The truth is a person – Jesus Christ – and He lives in me. I *choose* to yield to Him and let Him live His life in and through me instead of me living by my own choices.

My new *position* in Christ solves the problem of the "old" me – my old sin nature. I am now new. Knowing our position is powerful. Our position is IN Christ and He is in us! (Ephesians 2:4-9) Our *posture* remains one of humility, agreeing with God when He says we are a new creation and He sees us as holy and blameless. This is lived out in *presentation*. How are we going to present Jesus to the world around us as he lives His life through us? Are we presenting the nature and character of Jesus as He really is? Are we letting the expression of the Fruit of the Spirit be revealed as we interact with people on a daily basis? We are representing the Father, Son and Holy Spirit to those in our realm of influence. We must know our *position, posture and presentation* as we embrace our identity in Christ. Let's find out who we really are *in* Christ and just let Him *be* that in, for and through us. This is so much easier than trying to perform like a Christian, failing and feeling guilty in the process. Paul says there is "no condemnation for those who are *in* Christ Jesus" because through Jesus Christ we have been set free from the law of sin and death. (Romans 8:1-2)

THOUGHTS DEFINE OUR DESTINY

When I think like a sinner, I focus on my *behavior*, always failing and not measuring up. I think surely if I can make myself do the right thing everything will be okay. When I think like a saint – a new creation that is indwelt and empowered by His life – I am focusing on His Presence indwelling me and *being* who He says I am. Then my behavior begins to reflect who I already am *in* Him. At the end of this section I have included "Christ In Me Is…" and "In Christ I Am…," some declarative statements about our identity in Christ and who Christ is in us. Reflecting on, rehearsing and repeating these truths until you are habituated in them will change your life! Rehearsing these truths means to practice them until they become automatic in your thinking, feeling and behaving. When I began to learn to focus on having my mind renewed to agree with Him and let Him take His place *in* me, transformation took an accelerated turn.

> The way we live our life is determined by what we believe to be true about God, about others, and especially about ourselves.

The way we live our life is determined by what we believe to be true about God, about others, and especially about ourselves.

C. S. Lewis is quoted as saying "We are what we believe we are." [22] Perhaps you remember the story told in Numbers 13 when Moses sent men to spy out Canaan. The spies encountered not only an abundance of fruit and a land flowing with milk and honey, but residents who were giants and strong warriors. The majority took the position they couldn't take possession of the land because when they saw the men of great size they "became like grasshoppers in our own sight, and so we were in their sight." A powerful perspective that did not take into account God's equation for victory. *PAL: "Holy Spirit, what am I believing about myself that hinders your destiny for me?"*

If you *believe* you are a saint, you think like one, feel like one, and behave like one. The reverse is true. If you continue to believe you are a sinner, you will continue to think like one, feel like one, and behave like one. Continuing to have the mindset of a sinner is contrary to the mind of Christ, which is in you. (1 Corinthians 2:16) Eventually you will have built ungodly strongholds that will need to be torn down. (2 Corinthians 10:3-5)

A sinner mentality calls forth unworthiness, shame, false guilt, inadequacy, envy, perfectionism, legalism, and strife. A saint mentality calls forth victory, freedom, being more than a conqueror, being a joint heir with Jesus, holiness, righteousness, forgiveness, acceptance, love, peace, patience, gentleness, and self-control. You get the idea. When I accept myself as a sinner, my core identity is sin.

As a believer I am justified by faith…I am no longer identified as a sinner. In scripture, believers are referred to as brothers, children, sons of God, light in the Lord and saints – not as sinners. We have a new core identity. We are *IN* Christ. When we act otherwise, we must recognize it is the old nature making its appeal to us to sin. We can then confess and ask for forgiveness.

PAL: "Holy Spirit, what thought led to that behavior? Holy Spirit will you lead me to the truth?"

PAL: "Father, I have sinned against you by _____. Will you please forgive me? I receive your forgiveness. Holy Spirit what truth would you like to share with me about what thought(s) led to my sinful behavior? I want to receive your thoughts so I can renew my mind and be like Jesus. Thank you for helping me."

Because of the shift in my belief system I can now boldly say I am a saint who sometimes sins. When I sin I have provision made by Jesus's shed blood on the cross to confess and receive forgiveness and cleansing. (1 John 1:9). I want to see myself as God sees me – holy and blameless, forgiven and redeemed. I recognize that my spirit is brand NEW and my soul is going through a sanctification process where all the old way of thinking is getting torn down and replaced with the mind of Christ. I am being transformed by the renewal of my mind. (Romans 12:2) I am no longer defined by or a product of my past. I have a new identity IN Christ and He is empowering me to embrace and live in that new identity. I am a saint learning how to be a saint. I give you grace to do the same. We say frequently in our gatherings (we are habituating ourselves in this truth) "I am Dead to sin, Alive to God, and I'm Walking in newness of life!" I think we say it so much some of us wake up in the night saying it. That's what we want!

You know the old saying, "You can't give away what you don't have?" That was certainly true for me in pastoral care. With this understanding of our new nature that calls forth saints learning to be saints, our identity *in* Christ and our understanding of who He is, pastoral care definitely takes on a direction that can lead to deeper healing and lasting freedom. Asking the Lord Jesus to help me see people like He sees them enables me to know what He wants to impart and what He wants to heal. I can begin to ask the Holy Spirit what hindrances are blocking their true identity and help lead them to Jesus for healing. When I begin there I have more patience and compassion. Sometimes I have to remind myself who the real Enemy is and go to war with that Enemy – it is not "flesh and blood but against the rulers, authorities, the powers of this dark world and against the spiritual forces of evil in the heavenly realms." (Ephesians 6:12) The Enemy doesn't want any of us set free, but Jesus does – and He is definitely the Greater One!!

PRAYER of DECLARATION

To begin and continue to renew your mindset and identity from a sinner to a saint declare the following prayer:

"I renounce the lie that I am just a sinner, or just a sinner saved by grace. I acknowledge that I am a saint not due to any effort on my part but because of my redemption in Christ. I receive and appropriate my new identity in Christ as a saint and I choose to do so by faith. I ask you to fill me with Your Holy Spirit and enable me to live out my true identity as a saint so I may not sin. I choose to walk in the light that I may glorify You. I thank you for the gift of Grace: Your divine supernatural power that indwells me and empowers me to walk in newness of life. I pray this in the name of my Lord and Savior, Jesus Christ. Amen!"

CHAPTER 7

THE POWER OF CHOICE

"…Choose life in order that you may live…" Deuteronomy 30:19

"God's way is the best way. I am free to choose any way I want, but I'm not free to avoid the consequences of my choices. My life right now is the sum total of the choices I have made. I cannot choose what other people say and do, but I am free to choose how I respond to what others say and do that affect me. Right now, I am experiencing my life as a result of the responses I have chosen."
Pastor Ron Allen

TODAY, MY LIFE IS A PRODUCT OF THE CHOICES I have made over my lifetime. It is hard to embrace that truth, especially if we have had traumatic events in our lives when others have sinned against us and wounded us. We are ready to heal when we quit blaming others for our problems and begin to *PAL*: *"Holy Spirit what is in me that you want to change to be like Jesus? What fruit of the Spirit is missing in my understanding of the Exchanged Life? What patterns of thinking have brought me to this place of desperation and being stuck? What do you want to reveal to me?"*

This posture in no way says all the things done to you were okay, but it does bring you out of a problem-oriented mindset into a solution-oriented mindset. Now God can begin to do the work of imparting His perceptions about your choices and your situations, changing and transforming you to look like Jesus Christ.

Blaming others for the way we are is the way a victim thinks. If you find yourself thinking any of these thoughts, please consider reevaluating your position. *PAL: "Holy Spirit is there is another way for me to think about this situation/person?"* Realize that you do have the *Power to Choose* something different. You can choose what God says!

A victim says:

> *I am stupid.*
>
> *I am always wrong.*
>
> *I'll never be good enough.*
>
> *Why are they acting this way…they are sooo stupid, selfish, hateful, etc.*
>
> *God is mean and unjust in my situation.*
>
> *God is distant…there for others, but not for me.*
>
> *I'm not capable.*
>
> *I'm not as good as…*
>
> *My opinions never count, so I'll keep them to myself.*
>
> *I can't do this…someone else needs to do this for me. They are better at it. I'll just mess it up anyway.*
>
> *If they would just… then I could/would… (Excuses)*
>
> *This isn't my fault.*
>
> *I will never fulfill my potential.*
>
> *I will never fulfill my destiny.*
>
> *This won't work for me.*
>
> *I've always been this way.*

I will always be this way.

My whole family is like this.

I've never done it this way before…it won't work.

I already asked God for that and nothing happened and it never will.

I tried that once.

Sometimes you just have to learn to live with it.

If God doesn't heal me we will be planning a funeral.

I've never heard of anyone being healed of this.

This disease just runs in our family.

Habitually thinking in these ways releases negative feelings about others and ourselves. We begin to behave and talk like a victim. God says we are victorious and more than conquerors – not victims. (Romans 8:37)

It is very freeing to realize that other people do not get to define you. Your past failures, sins and disappointments do not get to define you. Your circumstances do not get to define you. Your Enemy does not get to define you. Your critics do not get to define you. Your friends and family do not get to define you. Only God, in His infinite wisdom, gets to define who you are and what you do in life.

When God created us, He created us as free moral agents with the power to choose. This is the function of the will. We all choose every day what we think, how we feel, how we behave, and how we talk.

I am convinced that our feelings and behavior are determined by our belief system. What we believe to be true is so powerful it can either lead us into our God-designed destiny or into dysfunction and destruction. This dynamic is explored further in the "*Ungodly Thought Patterns*" section.

Whether I am working through a personal challenge or listening to someone as a pastor, I try to keep these two formative questions in mind:

What kinds of thoughts are producing these feelings?

What kinds of thoughts produce this kind of behavior?

I do not go into sessions with the goal of changing their behavior to line up with Scripture. God isn't about fixing up our old nature so we can behave properly. He killed the old nature, got rid of it, put it in the grave. Then He created a new man. We are a new creation! We have His divine nature within us now. (Romans 6, 2 Corinthians 5:17, 2 Peter 1:4) My goal is to help the person change their thinking to line up with God's truth so their feelings, behavior and talk will look and sound like Jesus. Behavior is certainly important and we are not free to act any way we feel like. But as we are being healed, we must go to the root cause of the behavior for lasting transformative results. Self-control is one of the Fruit of the Holy Spirit. Jesus is available to be that in, for, and through us as we embrace His life exchanged for ours.

Sometimes we think it is too hard to choose God's way. It seems impossible. The truth is that without Him and His indwelling presence empowering us, it is impossible. Instead He partners with us to choose His way. Take a look at this scripture with me.

"This command I am giving you today is *not too difficult for you*, and it is not beyond your reach. It is not kept in heaven, so distant that you must ask, 'Who will go up to heaven and bring it down so we can hear it and obey?' It is not kept beyond the sea, so far away that you must ask, 'Who will cross the sea to bring it to us so we can hear it and obey?' No, the message is very close at hand; it is on your lips and in your heart so that you can obey it… "Today I have *given you the choice between life and death,* between blessings and curses. Now I call on heaven and earth to witness the choice you make. Oh, that you would *choose life,* so that you and your descendants might live! You *can* make this choice by *loving the Lord* your God, *obeying* him, and *committing* yourself firmly to him. This is the key to your life." (Deuteronomy 30:11-14; 19-20 NLT)

We can also make this affirmation along with the apostle Paul, "I can do all things [which He has called me to do] through Him who strengthens *and* empowers me [to fulfill His purpose—I am self-sufficient in Christ's sufficiency; I am ready for anything and equal to anything through Him who infuses me with inner strength and confident peace.]" (Philippians 4:13 AMP)

"I am the Vine; you are the branches. The one who remains in Me and I in him bears much fruit, for [otherwise] apart from Me [that is, cut off from vital union with Me] you can do nothing." (John 15:5 AMP)

Wow! That's the good news of the gospel of Jesus Christ. By ourselves, we are doomed. But with Jesus' presence indwelling us we are empowered to walk in newness of life. When we remain in His presence and allow Him to live His life in and through us, we will bear good fruit.

What an amazing encouragement for us. God gives us a choice between life and death, blessings or curses. What are you choosing today? Are you using the gift of the power of choice that will lead to blessings…or is your power of choice leading to curses in your life? What do you want? You have the power of choice!

You have the power of choice!

We get to choose every day whether we are going to respond to life according to the Spirit or according to the flesh. Will we allow Jesus to be the Fruit of the Spirit expressed through us in all of our situations and relationships? Paul says to the Galatians if you have begun in the Spirit why are you now trying to be like Jesus by walking in the flesh? (Galatians 3:3) It is a frustrating, impossible exercise! When we choose to follow Jesus and receive Him as our Lord and Savior, we commit to walking in newness of life. Paul is encouraging us that if we choose to begin in the Spirit, let's continue walking in the Spirit. That's the only way to become and stay free.

When God gave us the power of choice, He equipped us with the provision and the power to not only make a godly choice, but to apply the implications of the choice to our daily lives. It is the life of Jesus Christ living in and through us. "My old self has been crucified with Christ. It is no longer I who live, but Christ lives in me. So I live in this earthly body by trusting in the Son of God, who loved me and gave himself for me." (Galatians 2:20 NLT)

> God offers us gifts – so many gifts – and we get to choose whether to receive, embrace and apply them to life or reject them.

God offers us gifts – so many gifts – and we get to choose whether to receive, embrace and apply them to life or reject them. Let's choose life. SoulCare encourages people who are stuck and coming for help to make a decision to take responsibility for their life under the direction and empowerment of the Holy Spirit. Along with the Father, we invite everyone who comes seeking help to make the choice to learn to believe like Jesus believes so we can be and do what Jesus does.

Exercise your God-given power of choice to embrace life!

Remember…

God's way is the best way. I'm free to choose any way I want but I'm not free to avoid the consequences of my choices.

God is at work in my present circumstances to remove the wrong and impart the right, indwelling and empowering me so I can choose a willing heart towards Him as He forms the character and conduct of Jesus in me, so that the world may know the Father's love.

Pastor Ron Allen

CHAPTER 8

THE POWER OF CHRIST IN ME

I have been crucified with Christ; and it is no longer I who live, but Christ lives in me; and the life which I now live in the flesh I live by faith in the Son of God, who loved me and gave Himself up for me. Galatians 2:20

Christ In Me Is…
In Christ I Am…

I HAVE HAD SEVERAL PEOPLE TELL ME THEY USE the next sections *"Christ In Me Is…"* and *"In Christ I Am…"* for devotions. The truths in these scriptures are what we need to dwell on in our thought life so we believe, embrace and apply them daily. Using the tools of *Repetition* and *Rehearsal* with these scriptures will deepen your relationship with God and build your confidence as you learn how to walk as a saint. (See Chapter 20) They will become who you are. Realizing who Christ is in you and that He is in you 24/7 is a game changer. He truly is everything you need in every situation of your life. Knowing these truths helps you "see that His divine power has granted to us everything pertaining to life and godliness, through the true knowledge of Him who called us by His own glory and excellence." (2 Peter 1:3)

Take your time with each truth and meditate on it. *PAL: "Holy Spirit, would you help me see how You want to be this in me, for me and through me today?" "Holy Spirit, would you grace me to embrace this truth about myself that Your Word says is true? Would you help me see how I can apply it to my life today?"*

CHRIST IN ME IS...

The Creator of all things. (Colossians 1:16)

Holding All Things Together (Colossians 1:17)

The Head of the Church (Colossians 1:18)

The Alpha and Omega (Revelation 1:8, 22:13)

The Reconciler of all things in heaven and on earth (Colossians 1:20)

My Peace (Ephesians 2:14)

My Strength (Philippians 4:13)

My Portion (Psalm 119:57)

My Deliverer (Romans 11:26)

My Provider (1 Timothy 6:17)

My Healer (Luke 4:23)

The Great I AM (John 8:58)

The Bread of Life (John 6:35)

The Source of all Life (John 11:25, 14:6)

My Life (Colossians 3:4)

The Light of the World (John 1:1-9, 8:12, 9:5)

My Redeemer (Job 19:25, Isaiah 59:20, 1 Corinthians 1:30)

The Lifter of My Head (Psalm 3:3)

The Word (John 1:1, 14; Revelation 19:13)

The source of all the treasures of wisdom and knowledge (Colossians 2:3)

The Embodiment of the Fullness of the Godhead (Colossians 1:19)

The Author and Perfecter of my Faith (Hebrews 12:1)

ALL and IN ALL (Colossians 3:11)

My Advocate (1 John 2:1)

The Almighty (Revelation 1:8)

The Anointed One (Psalm 2:2, Daniel 9:25, Acts 4:25)

The High Priest (Hebrews 3:1)

My Banner (Isaiah 11:10, 12)

My Salvation (Luke 2:29-32)

The Bridegroom (Matthew 9:15, 25:1-13; John 3:29)

The Cornerstone (Matthew 21:42, 1 Peter 2:7)

The Good Shepherd (1 Peter 5:4, John 10:11)

The Chosen One (Isaiah 42:1, Luke 23:35)

The Christ (Matthew 1:16, 16:20, Mark 14:16, Luke 2:11, John 1:41, Acts 5:42)

The Lord (Luke 6:46, Acts 2:36, Romans 10:13)

The Great Physician (Luke 4:23, Matthew 9:12)

Eternal Life (1 John 5:20)

Everlasting Father (Isaiah 9:6)

Wonderful Counselor (Isaiah 9:6)

Prince of Peace (Isaiah 9:6)

The Exact Representation of God (Hebrews 1:3)

Faithful and True (Revelation 19:11)

Faithful Witness (Revelation 1:5)

My Foundation (1 Corinthians 3:11)

Friend of Sinners (Matthew 11:19)

Gift of God (John 4:10, 2 Corinthians 9:15)

Glory of the Lord (Isaiah 40:5)

The Heir of All Things (Hebrews 1:2)

The Holy One of God (Psalm 16:10, Mark 1:24, John 6:69, Acts 2:27)

Wisdom of God (1 Corinthians 1:23)

Our Righteousness (1 Corinthians 1:30)

Our Holiness (1 Corinthians 1:30)

Our Hope (1 Timothy 1:1)

Our Hope of Glory (Colossians 1:27)

Immanuel (Isaiah 7:14, Matthew 1:23)

The King of Kings (Revelation 17:14, 19:16; 1 Timothy 6:15)

The King over All the Earth (Zechariah 14:9)

The Lamb of God (John 1:29, 1:36; Revelation 5:6-13, 6:1, 17:14, 21:22, 22:1)

The Living One (Revelation 1:18)

The Living Stone (1 Peter 2:4)

The Lord of All (Acts 10:36, Romans 12:12)

The Lord of Glory (1 Corinthians 2:8)

The Lord of lords (Revelation 17:14, 19:16; 1 Timothy 6:15)

The Lord of the Sabbath (Matthew 12:8)

Son of Man (John 12:34)

Man of Sorrows (Isaiah 53:3)

The Master (Matthew 23:8)

Our Mediator (1 Timothy 2:5, Hebrews 8:6, 9:15, 12:24)

Our Intercessor (Romans 8:34, Hebrews 7:25)

The Bright and Morning Star (Revelation 22:16)

The Messiah (John 1:41, 4:25)

The One Who Is, Was and Is to Come (Revelation 1:4, 8)

The One Who baptizes us with the Holy Spirit (Mark 1:7-8)

The Only Begotten Son of the Father (John 1:14, 3:16;
     1 John 4:9)

The Radiance of God's Glory (Hebrews 1:3)

A Ransom for us all (1 Timothy 2:5-6)

Our Refiner (Malachi 3:3)

The Resurrection (John 11:25)

The Righteous Judge (Acts 10:42, 2 Timothy 4:8)

The Righteous One (Acts 3:14, 7:52, 22:14; 1 John 2:1)

The Rock (1 Corinthians 10:4, 1 Peter 2:8)

The Ruler of God's Creation (Revelation 3:14)

Our Savior (Luke 2:11, John 4:42, Acts 5:31, 13:23; 2 Timothy 1:10,
     Titus 2:13, 2 Peter 1:11)

The Teacher (Matthew 19:16, 23:10, John 11:28, 13:13)

The Truth (John 14:6)

The Vine (John 15:1)

The Way (John 14:6)

IN CHRIST I AM…

I am His possession. (Deuteronomy t 4:20, 7:6, 26:18; Exodus 19:5,
   1 Peter 2:9)

I am a royal priesthood. (Exodus 19:6, 1 Peter 2:9)

I am alive to God. (Romans 6:11)

All grace abounds towards me. (2 Corinthians 9:8)

All sufficiency is in me through Him. (2 Corinthians 3:5, Philippians 4:19,
   Colossians 1:15-20)

I am anointed. (1 John 2:20, 27, 2 Corinthians 1:21)

I am the apple of God's eye. (Zechariah 2:8, Psalm 17:8)

As He is, so are we on this earth. (1 John 4:17)

I am baptized into one Spirit. (1 Corinthians 12:13)

I am baptized into Christ and His death. (Romans 6:1-4)

I am being protected. (John 10:28-30, 2 Thessalonians 3:3,
   Deuteronomy 31:6, Psalm 46:1)

I am loved. (Romans 1:7, 5:8, 8:37-39, Ephesians 2:4-5, 1 Thessalonians 1:4,
   Zephaniah 3:17)

I am blameless in His sight. (Colossians 1:22, Ephesians 1:4, 5:27)

I am blessed with all spiritual blessings. (Ephesians 1:3)

I have comfort and bold access to the throne of God. (Hebrews 4:16, 10:19)

I am born again of God. (John 3:3, 1 John 5:18, 1 Peter 1:23)

I am bold as a lion. (Proverbs 28:1)

I am part of the Bride of Christ. (Ephesians 5:27, 2 Corinthians 11:2,
   John 3:29)

I was buried with Christ in His death. (Romans 6:4, Colossians 2:12)

I can do all things in Christ. (Philippians 4:13)

I am chosen. (Colossians 3:12, Ephesians 1:4)

I am part of a chosen generation. (1 Peter 2:9)

Christ indwells me with all his fullness. (Colossians 1:19, 2:9; Ephesians 3:17)

I am a co-heir with Christ. (Galatians 4:7, Romans 8:17)

I was created for good works. (Ephesians 2:10)

I am curse-free. (Galatians 3:13, Romans 8:2)

I am dead to sin. (Romans 6:6-11, Colossians 3:3, 2 Timothy 2:11)

I have died with Christ. (Colossians 2:20)

I am raised with Christ. (Colossians 3:1, Ephesians 2:6-7, Romans 6:4)

I am declared holy. (Colossians 1:22, 1 Corinthians 6:11, 1 Peter 1:16)

I am a disciple of Jesus. (Matthew 28:19, Luke 14:27, Acts 26:28)

I am enriched (in all knowledge). (1 Corinthians 1:5, 2 Corinthians 9:11)

I belong to God. (Philippians 3:12)

I am faithful. (1 Timothy 1:12, Revelation 2:10, Galatians 5:22-23)

I am a fellow-citizen. (Ephesians 2:19)

I am free. (John 8:36, Galatians 5:1, Acts 13:38-39, Luke 4:18)

I am free from sin. (Romans 6:22, 8:1-4)

He has freely given me all things. (Romans 8:32, 1 Corinthians 2:12,
     2 Peter 1:3)

I am a friend of Christ. (John 15:13, 15)

I am fruitful. (John 15:5)

I am gifted. (1 Corinthians 7:7)

I am a habitation of God. (Ephesians 2:22)

I have the mind of Christ. (1 Corinthians 2:16, Philippians 2:5)

God is at work in me. (Philippians 1:6, 2:13)

He is for me, not against me. (Romans 8:31, Psalm 118:6)

I am healed. (1 Peter 2:24, Isaiah 53:4, Psalm 103:1-5)

I am hidden in Christ. (Colossians 3:3)

I am highly favored. (Ephesians 1:3, 3 John 1:2, Proverbs 10:22)

We are His body. (1 Corinthians 12:27, Romans 12:5)

I am His workmanship. (Ephesians 2:10)

We are a holy nation. (1 Peter 2:9)

I am increasing in the knowledge of God. (Colossians 1:10, 2 Peter 3:18)

I am inseparable from the love of God. (Romans 8:35-39)

I am justified. (Romans 5:1, Galatians 2:16)

The Kingdom of God is within me. (Luke 17:20-21)

I am known by Him. (1 Corinthians 8:3, 13:12)

I am lacking in nothing. (Psalm 23:1, James 1:4)

I am the light of the world. (Matthew 5:14-16)

I am living and walking by faith. (2 Corinthians 5:7, Galatians 2:20,
     Hebrews 11:6)

I live by God's Word. (Psalm 86:11, Matthew 4:4, John 8:31-32, Ephesians 6:17)

I am a living stone. (1 Peter 2:5)

I am made in His image. (Genesis 1:27)

I am made rich in everything. (2 Corinthians 9:11, 6:10)

I am more than a conqueror. (Romans 8:37, 1 Corinthians 15:57, 1 John 5:4)

I am a new creation. (2 Corinthians 5:17)

I have a sound mind. (2 Timothy 1:7)

I am ordained. (John 15:16, Ephesians 2:10)

I am a different person. (1 Peter 2:9, Colossians 3:10, 2 Corinthians 3:18)

I am purified. (1 John 3:3, Hebrews 10:22, Ephesians 2:1-22)

I am filled with resurrection life. (Philippians 3:10, Colossians 1:29, Galatians 2:20, Ephesians 3:17)

I am redeemed. (Colossians 1:14, Isaiah 43:1, Ephesians 1:7, Romans 3:24-26)

I am the righteousness of God in Christ. (2 Corinthians 5:21, Romans 3:21-31)

I am a saint. (Ephesians 1:18, 2 Peter 1:4)

I am the salt of the earth. (Matthew 5:13)

I am sanctified. (1 Thessalonians 5:23-24, 2 Thessalonians 2:13, 1 Corinthians 1:30, 6:11; Hebrews 10:10)

I am saved. (Acts 16:31, Romans 10:9-10, John 3:16, 10:28-30; Ephesians 2:8, Hebrews 7:25)

I am seated with Him in heavenly places. (Ephesians 2:6-7)

I am a servant of God. (John 12:26, 13:12-15; Philippians 2:5-8, 1 Corinthians 4:1)

I share His authority. (Matthew 16:19, Mark 11:23, Luke 10:19, John 14:12, Acts 1:8, 1 John 4:4)

I am a sheep of His pasture. (Psalm 95:7, 100:3; Ezekiel 34:31)

I am a shining star. (Philippians 2:15)

I am a son of God. (Galatians 3:26, 4:6-7; John 1:12, Romans 8:14-16, 2 Corinthians 6:18, 1 John 3:1-2)

I am a son of light. (1 Thessalonians 5:5, Ephesians 5:8, John 12:36)

I am a steward of the mysteries. (1 Corinthians 4:1)

I am strengthened by Him. (Philippians 4:13, Ephesians 3:16,
    Colossians 1:11, 2 Corinthians 12:9-10, Isaiah 40:29, 31)

I am the fullness of life and godliness. (2 Peter 1:3, Colossians 2:9,
    John 1:16, Romans 15:29, Ephesians 1:23, 3:19)

I am the temple of God. (1 Corinthians 3:16-17, 6:19)

I am a vessel of glory. (2 Corinthians 3:18, Romans 9:23)

I am a vessel of honor. (Romans 9:21, 2 Timothy 2:21)

I am a citizen of heaven. (Philippians 3:20)

I am a slave of righteousness. (Romans 6:18)

I walk in newness of life. (Romans 6:4)

I am a warrior. (Psalm 18:39, 44:5; Ephesians 6:10-18)

I am wise. (Psalm 37:30, 1 Corinthians 1:30, James 1:5)

I am a witness. (Matthew 5:16, Acts 1:8, 4:20, 22:15; Romans 1:16,
    1 Peter 3:15)

I am an ambassador for Christ. (2 Corinthians 5:20)

I am forgiven. (Matthew 6:14-15, Ephesians 1:7, Colossians 1:14, 3:13)

"To You, oh Lord I bring my worship
And offering of love to You
Surrounded in Your holy presence
And all I can say is that I love You

Give ear to the groaning in my spirit
Hear the crying in my heart
Release my soul to freely worship
For I was made to give You honour

Holy, holy, holy, holy"

Craig Musseau, Mercy Publishing, 1992

PART 2

MINISTRY

CHAPTER 9

SoulCare

"Now may the God of peace Himself sanctify you entirely; and may your spirit and soul and body be preserved complete, without blame at the coming of our Lord Jesus Christ."
1 Thessalonians 5:23

THE SOULCARE PROCESS BEGINS WHEN WE RECognize we are stuck in our journey with Christ because of reoccurring habit patterns of thought, emotions and behaviors that produce ungodly fruit. Then we have an opportunity to demolish strongholds that hinder us from walking in the newness of life Christ has provided for us by His sacrifice on the Cross. Ungodly strongholds are spiritual fortresses of deceptive thought where demonic influences may hide and be protected. It is a perverted way of thinking that makes me a slave to the old me. Establishing godly strongholds provides a foundation of safety where God's thoughts can thrive and guide our thoughts, feelings and behaviors. We become established as a new creature, living and walking as saints.

Through focusing on a specific problem or heartfelt pain, SoulCare targets these areas of our lives for ministry:

Forgiveness
Generational Patterns
Word Curses
Vows
Bitter Root Judgments
Soul Ties
Judging God
Ungodly Thought Patterns
Healing Life's Hurts
Demonic Interference

A trained team (under pastoral supervision) prays and asks for a divine plan to systematically pray through the identified issue, targeting each area needing transformation and renewal.

The following biblical principles are included in prayers declared and embraced for each area of ministry:

Confession – agreement with God about our sin.

Repentance – changing our minds to agree with God and our intention to follow through with a change of behavior. The fruit of repentance is changed behavior – it requires action.

Forgiveness – an intentional choice to lay down our desire and requirement for any payment from or punishment for the offender.

Renounce – disowning the ungodly thought patterns, negatively expressed emotions and ungodly behavior and embracing what is godly.

Receive – embrace a gift from God to replace ungodly patterns.

Appropriation – the decision to put into practice the truth that has been revealed and received. God wants us to receive, apply and own the provisions, the realities and the victories of the Cross.

Declaration – a declarative statement based on God's truth about the ministry situation with an intention for change and growth.

The end result of ministering to the whole person is spiritual transformation. Transformation is the fruit of a renewed mind that is free from demonic interference. We are a community that is concerned, not only with learning and expressing God's gifts for ministry, but with growing and developing the Fruit of the Spirit in all areas of our lives. We want to clean up and grow up.

> We are a community that is concerned, not only with learning and expressing God's gifts for ministry, but with growing and developing the Fruit of the Spirit in all areas of our lives.

We like to say it this way at Heartland:

GOD IS AT WORK IN MY PRESENT CIRCUMSTANCES TO REMOVE THE WRONG AND IMPART THE RIGHT, INDWELLING AND EMPOWERING ME SO I CAN CHOOSE A WILLING HEART TOWARDS HIM AS HE FORMS THE CHARACTER AND CONDUCT OF JESUS IN ME, SO THAT THE WORLD MAY KNOW THE FATHER'S LOVE.

Pastor Ron Allen

We explored in *The Power of Forgiveness* (Chapter 4) the dynamic provision for each of the following targeted areas of ministry. Forgiveness flows from God to each of us, to each other and to ourselves.

Generational Patterns and Curses that have not been confessed can be a major stumbling block to breakthrough in our lives. Most of us don't like to think that we could be affected by our parents' and ancestors' sins; however, the Bible tells us that God "visits the iniquities of the fathers unto the third and fourth generations" (Exodus 20:5). Often we end up falling into the same sinful patterns that our parents struggled with (Please understand we are not blaming Mom and Dad to get ourselves off the hook!). What we have seen modeled is what we adopt as our own way to think, feel and behave. Our ancestors' choices can still affect us today. The good news is because of Jesus' sacrifice on the Cross, we can confess our sins and our ancestors' sins and break the power of curses and receive our inheritance as a citizen of the Kingdom of God. (Leviticus 26:40, Galatians 3:13) We can be free to make our own choices!

In connection with *Generational Patterns and Curses* we explore *Word Curses, Soul Ties, Bitter Root Judgments and Vows.*

All of us have beliefs that don't line up with God's truth. We call those *Ungodly Thought Patterns*, or personal beliefs that disagree with God's truth. These beliefs can hinder us from receiving lasting freedom in areas where we want to grow. How we think determines how we feel, which then affects our behavior. SoulCare places a high priority on discovering these beliefs and renewing them to agree with God so we see our lives and others from God's perspective. (Romans 12:2, Proverbs 23:7)

Gaining a new perspective is like getting a new lens prescription that enhances our ability to see more clearly. Sometimes we don't even know we aren't seeing clearly until we put the new glasses on our face and we can see so much better. We didn't know what we were missing. Paradigm shifts like this in the Kingdom of God move us from "old man" thinking to "new man" thinking when we begin to *PAL* for God's response to questions like *"What do you think about this? I've been thinking this way…is that ok with you?"* He loves to have dialogue with us and speak words of life to us that will draw us out of old habit patterns established in the old sin nature, so we can embrace a new way of living in the Spirit. "If you continue in My word, then you are truly disciples of Mine; and you will know the truth, and the truth will make you free." (John 8:31-32) Paradigm shifts in the Kingdom of God are normal because He is continually changing us from glory to glory. (2 Corinthians 3:18) Be ready for changes in your life as you follow Jesus!

> Paradigm shifts in the Kingdom of God
> are normal because He is continually
> changing us from glory to glory.

Many times painful situations from our past can hinder us from grow-ing and moving into the things God has for us. We adopt a perspective about the trauma/person/situation that is filtered through our woundedness, leaving us open and vulnerable to ungodly thinking. In *Healing Life's Hurts* we stand on God's promise that He is a God who "heals the broken-hearted and binds up our wounds." (Isaiah 61:1, Psalm 147:3)

We are especially vulnerable to the Enemy in times of trauma. Our defenses are down as we experience trauma in our physical bodies and souls. This is especially true of childhood trauma. As children we don't have much of the information we need to discern between a godly thought and a harmful, ungodly thought. We do not have the skills developed to process informa-tion correctly. Fear and doubt move into thoughts and allow fertile ground for ungodly strongholds that later have to be torn down.

One of the goals of SoulCare ministry is to identify and shut all of the open doors the Enemy might have to harass and oppress us in our walk as a new creation. This is *Demonic Interference*. The unconfessed Generational Patterns and Curses, unrecognized Ungodly Thought Patterns, and Life's Unhealed Hurts can create a dwelling place for the Enemy to hide and build strongholds. Strongholds exist because the Enemy has influenced thought patterns and reinforced them. Demons live in houses built of lies. Once the above areas have received ministry (recognition, confession, repentance, and renewal of the mind), the Enemy has no place to remain. He is left without a home! (2 Corinthians 10:5-6) With hindrances out of the way, renouncing and dismissal of the presence of demons is a much more fruitful process.

Three Scriptures are foundational to our understanding of ministering to the whole person:

> "The Spirit of the Lord God is upon me,
>   because the Lord has anointed me
>   to bring good news to the poor;
>   he has sent me to bind up the brokenhearted,
>   to proclaim liberty to the captives,
>   and the opening of the prison to those who are bound."
> (Isaiah 61:1, Luke 4)

Part of Jesus' mission was to heal the broken-hearted and set captives free. This describes every one of us to some degree at some point in our lives.

> "…Work out your salvation with fear and trembling;
>   for it is God who is at work in you, both to will and to
>   work His good pleasure." (Philippians 2:12-13)

This verse from Philippians describes grace at work…*God's supernatural indwelling presence that empowers us to walk in newness of life.* (This concept of grace was explored in "*The Power of Perspective*" Chapter 6.)

> "Is anyone among you sick? *Then* he must call for the elders of the church and they are to pray over him, anointing him with oil in the name of the Lord; and the prayer offered in faith will restore the one who is sick, and the Lord will raise him up, and *if he has committed sins, they will be forgiven him. Therefore, confess your sins to one another, and pray for one another so that you may be healed.* The effective prayer of a righteous man can accomplish much." (James 5:14-16)

This passage from James uses the word "healed" to mean both spiritual and physical healing. The Greek word is "*iaomai*" and means to "make whole, to free from errors and sins, to bring about one's salvation." [23] We are instructed to pray for the physically sick and to confess sins in order to be made whole. The word translated "salvation" (*sozo* in Greek) has a larger meaning than being saved from an eternity in hell. Jesus' provision for us includes the whole person.

> As a community we are learning to care for souls in a way that heals the broken-hearted and sets the captives free to walk in newness of life.

As a community we are learning to care for souls in a way that heals the broken-hearted and sets the captives free to walk in newness of life. (Romans 6:4)

PROMISES ARE CONDITIONAL

The gospel is simple, not complicated. But there are many promises of God we haven't even begun to put into practice or appropriate. As we embrace God's truth we get the hindrances from our past out of the way to experience the freedom we have been given through Christ's work on the Cross. This all is so that we can walk in the Spirit – that's Kingdom-of-God living!

2 Peter 1:2-9 beautifully describes a gift God has given us – His divine nature.

> "Grace and peace be multiplied to you in the knowledge of God and of Jesus our Lord; seeing that His divine power has granted to us everything pertaining to life and godliness, through the true knowledge of Him who called us by his own glory and excellence. For by these He has granted to us His precious and magnificent promises, so that by them you may become *partakers of the divine nature*, having escaped

the corruption that is in the world by lust. Now for this very reason also, applying all diligence in your faith supply moral excellence, and in your moral excellence, knowledge, and in your knowledge self-control, and in your self-control, perseverance and in your perseverance, godliness, and in your godliness, brotherly kindness, and in your brotherly kindness, love. For if these qualities are yours and are increasing, they render you neither useless nor unfruitful in the true knowledge of our Lord Jesus Christ. For he who lacks these qualities is blind or short-sighted, having forgotten his purification from his formers sins." (2 Peter 1:2-9)

God gives us the grace, His indwelling presence that empowers us to put the promises of the Gospel into practice through exercising faith and growing in character and conduct, to look like His Son Jesus Christ.

Promises are conditional. Most of the time God says if you will _____, then I will _____. The implication is if you *don't* _____, then I *won't* _____.

For example, Matthew 6:14-15: "If you forgive others for their transgressions, your heavenly Father will also forgive you. But if you do not forgive others, then your Father will not forgive your transgressions." Pretty clear and to the point!

One of my favorite examples of a conditional promise is from 2 Chronicles 7:14: "If My people who are called by My name humble themselves and pray and seek My face and turn from their wicked ways, then I will hear from heaven, will forgive their sin and will heal their land."

2 Corinthians 1:20 says to us that all the promises of God in Jesus are *yes* and amen. Until we say amen and agree with them, declaring them, and putting them into practice, they don't manifest themselves in our lives.

> "For as many as are the promises of God, in Him they are yes; therefore also through Him is our Amen to the glory of God through us."

To say "Amen" is to voice our agreement with God.

God's primary purpose for us as His children is that we be conformed into the image of Christ in character and conduct. (2 Corinthians 3:18) The first step in this process is to be "born again" or to be converted to think and be like Him. When we are born again, we "legally" become "holy" because God sees us through the eyes of the results of the Cross. (Colossians 1:22)

To be holy means to be separated, set apart, pure. God has two objectives in mind concerning holiness: to be pure and to be separated from the world to God. Peter tells us to *choose* to be like God in that he says "Be holy, because I am holy." (1 Peter 1:15-16) We also *begin* the process of *becoming* "holy" which is what the Bible calls sanctification.

PROCESS: SALVATION AND SANCTIFICATION

We *have been* saved, we *are* being saved and we *will be* saved.

Our concept of being "saved" is important to our understanding of how God works in our lives to sanctify us. The Greek work for saved or salvation is "sozo" and is found in the New Testament more than a hundred times. It means *"to be saved out from under the Devil's power and restored into the wholeness of God's order and well being by the power of God's Spirit"*.

A reading of Strong's Greek Lexicon and Vine's Expository Dictionary for "sozo" notes all of these meanings:

> *It means to be saved.*
> *It means to be healed.*
> *It means to be delivered.* [24]

It means to be provided for in every way. Salvation is for our whole being. It means all of these things at the same time. When we read about and talk about salvation for the believer we are encompassing all these provisions Jesus provided through His shed blood on the Cross:

Salvation
Healing
Deliverance

We experience salvation in all three tenses. The verb is the word used to express action. The verb tense is the form of the verb that tells when the action takes place. The past and perfect tenses tell us that the action took place in the past; that it has already happened. The present tense tells us the action is taking place now, in the present time. The future tense tells us that the action is yet to take place. [25]

Salvation in scripture is said to take place in all three of these tenses:

We *have been* saved. The work has been done.
> (1 Corinthians 6:11, Ephesians 2:8-9, 2 Timothy 1:9,
> Titus 3:4-7, John 5:24, 1 John 5:11-13)

We *are being* saved. Our salvation is progressive.
> (1 Corinthians 1:18, 1 Corinthians 15:1-2, 2 Corinthians 2:14-16,
> Philippians 2:12-13)

We *will be* saved. Jesus is coming again!
> (Romans 5:9-10, Mark 13:13, 1 Thessalonians 5:8, Revelation
> 2:11; 3:5, Revelation 2:10)

This Scripture puts some revelation on all three tenses of salvation:

> "Blessed be the God and Father of our Lord Jesus Christ, who according to His great mercy *has caused us to be born again to a living hope* through the resurrection of Jesus Christ from the dead, to obtain an inheritance which is imperishable and undefiled and will not fade away, *reserved in heaven for you*, who are protected by the power of God through faith for a *salvation ready to be revealed in the last time*. In this you greatly rejoice, even though now for a little while, if necessary, you have been distressed by various trials, so that *the proof of your faith*, being more precious than gold which is perishable, even though tested by fire, *may be found to result in praise and glory and honor at the revelation of Jesus Christ*; and though you have not seen Him, you love Him, and though you do not see Him now, but believe in Him, you greatly rejoice with joy

inexpressible and full of glory, *obtaining as the outcome of your faith the salvation of your souls.* (1 Peter 1:3-9)

Yes indeed, we have been saved, we are being saved, and we will be saved.

I like the way Chester and Betsy Kylstra say the "basic responsibility of the Holy Spirit is to promote, activate and energize the sanctification process in each of our lives." [26] We choose (remember we have the *Power to Choose*) to either cooperate or resist this work. We are all in process and need cleansing by the work of the Holy Spirit in our lives. Sometimes we get stuck…we find obstacles and barriers that keep us from getting past certain sins and patterns in our lives. Sometimes we need help from others in the body to pray for us. As referenced earlier in James 5:14-16, we are instructed to confess our sins and pray for one another so we can be healed. This is SoulCare in action!

It can be difficult for us to ask for help, even though we have fruit in our lives that is obviously not like Jesus. We may feel embarrassed or vulnerable. We may not know who is safe to trust. But I pose this question to ponder if someone is hesitating to reach out for help:

> *PAL: "Why am I trying to be a Christian if I don't want to be like Jesus?" "How desperate am I to be like Jesus?" "Do I want to pay the price of denying myself to be like Jesus in character and conduct?"*

God wants us to look like His dear Son, Jesus Christ. (2 Corinthians 3:18) We need to evaluate whether our desire to be like Christ is stronger than our fears of asking for help.

> Another *PAL: "Do I want to live the rest of my life like I am living right now?"*

If the answer is no, change is required. To be like Jesus is to let Him live His nature and character in and through us. The Exchanged Life! His life for ours. (Galatians 2:20)

We have misguided perceptions about receiving help, even though we find ourselves repeating behaviors that don't produce godly fruit. Some of those perceptions are:

> I am saved now, so I will reflect Jesus' image without intentionally working at it.

> I'm saved now, so my past doesn't affect me anymore. I can just forget about it.

These perceptions are a result of a misinterpretation of a truth expressed in 2 Corinthians 5:17. "Therefore if any man be in Christ, he is a new creature: old things are passed away; behold all things are become new."

People interpret this as "The Bible says I'm a new person now, my past is gone so I just need to forget it and move on." While this is true positionally, we have some work to do experientially in having our minds renewed and behaviors changed to reflect the nature of the One we are to be like.

We make ourselves hypocrites when we say things like, "Well I was made perfect when I was born again, so I don't need help." In reality our lives in no way reflect perfection. It produces legalism in a way that condemningly says, "Don't do as I do, do as I say". So how do we humble ourselves and ask for help?

Our self-talk produces condemnation, guilt and shame when we say we don't need help because we have been made new, but our daily lives reveal a different reality. The reality is our souls (our mind, will and emotions) need transformation from established habit patterns. The old habit patterns do not automatically change at our new birth.

After our spirits have been regenerated or made new, our souls go through the process of sanctification – being transformed into the image of Christ. We now deal with habit patterns of thought, feeling and behavior that have become automatic to us. We don't even think about them. We think, "This is the way I am" and "This is normal". Perhaps it would be helpful to read 2 Corinthians 5:17 this way, "All things have become new, all things are continuing to become new and all things will become new." This brings hope… it *is* possible to become more like Jesus every day! This reading recognizes a position made available because of the Cross and allows for the experience of the process that continues to make us new in our response to daily life. Our journey into wholeness is a continual, ongoing process.

By way of personal testimony, when I was five years old I was sexually abused. I was already a Christian at that time. I can witness that just because I was a Christian I did not automatically get over the effects and consequences of my responses and reactions to the abuse. Nor did I automatically get over it as I grew in my relationship with God. I have been healed as I have learned the importance of forgiving and learning how to think like God thinks. I am learning to ask for and embrace His perspective on the abuse and the abuser.

There is so much that is a part of the sanctification process that is continually leading us to a deeper understanding and experience of the Father's love for us. One consequence of the abuse for me has been difficulty trusting – trusting God, other people and at times even myself. I continue to grow in this area of my life because His grace is daily empowering me to walk in newness of life as I am being transformed into His likeness.

We take an active posture in becoming saved as we receive Him by faith. We are active in cooperating with the Holy Spirit, allowing the work of sanctification to make us more like Jesus Christ. We learn to engage in warfare, doing our part to put off the old man's nature and put on the new man's nature.

As we minister to the whole person, we begin to see how the way our ancestors thought and behaved affect us. Their emotional health might affect our thought and behavior patterns as well as our emotional health. We see how curses might have been activated through their disobedience to God. Sometimes we even say, "I'll never do what my parents did," not recognizing we are doing the same things. That's why taking an assessment of our family history is helpful. We *PAL*: *"Holy Spirit, what patterns of thought, emotional expression and behavior are in my life as a result of the influence of my ancestors?"*

We sometimes get a glimpse of how some ancestral patterns of behavior influence and cause deep hurts to the people we love the most. When the pressure to sin is yielded to, curses can be activated. This usually results in some form of abuse, abandonment or rejection that needs God's healing touch. While we can never undo or change what has happened, when the Holy Spirit is involved He releases a godly perspective that can change how we view what has happened. It's not about what has happened to us that will determine our future, but how we view what has happened to us and how we will walk in God's provisions of healing, salvation and deliverance. When we gain a godly perspective we gain the ability to walk in His provisions for freedom.

It's not about what has happened to us that will determine our future, but how we view what has happened to us and how we will walk in God's provisions of healing, salvation and deliverance.

Adopting ungodly patterns from our ancestors (entering into their sins) creates open doors for demonic interference. Demons are sent to rob, kill and destroy us. One of the ways they operate is to deceive us through ungodly generational patterns. Thought and behavior patterns keep getting stronger from generation to generation as they build momentum through habitual use. Strongholds that keep us from thinking from God's viewpoint are built and they must be destroyed and replaced. Continual, repeated sin allows for the presence of demons to continue the cycle that began with our forefathers.

If someone were to experience "deliverance ministry" without considering the generational patterns, ungodly thought patterns and life hurts that are not healed, the demonic might still have a legal position to stay and influence the person's life. Any progress made during deliverance would be difficult to maintain if the other areas in the person's life are not taken to the Cross, and healing applied as needed.

CHAPTER 10

GENERATIONAL PATTERNS AND CURSES

"You shall not worship them (idols) or serve them; for I, the Lord your God,
am a jealous God, visiting the iniquity of the fathers on the children, on the
third and the fourth generations of those who hate Me."
(Exodus 20:5)

THE SECOND COMMANDMENT RECORDED IN
Exodus 20:4-6 is not only an exhortation about worshipping and serving idols,
but describes the consequence for those who practice that behavior. An idol
is anything or anyone we put our trust in other than the Lord Jesus Christ. An
idol can be any thing or any person that becomes more important to us than
our relationship with Jesus Christ. God says when that happens He will "visit
the iniquity of the fathers on the children to the third and fourth generations."
The good news is there is provision for confession and repentance, not only
for our own sins, but for the sins of our forefathers. It is good to remember
that we can also receive and experience God's loving kindness because of our
forefathers who chose to love God and keep His commandments, even to a
thousandth generation! (Exodus 20:6, Deuteronomy 7:9)

We all have ancestors who have chosen to sin, be disobedient to God.
A propensity (a strong natural tendency to do something) to sin in the same

way can become a habitual pattern of thought and behavior without even recognizing it as sin. We think it's 'just the way we are' and it is normal. As we begin to learn about thought patterns and behavior patterns that don't produce godly fruit, we recognize there are some ways we sin because it has been set up (unknowingly) by our forefathers' actions. Someone needs to repent for the sin against God and break the power of the consequence of the curses activated by not obeying God.

The "iniquity" spoken of in Exodus 20:5 includes the influence or pressure to sin as well as the actual act of committing the sin. Some choose to yield to the pressure or temptation and some choose to obey God. The important thing to remember is that with the help of the Holy Spirit we don't have to yield to the sin; we can choose to say yes to God!

Strong's Hebrew Lexicon defines iniquity as having the following characteristics: being lawless, twisted, distorted, perverted, acting wickedly, to be depressed by calamities, unrighteous, transgressor of the law, being contempt of the Divine law. [27] This is a condition of the heart for which only God can bring freedom and healing. It requires confession (agreeing with God concerning the condition of our heart), repentance (changing our mind to agree with God), and asking for and receiving forgiveness and cleansing for our sinful condition.

In the Exodus 20 passage we see that the result of disobeying God is a curse; it's the penalty for sin. The New Testament reveals that when Jesus Christ shed His blood at the Cross, the power of curses was broken. To receive that blessing, each person must receive, own and apply what Christ did. We do this by making confession (agreeing with God) about our ancestors' sins and repenting for them. We can then take responsibility for our own actions and repent, receiving forgiveness and cleansing so we are able to walk in the newness of life for which Jesus died.

There is a model presented in Scripture for confession, repentance, and receiving forgiveness. Leviticus 26:20-25 is one passage where we see this pattern described. In the first part of Leviticus 26 the Lord has laid out the penalties for disobedience to Him and then in verse 40, "*If* they confess their iniquity and the iniquity of their forefathers, in their unfaithfulness which they committed against Me, and also in their acting with hostility against Me…42

Then I will remember My covenant with Jacob…Isaac…and Abraham as well…45 That I might be their God."

1 Peter 1:18-19 says it this way, "You know that God paid a ransom to save you from the empty (futile) life you inherited from your ancestors. And the ransom he paid was not mere gold or silver. It was the precious blood of Christ, the sinless, spotless Lamb of God." (NLT)

God requires us to recognize and repent of the sin of entering into the sins of our ancestors, forgive them for the sin and the consequences of their sins in our lives. Then we are in a position to receive the freedom Christ has paid the penalty for and apply it to our lives.

The principle of repenting for the sins of forefathers is also illustrated by Daniel (Daniel 9), Ezra (Ezra 9), and Nehemiah (Nehemiah 2, 9). This demonstrated principle is identifying with our forefathers in their sin, repenting on their behalf and for ourselves to the degree we have entered into the same sin. God has a jealous heart for us. He wants us to always return to Him so He can be the covenant making God He promised to be for us if we obey Him. Throughout the Scriptures we see this heart of the Father for His children – "Please won't you come back to Me, listen to Me, and obey Me. I want relationship with you!"

> ## "Please won't you come back to Me, listen to Me, and obey Me. I want relationship with you!"

Jesus himself became a curse so that we can be free. (Galatians 3:13) On the Cross, he took onto Himself ALL our sins, all our ancestors' sins and all the consequences or curses of those sins. We receive and take as our own the benefits of the Cross as we confess and repent of sin and begin to apply the promises and provisions to our own life. Curses can be broken through the provision of the Cross.

Many of us have a tendency to sin in the same way our ancestors did. It is easier to recognize patterns of alcohol or drug abuse, or sexual abuse than some other patterns. But if we intentionally take a look at our family history when we are frustrated about our current behavior patterns, we might find similar patterns that were instilled into our way of life as habitual patterns. When something is a habit, we don't think about why or how we do it, we just do it. Sometimes demons see vulnerability as a result of ancestral behavior that is an invitation for them to come harass and influence our thinking and behavior. The Enemy takes every opportunity to rob, kill and destroy our lives. We are all such creatures of habit that we learn behavior just by watching it modeled. The old saying, "Monkey see, monkey do" is how we all learn. And we tend to think it is normal behavior, so we don't challenge it until it disturbs our way of life and keeps us from being free.

Some of the more common types of curses we experience as a result of our ancestors' sins are all kinds of abuse, substance abuse, abandonment, divorce, diseases and illnesses, all kinds of fears and sexual sins.

Please understand we are not looking for ways to blame our ancestors for our conditions and choices. We are endeavoring to understand our own behaviors so we can take responsibility for them and change with the help of the Holy Spirit indwelling us. Along with the Apostle Paul we sometimes cry out "Why do I do the things I don't want to do?" (Romans 7:15) We want to understand the Kingdom of God reality that we are indeed dead to sin, alive to God and are empowered by the indwelling Holy Spirit to walk in newness of life. (Romans 6:4, 11) We are being transformed into the likeness of Jesus Christ. (2 Corinthians 3:18)

When we minister to the *Generational Patterns and Curses* in a person's life we are taking back the territory that the Enemy has taken over. Sin, when not repented of, leaves an open door for the Enemy to function, influencing thought and behavior patterns. When we as believers learn to appropriate (receive, own and apply) the work Jesus did on the Cross we are taking what legally belongs to us out of the realm of the influence of the Enemy. When disobedience is repented of and we are forgiven and cleansed there is no room for the Enemy to stay. He is crowded out. We are God's dwelling place and He has made a way for us to prepare and maintain a clean heart for Him. Repenting of and breaking off the effects of the curses/sins of our forefathers is a step in crowding out the Enemy.

GENERATIONAL PATTERNS DEFINED

When we talk about generational patterns (the Bible calls these patterns sins or iniquities of our fathers) we are talking about the resulting consequences of all the sins of our forefathers. We inherit tendencies and vulnerabilities from our ancestors that can pressure us to think, feel and act in the same ways.

Generational patterns are tendencies to sin against God in particular ways, following the examples of those who have gone before us.

The effects of these patterns continue until we meet the condition prescribed in Leviticus 26:40-46 - confession of the ancestors' iniquities, repentance for ungodly behaviors and a yielding to the commandments of God. Notice this Scripture does not ask us to take responsibility *for* our ancestors' sins, but to recognize and confess them.

It is important to note that we are *not* doomed to repeat the same sins as our fathers – we may be pressured or have a tendency to act in the same manner, but we are not forced to. We have a free will. We can choose. We are each responsible for our own sin. The Bible makes it clear each person dies for their own sin, or lives with eternal life if they confess Jesus as Lord and walk in newness of life. Even if we have the worst of ancestors, we are not doomed because of their sin. Our own choices determine our relationship with God and our future. We don't have to suffer for what they did if we choose to respond God's way.

In *"The Power of Choice"* (Chapter 7) we looked at this quote (which is slightly modified here) from Pastor Ron Allen. It fits here as we want to recognize even though we can be influenced by our ancestors' thoughts and behaviors, we still have the option to choose:

> "God's way is the best way. We are free to choose any way we want, but we are not free to avoid the consequences of what we choose. Right now my life is a sum total of my choices, so if I want something different I need to choose something different – God's way."

You may find yourself thinking – *this isn't fair*. I didn't make this mess – my ancestors did. Why should I pay for their stuff? It is hard to come to terms with the concept of inheriting a tendency to sin in certain patterns because of the choices of our ancestors, and having to pay a consequence as a result of their choices. God's nature is full of tensions we don't understand, such as the contrast between His mercy and His justice. He is both. We tend to want His mercy for ourselves but His justice for others, especially those who have hurt us. God will not deny His character and the laws He has set up to govern life. He provides mercy, but it comes as we meet His requirements. When those requirements are met, forgiveness and blessings and mercy prevail. Until then, the consequences of the iniquities of our forefathers are passed down from generation to generation.

God's justice results in the children being affected by the vulnerabilities passed down, as well as possible resulting consequences of curses put into action.

We are affected by our ancestry – both with blessings and curses.

We are affected by our ancestry – both with blessings and curses. The good news of the gospel of Jesus Christ is that there is a provision because of what He did on the Cross to set us free from all sin and curses. We are in a position to receive, apply and practice the provisions and promises of God.

You may say Jesus broke the power of sin and there are no more curses. Aren't we supposed to forget the past and just move on?

Jesus did take on the sins of the world and pay a debt we could never pay. We are free from the curses of sin. We are free to choose an exchanged life – it is now the life of Christ living in us, not our old sin nature. (Colossians 2:14, Galatians 2:20)

I would pose this question: If there are no more curses and the power of sin has been broken, why isn't your life perfect? While it is true we *have been* set free, we *are also being* set free and will *continue to be* set free. An important issue to address is the principle of sanctification – the process that occurs after we are "born again" and our spirit is made brand new. Our souls (mind, will and emotions) now go through a process of being made like Jesus in character and conduct. Paul addresses many issues of Christ-like character that are possible only as we understand, believe, receive and put into practice the new nature of the indwelling Christ. Along the way we have developed habit patterns of thought, feelings and behaviors that don't change overnight (some passed down from our ancestors). Habit patterns of thought become strongholds in our lives. Strongholds can either be godly or ungodly. When they are ungodly we must demolish them and replace them with God's way of thinking. (2 Corinthians 10:5)

We are saints learning how to be saints.

We are saints learning how to be saints.

That means knowing who Christ is and who we are in Him and letting Him live His life in and through us. We are learning to appropriate (put into practice) all that Jesus did for us on the Cross.

I have addressed the issue that salvation is so much more than being saved from an eternity in hell, apart from the presence of God. Knowing the provisions of the Cross enables us to stay in His Presence and appropriate those provisions as we learn how to walk in the Spirit. Being transformed into His image is possible because of the gift of salvation – *being saved out from under the Devil's power and restored into the wholeness of God's order and well-being by the power of the Spirit.*

When we recognize, confess, repent and release forgiveness to our ancestors, we receive by faith the provision to live as new creations. (2 Corinthians 5:17) We break the power of the effects of our ancestors' iniquities and embrace the reality that the promises in God's Word are true and available to us. We can activate this reality because we base it on the truth of God's Word and His nature.

Generational Patterns and Curses can be perpetuated through several ways, allowing cycles of thought, emotional expression and behavior to continue.

Sometimes these sinful patterns are in motion through our genes. Sometimes there are family histories that carry certain physical ailments. Sometimes the genes are actually altered, causing affliction and pain from generation to generation. It is worth asking God if any of these conditions are caused by a generational curse. *PAL: "Holy Spirit, are any of my current challenges caused by a generational curse?"*

We all grow up in an environment in our families where we develop thought and behavior patterns. Emotional and spiritual health are influenced by generational patterns.

Emotional and spiritual health are
influenced by generational patterns.

One of God's Laws is the Law of Sowing and Reaping. Our actions put into play a future harvest. What we sow is what we reap. Everything reproduces after its own kind. Sometimes one can easily see patterns of violence, substance abuse, co-dependency and occult involvement from one generation to the next.

Demonic activity is another avenue for generational patterns being repeated. Transference of demonic activity from one generation to another needs to be considered when ministering to the whole person. This often occurs when the occult is involved and a ritualistic ceremony is performed.

The following is an example of a prayer to minister to *Generational Patterns and Curses.*

PRAYER FOR GENERATIONAL PATTERNS AND CURSES

1. Father, today in agreement with you, I ***confess*** the sins of my ancestors, my parents, and my own sins of _____, including _____, _____, etc. I ***repent*** on their behalf and declare I am willing to allow you to help me change the thought and behavior patterns they had that have influenced my life. (*PAL: "Holy Spirit are there any other sins you want to make me aware of that need to be confessed? Adjust prayer as you listen, if necessary.)*

2.

   a. Right now I am choosing to ***forgive*** (let go of and willingly release them from any debt I think they owe me) my ancestors as well as all others who may have influenced me.

   (Ask this question to help you identify your thoughts that have kept you tied to them because of lack of forgiveness. *PAL: "Lord Jesus what do I think they owe me?"* As long as we have a expectation for something before we can forgive from the heart we keep ourselves connected to them - i.e. an apology, some form of retribution, admittance of wrong.) Forgiveness is a willingness to let go of the debt owed with no expectation of anything given in return.

   If you never say you are sorry, if you never admit your sin, if you never pay me back I declare you are forgiven.

   b. Father, I recognize there are **consequences** in my life today as a result of their sin. These consequences are _____, _____, etc. (*PAL: "Holy Spirit what are the thought patterns, behavior patterns, emotional response patterns that are part of my life as a result of their influence?)*

   I **forgive** them for these consequences, too. Their account with me is erased.

3. I ask You to **forgive me** Lord for these sins. I have yielded to them and have formed an ungodly perspective that has influenced my feelings and

behavior. I am ready to take responsibility for my own behavior and recognize it as sin. *Would you please forgive me for sinning against you, Father?* (*PAUSE AND LISTEN to hear Him tell you He forgives you.* We know as a Biblical principle that when we ask for forgiveness God forgives. It is important we hear Him speak personally to us that He forgives us – now in this moment. This somehow helps make this amazing dynamic in our relationship with God personal and real.)

4. Now, Father, because You have forgiven me, I want to agree with You and say **"I forgive myself."** I will stop disagreeing with You by beating myself up, blaming myself, shaming myself and holding myself hostage to false guilt. Since you have declared me forgiven, I agree with You and say "_____ (your name) you are forgiven."

5. I *renounce* the sins and curses of _____. I break the power of these sins and curses from my life and the life of my descendants through the redemptive work Christ has done on the Cross.

(Renounce means to say I recognize this thought, feeling, and/or behavior as ungodly and I don't have any space for you in me anymore. You have to stay away from me. I will not entertain you anymore. It means to **disown** and to **forbid the approach** of the things disowned. You give it up and speak it out that it has to stay away from you. It is a very powerful word that is used only a few places in scripture, depending on the translation. 2 Cor 4:2)

Speaking to the thought and feeling patterns say, "I recognize you now. You are not of God and I disown you. I forsake you. I forbid you to come into the realm of my thought processes. I declare there is no longer any space available to you in me. Instead I will think _____." *PAL: "Holy Spirit what do you want me to think instead?"* _____ "Thank you for that renewing thought. I receive it, embrace it and will put it in to practice whenever I am tempted to think the old way." (This godly thought becomes the weapon to maintain your progress.)

6. Father, today I have received freedom from these sins and resulting curses as you have forgiven me. (*PAL: Holy Spirit in place of the consequences of these sins, what would you like to give me today?*" _____ "Thank you for your gifts of _____, _____, etc. I receive them with a grateful heart and will, with the help of the Holy Spirit, apply them to my life."

CHAPTER 11

WORD CURSES

"Words kill, words give life;
they're either poison or fruit—you choose."
Proverbs 18:21 The MSG

"You're just a stupid preacher's kid!"

"Oh yeah? Sticks and stones may break my bones, but words will never hurt me."

Did you ever say these words on the playground at recess in reply to hurtful words spoken to you? This old Scottish nursery rhyme is anything but the truth. I said those exact words in response to the taunt I was called a stupid preacher's kid. Oh, how it hurt! I suspect I said it to help cover up the hurt I was actually experiencing and didn't want the perpetrator to know they hit their mark. I cringed inside but kept up a brave front externally to save face. The tears came later. The truth is, words do hurt – they wound the soul in ways that can hinder our path to freedom and wholeness. They can wound our perception of ourselves, others and God.

I carried these hurtful words with me into adulthood until I learned to ask Jesus if they were true. I forgave those who said the words and for the influence they had on my perception of myself. Then I heard the healing words of Jesus: "Carolyn Ruth, you are a preacher's kid, but you are not stupid. And remember - you are *My* child and you have My wisdom abiding in you to use whenever you need it." When you hear your Creator speak healing words to you, your soul wound is healed. Your perception of yourself, others and God changes.

I have a husband who is very intelligent and can remember things he read in books years ago, quoting and using them in sermons and conversations. I fell into a trap of comparing myself to him and would think to myself "I am so stupid…I can't do ____." Can you see how the curse spoken in childhood still affected me in adulthood? I lived under that lie until I learned to stop that thought and remember the weapon God gave me when He told me I had His wisdom abiding in me and could access it at any moment. Living your life based on a lie is crippling and ungodly. When God speaks truth to you, embrace, receive and apply it! Changing your thoughts will change your life!

Changing your thoughts will change your life!

Curses are usually expressed in words. Words can be spoken, written or inwardly spoken in our thoughts. We know from Scripture that our words have the potential to bring life or death, blessings or curses.

> "The tongue can bring death or life; those who love to talk will reap the consequences."
> (Proverbs 18:21 NLT)

> "Some people make cutting remarks, but the words of the wise bring healing." (Proverbs 12:18 NLT)

> "Gentle words are a tree of life; a deceitful tongue crushes the spirit." (Proverbs 15:4 NLT)

"In the same way, the tongue is a small thing that makes grand speeches. But a tiny spark can set a great forest on fire. And among all the parts of the body, the tongue is a flame of fire. It is a whole world of wickedness, corrupting your entire body. It can set your whole life on fire, for it is set on fire by hell itself. People can tame all kinds of animals, birds, reptiles, and fish, but no one can tame the tongue. It is restless and evil, full of deadly poison. Sometimes it praises our Lord and Father, and sometimes it curses those who have been made in the image of God. And so blessing and cursing come pouring out of the same mouth. Surely, my brothers and sisters, this is not right!" (James 3:5-10 NLT)

Curses can be invisible barriers to us receiving healing. They can operate without our recognition. This causes us to stumble and never quite reach the breakthrough we desire.

CURSES DEFINED

The concept of curses is found throughout the Scriptures. In the context of our discussion, a curse is *a penalty that is activated when one chooses to disobey God.*

> A curse is *a penalty that is activated when one chooses to disobey God.*

Merriam-Webster Dictionary defines curse as "an invocation for harm or injury to come upon another". [28]

Derek Prince defines curses as "words spoken, with some form of spiritual authority, (either good or evil), that set in motion something that will go on generation after generation. Behind the words is a spiritual power: God or Satan." [29]

THE FRUIT OF DISOBEDIENCE: CURSES

A curse is a result of a penalty for sin that comes as a result of disobeying God.

God promised the children of Israel that if they heard His commands and obeyed, blessings would follow. He would make them the "head" and not the "tail". (Deuteronomy 28:13-14) He also told them disobedience would result in them being walked on, dragged around and underneath – the position of the "tail." If you find yourself in a position where you are continually being broken down, oppressed, in poverty, never getting ahead, or continually sick you might suspect that you are living under a curse.

PAL: *"Holy Spirit, is there a curse over my life that is working to stop me from being prosperous, healthy and productive? What do I need to know about this in order to break its power and be free?"*

There is a spiritual power behind a curse that sets a person up for failure. It is important to note that while obedience releases blessings, disobedience releases curses – a penalty for breaking God's commandments. (Genesis 22:18, Deuteronomy 27-28)

This spiritual power can operate through words, as mentioned, as well as through physical objects. There is a warning accompanying the Second Commandment in Exodus 20 that forbids the making of any kind of idol or image to worship. If the commandment is broken and idols are worshipped the Lord punishes the children for the sin of the fathers to the third and fourth generation. Breaking this commandment released a curse on the generations.

My husband and I were speaking at meetings in Australia several years ago. One afternoon someone from the parish in which we were ministering stopped by with a gift for me. Our hosts looked a little hesitant as the gift was presented, but didn't say anything. I opened the beautiful package to find a gold necklace. I put it on. Almost immediately I got a headache. After the gift-bearer left I felt so poorly I went to my room to rest. I called my husband in to pray for me. I could hardly move and the headache was excruciating. Our hosts came in to pray with us. It was then they said they had questions about the gift, as the person had been involved in the occult. That necklace had some kind of curse on it and when I put it on it affected me physically. As soon as I took it off I was immediately well. To this day we don't know what was spoken over that necklace, but it definitely was not blessings. I did not keep that gift!

> ## Curses are real and the Enemy will use any means he can to stop us from doing kingdom work and living in freedom.

Be aware that curses are real and the Enemy will use any means he can to stop us from doing kingdom work and living in freedom. Curses are words that have supernatural power to release destruction. They can be spoken, written or used through physical objects that have been spoken over. Until they are recognized and renounced, they have the potential to stay effective from generation to generation.

Curses are not just random happenings. They are a result of someone releasing them over us. Sometimes we release them over ourselves through disobedience. Sometimes we speak words that have a negative consequence. Responding to God in humility is the only way we can recognize, repent and renounce the curse in operation, breaking its legal right to function. Proverbs 26:2 says there is a cause for every curse: "Like a fluttering sparrow or a darting swallow, an undeserved curse does not come to rest."

Curses can be generational or self-imposed. We need God's wisdom to sort them out. For sure, breaking the first two commandments provokes a curse from God.

It is a good thing to PAL: *"Holy Spirit, have I put any other gods before you? Do I have any idols I have put between you and me?"*

SOURCES OF CURSES

Some indicators that a curse is at work can be mental and emotional break-downs, repeated or chronic illness, barrenness or repeated miscarriages, mar-riage breakdown as a pattern in families, continuing financial or material insufficiency, being accident prone, and a family history of suicides or unnat-ural deaths.

Other activities or mindsets that allow a legal right for a curse to oper-ate in our life are injustice to the weak and helpless (Deuteronomy 27, Isaiah 58:6-12), wrong sexual practices (Deuteronomy 27:20-23, Leviticus 18:22), anti-Semitism (Genesis 12:1-3), legalism and carnality (Jeremiah 17:5-6, Galatians 3:1, 3, 10; 5:19-21), stealing, perjury and robbing God (Haggai 1:3-5.9; Malachi 3:8-12, 2 Corinthians 9:7).

Sometimes curses operate through authority figures in our lives, both naturally (parents, teachers, government, military) and spiritually (husbands over wives and children, pastors). God has absolute authority, but He delegates authority in different arenas. Not all authority operates in godly wisdom and at times releases curses rather than intended blessings. Just because authority is abusive doesn't mean its effect is canceled. Abusive authority releases power as well as correctly-used authority.

If things are not going well in your life and you suspect a curse might be working, the best approach is to ask the Holy Spirit to give you wisdom. Your end goal is to be free from the curse, not to blame someone for releasing it on you. In fact, forgiveness for the source of the curse is key to freedom.

SELF CURSES

If we believe that our words have the power of life and death, we need to take caution of the words we speak over and about ourselves. Our own words can come back upon us like judgments, cursing our well-being.

Jesus said "I tell you that every careless word that people speak, they shall give an accounting for it in the Day of Judgment. For by your words you will be justified, and by your words you will be condemned." (Matthew 12:36-37)

Careless words, words not planned are harmless, right? Surely they can't affect us. Wrong. "I really didn't mean it" doesn't take away the power of the words.

Peter cursed himself after he denied Jesus three times. He probably had no idea what effect his words would have on himself. Peter experienced a falling away in his relationship with Jesus. (Mark 14:66-72)

When we start listening to our self-talk we begin to hear curses instead of blessings more than we like.

I will never be able to _____.

I can't _____.

I just know my husband will have an affair on me.

I know I'm going to fail at _____."

I'm getting sick. My sister and my mother died of cancer, so I probably will too.

I'll never amount to anything.

I'm really stupid.

Nobody wants to be around me.

I'll always be poor.

I'll never change.

I will always be insecure.

I could never speak in front of people.

I could never prophesy.

I'll always be left out.

I'll always be the last person chosen.

You're just driving me crazy.

Good things happen for everyone else, but never for me.

These and many more statements release power to make them a reality. When said repeatedly they develop a stronghold. Let's learn to speak wisely! *PAL: "Holy Spirit what words have I spoken over myself that have released a negative consequence affecting my current life?"*

We invoke curses against ourselves when we make pledges or oaths in joining secret societies. Some pledges are totally inconsistent with Christian faith and put us in a bind. *PAL: "Holy Spirit have I made an oath or pledge that opened the door to a curse in my life?"*

We have prayed prayers renouncing and breaking the curses resulting from family lines participating in Masonic Lodges. This is a prime example of a generational curse in operation even though the person might not be a participant.

Get rid of any physical objects you have related to the lodges or secret societies. Power can be released through those objects as well, as discussed previously.

Scriptural covenants, oaths and pledges release blessings. Ungodly oaths and covenants release curses.

CURSES FROM OTHERS

If someone else has cursed us with a spoken word, that power holds us until we forgive the person and renounce and break the power of the word spoken. God always has a truth to overcome a lie, a blessing to overcome a curse.

> God always has a truth to overcome a lie, a blessing to overcome a curse.

The power in a curse that is released from someone else usually doesn't take hold unless that person holds some kind of authority over us, relationally or spiritually. People are sometimes dedicated to satanic and/or occult organizations and causes. Until the curse is broken it will operate from generation to generation.

Curses from our primary care-givers, parents or others, stick like glue to our inner beings.

"You'll never amount to anything."

"You are just like _____. You're headed down the same path he/she went."

"You are a failure."

"You're nothing but a junkie. You'll never make it in life."

"You'll never hold a job."

"I wish you'd never been born."

"You should have been a girl/boy."

"You're just weird."

We tend to believe statements like this and they operate like curses, keeping us in bondage to lies as we live our lives based on them.

THE BIG EXCHANGE

It is amazing what God has offered to us and many times we do not receive and appropriate His provision. In this case, He is offering blessing instead of curses and a way to move into blessings from those curses.

Jesus made the way. Galatians 3:13-14 "Christ redeemed us from the curse of the Law, having become a curse for us – for it is written, "Cursed is everyone who hangs on a tree" – in order that in Christ Jesus the blessing of Abraham might come to the Gentiles, so that we would receive the promise of the Spirit through faith."

All the consequence of sin that should have been ours was put upon Christ. He became the curse for us.

He provided The Big Exchange:

His healing for our broken hearts and bodies.

JOURNEY INTO WHOLENESS

His peace for our turmoil.

His righteousness for our sin.

His life for our death.

His riches for our poverty.

His glory and acceptance for our shame and rejection.

Curses are real. God would not have made such a costly sacrifice if there were nothing to curses. We receive blessings because He was made the curse. The Big Exchange indeed!

PRAYER FOR WORD CURSES

1. Lord Jesus today I am choosing to **forgive** _____ ('myself' if it is a self-curse) for cursing me with the spoken word, by saying _____.

2. I also **forgive** _____ for their part in influencing my acceptance of this curse and reinforcing its power in my life. *PAL: "Holy Spirit is there anyone who has influenced and reinforced this curse to operate in my life?"*

2. I ask you to **forgive me** Lord for receiving this curse and living my life based on it. I **repent** and am ready to change how I think so I can walk in freedom. *PAL: "Father, would you please forgive me?"* Thank you for forgiving me. I receive your forgiveness.

3. I **renounce** and break the legal right and power this curse has had in my life based on the shed blood of Jesus Christ and His finished work on the Cross. I release myself from all sources of every curse and every evil influence over my family and myself.

With your help I will put in to practice the power of the Cross that cancels all judgments and stops the work of all demons associated with this curse.

4. *PAL: "Holy Spirit what would you like me think instead of this curse? What is your Truth?"*

CHAPTER 12

VOWS

When you make a vow to God, do not be late in paying it; for *He takes* no delight in fools. Pay what you vow! It is better that you should not vow than that you should vow and not pay. Do not let your speech cause you to sin and do not say in the presence of the messenger of God that it was a mistake. Why should God be angry on account of your voice and destroy the work of your hands?
Ecclesiastes 5:4-6

VOWS ARE VERY IMPORTANT TO GOD. HE TAKES them seriously. We can make a vow to God or we can resolve to do (or not do) something ourselves. Vows are promises that are consciously and deliberately spoken. They are usually about ourselves and they lock us into a behavior that often keeps us from experiencing emotional freedom and healthy relationships with others. The word "never," is usually found in a vow.

Some examples of vows:

"I will never be like my mom."

"I will never let another person control me."

"I will never have any friends."

"I will never do this right."

"I will never measure up."

These vows can hinder our relationships with others as well as God. When we vow to never let another person control us, sometimes that is transferred into our relationship with God. This mindset hinders our ability to surrender control to God.

In contrast to a judgment, which is a statement or thought about others and is an opinion made about them, (i.e. "You are so controlling"), a vow is personal and is a statement made about what you personally intend to do. Vows like the examples previously given will have negative consequences in our lives. The power of life and death are in the tongue and we reap what we sow with our words. (Proverbs 18:21)

PRAYER FOR VOWS

1. Today I choose to **confess** and **repent** of my sin of vowing _____.

2. I **forgive** _____ for their influence in my making this vow.
   PAL: "Holy Spirit, did someone influence me in any way as I made this vow?"

3. I ask you to **forgive me** Lord for making this vow.
   PAL: "Father, would you please forgive me?"
   Take a moment to soak in His answer. Then say:
   Thank you Father for forgiving me. I receive your forgiveness.

4. Because you have forgiven me, I now choose to **forgive myself**. I will no longer hold myself hostage for making this vow and sinning against God. _____ (put your name here), you are forgiven. (The person is speaking to his or her own soul, like David did in Psalm 42. It is powerful to hear yourself speak truth out loud.)

5. I **cancel** and **renounce** the legal power of my vow, and all legal rights and power I gave to demons to carry out this vow in my life.

VOWS

6. Lord Jesus I **receive** your freedom from this vow and its consequences. (*PAL: "Holy Spirit, what consequences am I living right now as a result of this vow?"*)

7. I declare in the power of the Holy Spirit that _____. (*PAL: "Holy Spirit, what do you want me to replace this vow with?"*)

CHAPTER 13

BITTER ROOT JUDGMENTS

"See to it that no one comes short of the grace of God; that no root of bitterness springing up causes trouble, and by it many be defiled."
Hebrews 12:15

"Judge not, that you be not judged. For with what judgment you judge, you will be judged; and with the measure you use, it will be measured back to you." Matthew 7:1-2

"Do not be deceived, God is not mocked; for whatever a man sows that he will also reap." Galatians 6:7

WHAT IS A BITTER ROOT JUDGMENT? HOW DO we get them? How do we know we have them?

Do you ever wonder why you find yourself in the same sorrowful, hurtful situation again and again? Do you ever feel like you get over one hurt, only to experience another similar situation? Do you seem to repeat the same cycles of hurt or failure in your relationships or business affairs? Does it feel like you have a "Kick Me" or "Abuse Me" sign on your back? How is it possible to have a

"Kick Me" sign on your back and not even know it? How did it get there? How do you recognize you have a kick me sign on? How can you get it off?

Basically that "kick me" sign is on our backs as a result of making judgments about people (dishonoring them) that result in us forming a belief system that disagrees with God.

The scriptures quoted above show us how important it is to watch how we think and talk about people. Bitterness is a feeling of deep bitter anger and ill will, resentment and cynicism. Bitter is defined as a sharp, unpleasant, painful or stinging sensation. No wonder we are warned in Hebrews 12 to not let them take root in our hearts. A root is the part of the plant that is buried deep and gains nourishment from the soil in which it is planted.

If the soil of our heart is tainted with bitterness, anger and resentment, we will grow fruit that is bitter, angry and resentful. You have probably heard it said, "If you grow good fruit, you have a good root. If you grow bad fruit, you have a bad root. If you have the fruit, you have the root!"

We can repent for bad fruit but will not see a change until the root is exposed and uprooted. Roots continue to produce a crop.

What we sow is what we reap in kind. Once we make a judgment about a person, the law of reaping and sowing is in effect and until confession and repentance break the cycle we are basically wearing that "kick me" sign inviting the same judgment upon ourselves that we have made about someone else. When judgments are not repented of and broken they can become a stronghold.

Bitter root judgments are opinions and conclusions made about another person without God's perspective that allow negative feelings and behaviors to be expressed as a byproduct of that judgment.

These judgments usually assign motive to the other's character without checking the validity of their intentions. If we were to choose to check out what they intended with their words or actions we would *PAL: "When you said or did _____, I thought _____ and I felt _____. Is that what you wanted me to think and feel?"* Often they are shocked you came to that conclusion and are able to express what they want for your relationship to be healthy. Erroneous perceptions defile not only yourself, but others.

> If we allow a bitter root to take seed
> in our hearts as a result of a judgment, it
> will grow into a bitter root stronghold.

A stronghold is a habit structure of thought. If we allow a bitter root to take seed in our hearts as a result of a judgment, it will grow into a bitter root stronghold. Judgments and strongholds open the door for curses to have an effect in our lives. Strongholds exist in our souls and cause us to agree with the Enemy instead of God. As we will learn in this book, strongholds must be recognized, repented of and torn down, and replaced with Godly patterns of thought. This is part of our transformation process. (2 Corinthians 10:4-6)

HOW DO BITTERROOT JUDGMENTS GET STARTED?

God has designed the universe in such a way that basic laws govern it. Some of the moral and spiritual laws are:

Law of honoring our parents.

Law of judging.

Law of sowing and reaping.

Law of becoming what we judge in others.

One of the most basic laws mentioned in Deuteronomy 5:16 is "Honor your father and mother, as the Lord your God has commanded you, that your days may be long, and that it may be well with you in the land which the Lord your God is giving you." This law is broken often and never repented of, so we continue to reap the consequence of a broken law. Our parents are the first people we have an opportunity to judge.

Whatever area we don't honor our parents in, is the area of life that will not go well for us. When we judge someone, even if the judgment is true, the law declares that the measure you give out is what you must receive and it goes into effect. (Matthew 7:1-2)

Judgments are seeds sown that by law will grow and be reaped. The longer it stays hidden the larger it will grow and the more abundant the fruit will be.

There is a distinction between judging and discerning that is important to note: judging is holding someone guilty for something; discerning is identifying a concern for intercession. The difference is in the attitude I take when I recognize the truth about someone or a situation. *PAL: "Holy Spirit, have I judged this person by thinking/saying _____? Would you please help me embrace your perception about them so I can agree with you in prayer on their behalf?"*

The Law of Sowing and Reaping is a Kingdom of God dynamic we will never change. The Laws of Sowing and Reaping are found in Galatians 6:7-10:

We reap what we sow.

We reap the same in kind as what we sow.

We reap more than what we sow.

We reap bountifully, if we sow bountifully.

We reap in a different season than when we sow.

God didn't make laws to govern the universe to be mean to us. They are for our wellbeing. His kingdom principles are meant to sanctify us, to cause us to mature in our character and conduct to be like Jesus. It is a kingdom principle that sowing demands increase. So in order to reap a bountiful harvest that is how we must sow. We get into trouble when we sow the wrong crop, not knowing what the consequences or the resulting crop will be. There is a way to break the cycle of sowing judgments that result in bitter root judgments or strongholds – recognition and repentance.

If you judged a parent for being controlling, harsh and legalistic you have set yourself up to be controlled by someone. This judgment will leave an open door that will draw to you people who are controlling, harsh and legalistic. Do you find yourself acting in ways you don't want to around certain people? They are drawing on something that is in you. There is a root. If you think about it, some of the people you find in your life are placed there by God to knock off the rough edges. Those people are your grace growers. When you partner with the Holy Spirit to respond to them like Jesus wants to, the gift of grace grows and matures and becomes part of your new nature.

Bitter root judgments are the most common, basic sin in our relationships. They begin the foundation for reaping a harvest of whatever and whomever we have judged.

Jack Frost [30] and John and Paula Sandford [31] present these simple laws in their teaching about Bitter Root Judgments. They affect all of life:

> Life goes well for us in areas we honored our parents. It does not go well for us in the areas we dishonored (judged) them.

> We receive harm in the same areas of life in which we have meted out judgment against others.

> We will reap what we have sown, both for good and for ill.

When we have a habit pattern of thought that has evolved into a stronghold and it has not been recognized and repented of, the necessity to reap the bitter judgment guarantees someone will come along to fulfill the law of sowing and reaping. We also need to realize that other people's bitter roots can defile us when we have a negative root system upon which to build. Sometimes we reap through another; sometimes we reap our own actions and thoughts.

Romans 2:1 says, "You are without excuse, every man of you who passes judgment, for in that you judge another, you condemn yourself; for you who judge practice the same things." When we judge another we doom ourselves to do the same thing. (i.e. I'll never act like my mom. I will never discipline like my dad. I'll never be legalistic like my childhood pastor.)

For every action in life we will reap a result.

For every action in life we will reap a result. No law of God is an inert, dead thing. A key *PAL* question is: *"Holy Spirit who have I judged and how have I judged them that has resulted in these negative consequences in my life today?"*

When you have heard from God concerning those you have judged, repent and ask forgiveness. Break the cycle of reaping the bad seed you have sown through the provision made by Jesus on the Cross. There are some suggested prayers to pray for bitter root judgments at the end of this section. Please let God search your heart and do an honest assessment before Him. (Psalm 139:23-24)

HOW DO I KNOW I HAVE A BITTER ROOT JUDGMENT?

In his work *"The Importance of Forgiveness"* John Arnott says: "If repetitive, negative fruit is in your life, there is usually a judgment rooted in bitterness, anger or hurt, that is allowing the Enemy access. Keep in mind that it will not be in every area of your life, but it will be in the areas where you have been hurt and wounded."

The following questions will help you as you evaluate if you have a bitter root judgment.

PAL:

> *"Holy Spirit, do I have a firmly fixed negative attitude and feeling about this person? Do I believe the worst about them instead of the best?*
>
> *Do I look for them to fail and be punished? Am I upset when they are blessed?"*
>
> *"When I think about a certain person do I tense up and get a frown on my face?"*
>
> *"Am I constantly pestered with negative thoughts about anyone?*
>
> *"Am I duplicating things I saw modeled in my parent's or someone else's life?"*

"Am I pushing aside an issue in my life the Holy Spirit has spoken to me about because I feel helpless to deal with it?"

"Do I find myself acting in ways I shouldn't toward someone and don't know why?

"Am I constantly thinking negative things about myself… that I'm not important to someone even though nothing has been implied or said?"

"Do I have a behavior or attitude that I said I would never be, do or act like?"

We are not free to avoid the consequences of our choices in judging. But we can make the choice today to ask the Holy Spirit to reveal what is in our hearts concerning bitter root judgments so we can break the cycle, start planting Godly seeds, and reap a good harvest instead of a bad one.

PRAYERS FOR BITTER ROOT JUDGMENTS

Father, in the Name of Jesus, I ask you to make me whole and fully healed so I can look more like your Son, Jesus. I need to be close to You. Thank you for helping me to recognize that my responses to people and to circumstances in my life have allowed sinful behaviors to be expressed in my relationships.

Thank you Father, for teaching me that if I don't release forgiveness to others, to You and to myself, you won't be able to forgive me when I need it…And I'm in need of it quite often. I don't want to pay the consequence of not having You forgive me, of not being in a place where you can protect me and provide for me. So I'm willing to do whatever you ask of me to bring a release of freedom in my life.

I'm really tired of living in unbroken cycles of sinful behavior. Would you continue to bring revelation in my life of these cycles and how they began in my life? My heart is broken when I see the grief my sinful behavior causes you and for the hurt I have caused and continue to cause those I dearly love. I'm coming to you, asking you to bring to light those things that have been hidden, to expose the roots that have been supporting bad fruit in my life. I give you permission to expose the deep places in my heart. I am ready to repent and change.

PAL: "Holy Spirit, what cycles do you want to identify in my life? What roots do you want to expose that are bearing bad fruit?"

Father, as you bring to my mind those I have judged, I will choose to release and forgive every one, whether I "feel" like it or not. I will choose to forgive them, even for the times they have hurt me and caused pain in my life. I will let go of all judgments I have made about them. I ask you to expose the defense mechanisms that have enabled me to keep justifying my behavior. Expose areas of deception that have enabled me to think I am right, causing me to live in stubbornness. I give up my "right to be right" and ask you to heal the unmet "needs" that cause me to strive to be right. I am ready to quit blaming other people for my problems. I take responsibility for my own thoughts, attitudes, feelings and behavior.

PAL: "Holy Spirit, what kinds of behavior am I justifying and/or rationalizing? What are my defense mechanisms?"

Thank you for giving me the Holy Spirit to lead me into all truth, and giving me the capacity to forgive. Father, in the Name of Jesus, help me discern your truth and walk in it. Thank you for Your death on the Cross that allows me to have freedom and healing. I desire to walk in that freedom and healing.

I am ready to take responsibility for breaking your commandments that tell me to honor my father and mother, and to not judge other people. I now realize that when I break one of your laws it sets into motion a curse to gain a foothold in my life: I will reap what I have sown. Today I am asking that the power of the curses in my life be broken. Would you help me begin a process of planting good seeds that will result in blessing?

PAL: "Holy Spirit, what are some blessing seeds I can plant today?"

Father, because you have forgiven me, I will forgive myself as I need to and release myself from accusations, judgments and self-hatred. I choose to accept myself as you created me, because you love me. You even love me as much as you love your Son, Jesus. So I will love myself too. I will love your special creation. Thank you for not giving up on me.

PAL: "Holy Spirit, what judgments have I made against/about myself?"

Father, in Jesus Name, I ask you to **forgive me** for **judging** my _____ (father, mother, siblings, friends, teachers, spiritual authorities, spouse, children).

I **confess** that I judged _____ for _____.

PAL: "Holy Spirit, how did I judge _____?"

Forgive me for planting seeds of bitterness, criticalness, harshness, legalism, hatred, and anger.

PAL: "Holy Spirit, what other seeds did I plant?"

I **release** _____ from all judgments and ask you not to hold anything to _____'s account for the harmful ways he/she/they treated me. I **forgive** him/her/them. I **cancel** the curse these judgments have caused in my life, the cycles of dysfunctional behavior that have resulted in my life.

PAL: "Holy Spirit, what dysfunctional behaviors are in my life as a result of my judgments?"

Would you help me pull up these ungodly behaviors by the root so I won't have to keep reaping from them? I **forgive myself** for making these judgments and for causing a harvest of bad fruit in my life.

Please give me understanding to discern the behaviors and recognize the hurt I have caused others because of it. I **repent** for causing Your heart to hurt and for hurting others.

PAL: "Holy Spirit, how has my sinful behavior hurt others? Do I need to ask forgiveness from anyone because of this sinful behavior?"

Please help me change my behavior so I will have good fruit in my life. I really need your help to do this.

Please help me disown ungodly thought patterns I embraced as a result of bitter root judgments. As I begin to embrace what is true from your perspective, help me make it part of my daily experience. Help me begin to respond to people in my life as the new creation you have made me to be.

I'm calling on your name, Lord Jesus Christ, to deliver me, set me free and heal me. Please help me be totally available to you and unavailable to the evil one.

Help me be consumed with the things you are consumed with, to see things from your perspective.

DECLARATION

I am serious about living this new resurrection life with Christ, so I will begin to act like it. I will look up, keeping my eyes fixed on Jesus Christ, the one who is causing me to look more like Him. My old life is dead. My new life is with Christ in God the Father. I am killing off all the old ways of living that were leading me on a path of death. I am going to let Father God shape my feelings, thoughts, attitudes and actions. I am choosing life. I am ready to let Father God give me new clothes…clothes of kindness, humility, quiet strength, discipline and love. With the Holy Spirit's help I will be even-tempered and quick to forgive. I am determined I will never be caught without love. Everything I do I will do in the name of the Lord Jesus Christ, thanking God the Father for a life lived in freedom.

CHAPTER 14

SOUL TIES

"Now it came about when he had finished speaking to Saul, that the soul of Jonathan was knit to the soul of David, and Jonathan loved him as himself."
1 Samuel 18:1

FIRST, LET'S SAY WE CAN HAVE GODLY SOUL TIES in our relationships. Spouses, parents and children, and healthy friendships that are developed with Godly boundaries enjoy being connected spiritually, emotionally and physically (spouses). Relationships built on Godly principles will produce good fruit.

Spiritual, emotional and physical (sexual) connections that have been damaged by dysfunctional family and relationship patterns, control and ungodly influence are ungodly. As these are recognized they can be broken through confession, forgiveness and renouncing. As they are broken, we have the opportunity to develop a Spirit-led relationship with the freedom for each person to maintain their power of choice and identity.

SOUL TIE DEFINED

An ungodly Soul Tie is an unhealthy emotional, spiritual or sexual connection between two people in which one person (or both) submits to the control or manipulation of the other.

QUESTIONS TO ASK TO DETERMINE IF YOU ARE INVOLVED IN AN UNGODLY SOUL TIE

Who do you often think of when you need to make a decision and-wonder what they would do/say, or what they would think of your decision?

Am I free to be myself (without this person's control) and fulfill my destiny?

Is this relationship inhibiting or holding me back in any way? Am I bound or controlled by what this person thinks or feels about me?

Am I afraid to make a decision without this person's approval for fear of rejection or anger?

Does this person control how I think, feel and act?

Do I want this person's approval above God's approval? Do I long for their approval?

Is my behavior controlled by their behavior? (i.e. when they are angry do I pull back in fear and become paralyzed?)

What fruit has developed as a result of my relationship with _____?

Godly soul tie fruit: love, blessing, honor, closer to Jesus, free-dom to be yourself.

Ungodly soul tie fruit: resentment, anger, strife, jealously, control, manipulation, bitterness, hatred, co-dependency, confusion.

Have I had sexual relations with someone that is not my spouse?

This is a major area needing ministry. Many people have had sexual relations outside of marriage, some pre-Christian, some not. All sexual intimacy results in a spiritual tie that needs to be repented of and broken.

This is important because we are a spiritual being in a physical body. God designed us as man and woman to come together in marriage and become one – we are knit together spiritually as well as physically. (Genesis 2:24) It is a mystery we cannot understand.

Everyone we have physical relations with we bind ourselves to them in some way. We are connected to them and when we move on to other relationships that bond stays inside us.

This causes a lot of confusion and at times a 'sense' that someone else is present as we begin new relationships. Part of them actually is.

We don't want pieces of ourselves attached to anyone other than the person God has for our life partner. We want to be totally available for each other as we come to a marriage relationship.

When we sin sexually, we defile our own body. (1 Corinthians 16:15-17)

> Ungodly soul ties hinder your ability to be totally free and move in the destiny God has planned for your life.

Ungodly soul ties hinder your ability to be totally free and move in the destiny God has planned for your life. Learning to recognize these ties is the first step toward being set free from the effects of them on your life.

As we have prayed with many people to break ungodly soul ties, people actually feel the weight of the tie drop off them. They begin to sense freedom while they didn't even know they were bound. Many describe it as a 'clean' feeling. We have prayed with people who have had as many as one hundred ungodly sexual soul ties. It may seem laborious to pray through that many, and most likely they will not remember all their names, but many can see faces. Asking the Father to bring to remembrance all that is necessary in order to be free and clean is worth the freedom experienced in the end.

Some people report after praying that they feel something being "cut" from them and they experience a sort of "lost" feeling. We ask God to fill their hearts with what He wants to do in the relationship that has been hindered by ungodly soul ties. (*PAL: "Holy Spirit what do you want this relationship to look like? How do you want me to relate to them? What is the first boundary you would like me to start practicing? When I start to feel controlled and manipulated what do you want me to say/do?"*)

In addition to having ungodly soul ties to people, we have experienced ministry situations where people have had an ungodly emotional and/or spiritual connection to objects (attachments to sentimental things that they 'can't get along without', memoirs from old affairs), and to institutions and even doctrines. One must listen carefully to the Holy Spirit while you pray, as He is the One who searches the deepest places of our being and knows the deep things of God that will set us free. (1 Corinthians 2:10-13)

PRAYER FOR UNGODLY SOUL TIES

Father, I **confess** all emotional, physical and spiritual ungodly connections and soul ties with _____.

I agree with you that I have been trying to please _____ in our relationship more than you, and that is sinful. They have come between you and me. (*PAL: "Holy Spirit, what are the signs that I have allowed _____ to come between you and me? I want to change those patterns."*)

I **forgive** _____ for their part in my ungodly soul tie.

I ask you to **forgive** me for my sin resulting in ungodly soul ties. Would you please forgive me? (*Pause and listen to hear the Father's voice tell you that you are forgiven.*)

Thank you for your forgiveness, Father. I receive it.

I **renounce** (disown) and break all ungodly soul ties. I release _____ and myself. I will bind myself only to you, Lord.

I **renounce** and **cancel** the assignments of all demons associated with these ungodly ties.

With the help of the Holy Spirit I will be alert and recognize the warning signals to involvement with ungodly soul ties and renounce (disown) them before I think the thoughts that will lead me to ungodly behavior. (*PAL: "Holy Spirit, what are my warning signs? What are my weapons to overcome them?"*)

In the Name of Jesus I pray, Amen.

(Note: warning signals can be patterns of thought, feeling or behavior in which you have habituated yourself. Identify those and ask the Holy Spirit to help you be aware of them so you can take them obedient to Christ immediately. Then embrace and declare the thought (your weapon) Jesus wants you to have about the relationship.)

CHAPTER 15

BLAMING AND JUDGING GOD

"People ruin their lives by their own foolishness
and then are angry at the Lord."
Proverbs 19:3 (NLT)

"People ruin their lives by their own stupidity,
so why does God always get blamed?"
Proverbs 19:3 (MSG)

THERE HAS BEEN A THOUGHT PRESENTED THAT
encourages one to "forgive" God for what He has done or not done for/to you.
This has no biblical foundation. God does not sin, period! It is not in his nature
at all. When we are disappointed with God we need to come to the recognition
we are upset or angry with Him and we live out of sorts, causing a distance in
our intimacy with Him. That has been our choice, and in reality anything that
separates us from God is harmful to us.

We can follow the examples in Scripture of expressing our disappointment, hurt, frustration and anger, but need to take responsibility for living in
disagreement with God about who He is…He is for us, not against us. He only

has our best interests at heart, even when we do not understand His actions or lack thereof.

The following prayer is crafted to enable us to express our feelings and thoughts in a helpful manner, helping us get back on track in our relationship with God so we can gain His perspective to replace our hurt and disappointment.

PRAYER OF REPENTANCE

Father, today I am beginning to **recognize** that I am angry with you and I blame you for not coming through for me like I wanted you to. I was expecting you to _____ and I was disappointed when that didn't happen. In my thoughts I have been accusing you of being (faithless, mean, not there for me, loving others more than me). These thoughts leave me feeling abandoned, betrayed and left out.

Please **forgive me** for thinking these thoughts about you. I know you are not any of those things because your Word declares a different nature. I declare that you are a good God and that your plans for me are good and you have a future for me.

You gave me the opportunity to exchange my old sinful life for Your life. I have received that gift and will step in to the provisions you have given me through your Son Jesus Christ's sacrifice on the Cross.

I take responsibility for my sin against you, **repent** and ask you *"Would you please forgive me?"* (Pause and Listen for His answer to you.) Father I receive your forgiveness and thank you for it. Thank you for forgiving and cleansing me.

PAL: *"Father, is there anything you would like to say to me? What would you like for me think about the disappointment/hurt I experienced when _____?"*

Declare this truth: You are a good Father to me!

CHAPTER 16

UNGODLY THOUGHT PATTERNS

"Be transformed by the renewing of your mind"
Romans 12:2

Everyone has a belief system. Scripture says:

"As a man thinks in his heart, so is he." (Proverbs 23:7 AMP)

"It is by believing in your heart that you are made right with God, and it is by confessing with your mouth that you are saved." (Romans 10:10 NLT)

UNGODLY THOUGHT PATTERNS DEFINED

Ungodly thought patterns are lies we believe to be true about God, others and ourselves.

Every ungodly thought we embrace places us in agreement with the father of lies. He uses that agreement to rob, kill and destroy us. (John 10:10) The best defense to a lie is the truth. For every lie we have believed, God has a truth to overcome it. God is our Father, and He cannot lie. (Numbers 23:19) It is important to know your thoughts produce your emotions and lead to your behaviors. It may be your intention to grow the Fruit of the Spirit, but if you have thoughts contrary to God's truth, you will grow ungodly fruit.

Thoughts produce your emotions
and lead to your behaviors.

God's truth is not seen by the natural man, but by the spiritual man. Our spirit, once born again, knows God's transforming power. "But a natural man does not accept the things of the Spirit of God, for they are foolishness to him; and he cannot understand them, because they are spiritually appraised. But he who is spiritual appraises all things, yet he himself is appraised by no one. For who has known the mind of the Lord, that He will instruct him? But *we have the mind of Christ."* (1 Corinthians 2:14-16)

Jesus is our model. He is the Way, the Truth and the Life. (John 14:6) We learn God's truth from His Word and by abiding in Him. (John 15) If you have not yet decided to follow Jesus, take this opportunity to pray this prayer to begin your journey into wholeness with Him:

"Lord Jesus, I recognize I am broken and I need you in my life to save, heal and deliver me. I have sinned against you and others and I ask you to forgive me. Will you please forgive me? Thank you for forgiving my sins and washing me clean. I want you to be my Lord and Savior. I ask you to indwell and empower me with your Holy Spirit. I give you my life and exchange it for yours. Please live your life in and through me. In Jesus' name I pray. Amen."

What you think (believe to be true) will shape your future. What you think affects every area of your life. You must learn to submit every thought immediately to the scrutiny of the Holy Spirit or you risk allowing your thoughts to control you. If you are experiencing emotions that affect you negatively, you can change that effect by changing what you think. *PAL: "What thought is producing this emotion? Is this thought Godly? What thought do you want me to have concerning this God?"* If your expressed behavior is not the Fruit of the Spirit, ask the same set of questions, inserting behavior in place of the word "emotion".

146

What you believe about the sanctification process (being transformed into the likeness of Jesus Christ) affects your life. As we discussed in "*The Power of Perspective…Saint or Sinner,*" if you believe you have the nature of a sinner you will continue to sin. If you believe you have been forgiven and cleansed from sin and are now a saint, you will embrace and receive the nature of God who lives in you, empowering you to walk as a new creation. (2 Peter 1:4, Romans 6) You will become what you think you are. Be careful what you dwell on because you will get more of it.

You will become what you think you are.

As a byproduct of the renewing of your mind to agree with God, your mind, will and emotions are transformed. The Fruit of the Spirit will grow and change you from the inside out. When you *recognize* a thought you have embraced that does not agree with God's truth, you can, with the help of the Holy Spirit, agree with Him (confession), *repent* (change your mind about what is true), and go through a *renewal* process that includes *repetition* and *rehearsal* (practice). This "*5 R's*" *Activation* is described in Chapters 16 and 20.

Ungodly thought patterns are wrong attitudes and motivations that protect and defend the "old man" that in reality died in Christ. However, your mind was not erased at your new birth, and the influence of the old sin nature is still at work until lies are exposed and replaced with the truth. Comparing your thoughts to God's thoughts in His Word will expose the lies. Sometimes you think the way you believe is normal. You think it is just your personality or the way you are. You rationalize by thinking "I've always been this way, it's the way I was raised, it's the way my family is…etc."

This process of renewal and transformation takes time. You must remember the journey into wholeness is a process…you *have been* saved, you *are being* saved and you *will be* saved. This concept was addressed in "*Pastoral Care Foundations.*" (Chapter 1) Having your mind renewed to think like Jesus is an important part of this process as you begin to think (believe), feel and act like Jesus. You are sanctified by the truth. (John 17:17) You are also being transformed from glory to glory (2 Corinthians 3:18), and your righteousness in God is being revealed from faith to faith. (Romans 1:17)

> *Your capacity to exercise faith is limited to your belief system.*

What you believe to be true about healing is crucial. If you think the gift of healing is no longer a valid gift, you limit what you will experience when you need healing. *Your capacity to exercise faith is limited to your belief system.* This truth affects every principle and promise in the Bible. When you exercise faith you are putting your full confidence in God's power and His faithfulness.

Lest you think you are alone on this journey, everyone has patterns of thought that do not agree with God's truth. These patterns of thought are what keep us from looking like Jesus. The goal of our Father is for us to look like Jesus. (2 Corinthians 3:18) *Every* thought you have affects your behavior. You need to be ruthless with thoughts that do not agree with God. You must demolish and replace them. (2 Corinthians 10:3-5)

There is a school of thought that says it doesn't matter what you believe as long as you are sincere about it. You could sincerely believe the law of gravity doesn't exist, jump off a high building to test it and be dead wrong. You sowed a bad seed when you believed the Law of Gravity didn't exist and reaped a bad crop (death). Scripture says, "If you believe on the Lord Jesus Christ you will be saved (Acts 16:31), and if you confess with your mouth that Jesus is Lord and believe in your heart that God raised him from the dead, you will be saved. It is with your heart you believe and are justified and it is with your mouth that you confess and are saved." (Romans 10:9-10) Those are beliefs that agree with God. When you believe those truths, you are sowing good seed and will reap a good harvest. The principle of sowing and reaping is a given in God's Kingdom. For this principle to work to your benefit, you must embrace it as truth in your belief system and behave accordingly. Godly thought patterns produce godly fruit. We always reap a crop based on what we sow. *Belief systems are like seeds planted in our hearts that will reap a harvest.*

> ## Belief systems are like seeds planted in our hearts that will reap a harvest.

We are planting seeds of thought all the time. Since we become what we think, if you don't like who you have become, get some new thoughts about yourself. *PAL: "What thought produced this emotion? What thought produced this behavior? What thought processes led me to this place in my life? Holy Spirit, what am I thinking about myself that disagrees with you?"* These questions will help you evaluate your belief system and assess points of agreement and disagreement with God.

> ## If you don't like who you have become, get some new thoughts about yourself.

All of us have some core beliefs we grew up with and accepted as truth without even thinking about them. We don't question many of our assumptions about our value systems…after all they must be true because our parents told us, our family lived them, our culture shaped us by them, and our experiences reinforced them as truth.

Boys don't cry…Girls don't fight.
Don't tell family secrets – it's no one else's business.
Good Christians don't feel that way.
You're just different than everyone else. Get over it and get on with life.

You will never be accepted and loved for who you are.
You will never have enough money.
Good Christians don't drink, gamble, play cards, etc.
Good marriages don't ever experience fights.

You face a challenge when ungodly thought patterns *appear* to be true based on facts in your reality, yet they are not true based on what God says. *God's truth always trumps your facts.* These kinds of thought patterns are usually hidden from us for what they are. That is what a good deception is and that is the way the Enemy works. You can sincerely believe you are totally alone and no one loves you. God says, "I will *never* leave you nor forsake you," and "I love you with an everlasting love." (Hebrews 13:5, Jeremiah 31:3) Until the lie is recognized, you live your life based on it and continue in a pattern of sinful thinking, feeling and behaving until confession, repentance and renewal are embraced.

God's truth always trumps your facts.

Some of the thoughts or perceptions you might have of yourself that appear to be facts in your reality:

> *I am just a big mistake. I'm flawed beyond anyone's ability to fix me and will never amount to anything.*

> God's truth: I chose you before the foundations of the world. (Ephesians 1:4) I have plans and a future and a hope for you and it is good. (Jeremiah 29:11)

> *There are so many challenges in my life right now I am too overwhelmed to function and I will not make it. I cannot do this.*

150

God's truth: While it is true you are facing challenges,
with God's Presence and help you are an overcomer.
He never leaves you alone without a way to go
through adversity. (Deuteronomy 31:6, Hebrews 13:5)

You don't live in denial of what is happening, but you do reach for the "more" of God's perspective on your situation. His ways and His thoughts are higher than ours and they are the best way to live life. (Isaiah 55:8-9)

THOUGHT DEVELOPMENT CYCLE

Your beliefs get reinforced by your experiences, what you experience reinforces your beliefs and so a cycle begins and continues. "Look at what has happened to me. I have been betrayed *again*. It proves that my belief and my expectation that I will always be betrayed is true."

Beliefs result in expectations, expectations shape your reality and your reality (the facts) influences your beliefs. When you are caught in an ungodly cycle that results in ungodly results/behavior you must break the cycle and begin a new cycle that will lead to godly results.

Repeated experiences reinforce repeated thoughts and build strongholds. Repetition is a powerful force that can be used for good or ill.

There is a battle going on for our minds. The Word instructs us to be transformed by the renewing of the mind. (Romans 12:2) The Enemy does not want us to learn to think like God. He infiltrates our lives by suggesting erroneous perceptions to the struggles we face in life. He deceives us by burying the ungodly thought patterns deep in our belief systems that are distorted by generational tendencies and hurts and wounds we experience. Once we are born again, we have weapons with which to fight the Enemy and we learn to take the territory of our mind by agreeing with God.

"Remember, if you believe a lie long enough it will become truth to you. As it becomes your reality, you are faced with life choices that can lead you into a lifestyle of sin and disobedience. Sin left unrepented creates a place of darkness in your life, in your mind, and, worst of all, finds its place into your heart, causing you to respond to your pain by either hurting others or refusing to allow others access to your heart." [32]

Ungodly strongholds are lies that are the fruit of all the choices of your thoughts, feelings and behaviors regarding events in your life. A hurtful event occurs, you form an opinion about God, others or yourself. What you believe to be truth guides and forms your reality.

> ## What you believe to be truth guides and forms your reality.

The cycle of thought development looks something like this:

What you believe is either the truth or a lie. When an event occurs, you respond or react out of that belief. If you have believed the truth, a positive emotional response arises. If you have believed a lie, a negative emotional response arises. You have an opportunity to choose whether you will walk in the Spirit or in your flesh. Fruit will be evident in your life as a result of your choices: sweet or godly fruit is a result of believing truth; bitter or ungodly fruit is a result of believing a lie.

If you have made an error in your judgment about God, others or yourself and it is not corrected, you begin to make decisions about life based on that error. Erroneous thoughts lay a foundation that will produce expectations for a predetermined outcome. Similar hurts and wounds continue to happen that will reinforce the ungodly thought on which you have based your life.

SUMMARY OF THE THOUGHT DEVELOPMENT CYCLE

I think _____ about this event _____.
When I think _____ I feel _____.
When I feel _____, I behave _____.

The fruit of my behavior is _____ (godly/ungodly).

A similar event happens. I think, "This is happening again. I will feel and behave the same way. It's the way it is. My life will never change. This always happens to me." A stronghold is built. My ability to adopt a different perspective is hindered because of my belief and expectation that the same things will be my reality.

Sometimes when I am struggling with behavior I don't want, in my frustration I reach out to Jesus and *PAL: "Here is what I am thinking, Jesus. Is it okay with you for me to think this?"*

If you can learn to assess your thoughts as soon as you have them, you can ask the Lord these questions before the thought has an opportunity to go into long-term memory and increase the possibility of a stronghold.

PAL: "Holy Spirit, is there another way for me to look at this event?" "Is this thought in agreement with your thoughts?" "How do you want me to think about this event?"

Some questions to ask of yourself concerning this event: *"What do I believe to be true about God, others, and myself in light of this event?"*

PAL: "Holy Spirit, are these perceptions true? What needs to be changed?"

If you have adopted a lie upon which to base your life, you will need the help of the Holy Spirit to recognize it and change it. Observing ungodly fruit in negatively expressed emotions and behavior can expose lies. You can *PAL: "Holy Spirit, what thoughts in my life are producing this negatively expressed emotion and/or behavior?"*

For example, I was sexually abused as a small child. Even though I repressed the memory until my mid-30's I formed some perceptions about parental protection and men that affected me. I adopted the view that if God and those who were in place to keep me safe weren't going to be on duty, then I would have to do it for myself. I created a wall around my heart that didn't let people in to help when they could or wanted to. The beliefs I formed in response to the abuse were:

> *God doesn't care and isn't always on duty to protect me.*
> *God is mean, not just.*
> *I have to be strong for myself and not depend on anyone.*

I began to look at other people with a heart of mistrust, assigning motives to their actions without checking out their accuracy. I expected them to let me down, so I didn't even try to depend on them. My behavior in response to these experiences and expectations was to isolate myself, not only from other people, but from intimacy with God. You cannot be close to someone you don't trust or if you have made a character diagnosis labeled "Untrustworthy". Sadly for me this included God. It was hard to admit but I didn't trust Him.

Over and over again in life experiences, people I wanted to be able to depend on would let me down and I would say to myself, "What else can I expect? People are just this way. I can't depend on them." My expectations of being let down allowed me to isolate myself and the next hurtful experience of betrayal, rejection or abandonment reinforced my perception so I lived my life based on the lie – "God will not be there for me. Other people will not be there for me. Take care of yourself."

God's truth is: His nature is faithfulness. He is the Faithful One. He loves me and is always with me. My healing process began when I began to see and experience God's true nature as The Faithful One, and quit blaming Him for something He didn't do. I also needed to gain a perspective of the effects of sin in a fallen world. I began a process of learning how to see God's truth about other people who let me down: People will let me down. I am to put my trust in God and His faithfulness and depend on Him to take me through challenges in relationships when I am let down. God will show me who is trustworthy.

Gaining a perspective of the circumstances in the life of the person who let you down can be helpful.

PAL: "Holy Spirit, is there anything you would like me to know about this person that will help me understand what has happened? What would you like for me to think about him/her?" Having a revelation of how God sees a person does not excuse their behavior. It frees you to focus on giving the gift of forgiveness and allows the Holy Spirit to speak words that will heal your heart.

While it is true we are each responsible for our own sins, we struggle with life when we become the victim of someone else's sin. When this occurs through trauma and negative experiences in childhood, we are not responsible for their sin, but for our response to the sin committed against us. The gift of the grace of God that empowers us to walk in forgiveness heals us.

The gift of the grace of God that empowers us to walk in forgiveness heals us.

"If the ultimate cure (for wounded souls) is grace, then the ultimate cause of the behavior is the failure to understand, experience, and live out grace at every level of our lives." [33] Learning to receive grace as a gift touches every area of our lives, whether it is our sin or our response to sins against us.

Recognizing the ungodliness of the expression of your feelings and behavior is one of the first steps to recognizing the lie you have believed that has grown a bad crop of ungodly fruit.

Thoughts formed about our deep wounds and hurts are a primary source of ungodly thought patterns.

PAL this question to assess if you have a hurt or wound about which you have adopted an ungodly thought: *"Where do I allow my mind to rest concerning hurts and wounds I have received?"*

Your belief system is developed from those thoughts. Memory lies in every cell of the body – not just the mind. We respond to sight, sounds and smells as well as thoughts in the mind.

Some thoughts that will lead to ungodly conclusions:

I'm not important enough because my Dad/Mom don't have time for me.

Significant people won't be there for me when I need them.

Men cannot be trusted.

Women are manipulators.

Authority figures cannot be trusted.

No one is going to protect me so I will do it for myself.

I have to protect myself from being abused and taken advantage of.

I will never let my guard down, I will just get hurt.

If you are repeatedly told, "Just shut up," you might come to these conclusions that are ungodly thought patterns:

Things would be better if I hadn't been born.

My life is a mistake.

I'll keep my mouth shut and my feelings to myself. I get into trouble when I share them, so I'll stuff them and hide them.

What I have to say is not valuable. My opinions don't matter. I have no voice.

The repetition of similar hurts reinforces all these beliefs.

Childhood abuse causes very deep hurts and wounds. David Seamands points out, "Your childhood is the time of life when God desires to build the rooms of the temple in which He wants to live when you are an adult."[34] When we understand a stronghold as a house built of lies, we see the importance of beliefs that are formed during childhood. The Enemy of our souls makes sure to deceive us through hurts, wounds and abusive events. Children are vulnerable and readily form opinions that may or may not agree with truth.

Parents, do every thing you can to help your children form godly thoughts. Teach them the Word of God and have discussions with them to help them understand how they can apply the Word in their life. Talk to them about their daily hurts, what opinions they have formed and how they feel. Lead them in prayers so they grow up knowing they have a Father who loves them, cares about them and heals their hurts.

Deep hurts and wounds are burned into your mind because of their intensity. The healing power of Jesus is needed for you to adopt God's thoughts about what happens to abused children. Abusing children is never okay with God. (Mathew 18:3-6)

*Traumatic experiences we had in early childhood that continue
to rule in our thoughts and emotions today usually produce
ungodly thought patterns.*

From the family you were raised in, the churches you attended, the neighborhoods you grew up in, the communities you belonged to, the friends you had - all of these environments influence the belief systems you adopt and live out.

Your environment isn't all that shapes you because we all interpret the world in which we live in a different way. Take a look at your own family – how different and unique are siblings, cousins, aunts and uncles? Each was raised in the same environment but adopted different perceptions to the same stimuli. How about Jacob and Esau in Scripture? They certainly had two different belief systems and yet were born into and raised in the same family.

Sinful patterns of thought are sometimes passed down the family line. The same ways of thinking that have plagued families for generations often result in families sharing core ungodly thought patterns. For instance, if pre-marital sex is common in a family line, there is usually an ungodly way of thinking about the nature of sex, marriage and/or the value of women. Some families do not have a value in saving sex for marriage and premarital sex is accepted as normal behavior. But following this behavior results in curses and consequences because it is not God's design.

Violence in family lines can result in rationalization and normalizing of violence and ungodly thought patterns, as well as the victims' beliefs about self-worth. These kinds of behaviors that are the result of wrong thinking are sometimes hard to identify when you are caught in the cycle. It may take help from another to assess the cycle and bondage in which one is trapped.

Many of the ungodly thought patterns we have about God, others and ourselves are a result of traumatic experiences. One of the biggest tragedies is what happens when beliefs are planted during traumatic experiences. Most perceptions adopted during trauma are not God's thoughts and perceptions. The demonic realm takes advantage of vulnerability during these times and plants seeds of thought that lead us away from God's truth in order to rob, kill and destroy our destiny in God. These are some examples of thoughts formed as a result of trauma. If not recognized as ungodly thought patterns, they will develop into strongholds and your life will be based on them instead of God's truths:

> *I will build a wall so thick to protect myself no one will be able to reach me.*
>
> *I will never let anyone really know me.*
>
> *I can't trust men no matter who they are…they will always take advantage of me. No one was there for me, not even God. I can't trust anyone. I have to take care of myself.*

> *We misjudge other people's intentions toward us and form ungodly thought patterns.*

You can form an ungodly thought pattern by the way you think a person loves or rejects you. We all tell ourselves a story about every interaction and experience we have.

We all tell ourselves a story about every interaction and experience we have.

A child might resent parental authority that tells him not to do things that will harm him: "Don't play in the street." "Don't touch the stove, it is hot." "Don't play with matches." The child might think, "They just don't want me to have a good time." "They are punishing me unfairly."

My parents loved me deeply. They showed their love by providing shelter, food, clothing and family. Dialogues from the heart were missing. Emotional connection was missing. Legalistic rules dominated my childhood home. I was unable to connect with their love. They thought they were protecting me from harm by not allowing certain activities, but I formed the opinion they were cold and uncaring and didn't want me to have any fun. I remember going to high school when everyone was talking about this awesome new group called "The Beatles." I was so embarrassed. We were not allowed to listen to the radio so I had no clue what all the rage was about. My parents thought they were protecting me, but I thought they were just behind the times and mean. As an adult I can appreciate their point of view and realize that I was protected from a lot of things others experienced. But the damage was done in my soul - I misinterpreted their love for me.

PAL: "Holy Spirit, when _____ said/did _____, I thought _____. Is that what I should be thinking?" You might need to ask the person involved if that is what they intended for you to think. *"_____, when you said/did _____, I thought and felt _____. Is that what you intended for me to think and feel?"*

When you misinterpret hurts you can make inner vows that result in ungodly thought patterns.

Vows become harmful to your relationships and to how you think about yourself.

> *I will never do what my parents did to me. They were_____.*
>
> *I will never trust God again. He wasn't there for me. He let me down. He helps other people, but not me.*
>
> *I will never open my heart to you again – you have hurt me too deeply.*

Inner vows are like fish hooks – as long as you and every one else leave them alone they don't hurt. When someone tries to remove them you react because it hurts. "Change happens when the pain of staying the same is greater than the pain of change." [35] There comes a tipping point in our desperation to be healed. A choice to change has to be made. It can be and sometimes is painful to change.

When we embrace word curses spoken over us we form ungodly thought patterns.

All of us experience word curses or word blessings. The power of life and death is in the tongue. (Proverbs 18:21) When we receive blessings our spirit thrives and we are empowered to walk in that blessing. When curses are spoken over us and we receive them as truth, we embrace ungodly thought patterns and live our lives based on lies. (See *"Word Curses,"* Chapter 11.)

You must remember… hurt people hurt people. We all need blessing and affirmation. Blessed people need to remember to bless others. What you give away you receive more in like kind. It is a principle of sowing and reaping. What do you need more of? Give some away! If you need encouragement, encourage others. If you need verbal appreciation, appreciate others verbally.

False doctrines and teachings form ungodly thought patterns.

One of the most harmful doctrines is legalistic, pharisaical teaching that if you just follow the rules and perform you will be okay. Somehow that never works out because you can never seem to perform well enough. There is always another horizon to conquer. The way to God is not through works and a set of do's and don'ts. You do not have to strive to be a better person. You are saved by faith and you become more like Jesus because He has gifted you with His presence and His power that enables you to walk in the Spirit, not in the flesh. Too often you find yourself in a performance trap.

Do you find yourself saying things like, "I ought to, I should, I wish I would have, I could have, I tried but… No matter what I do, it isn't enough"? David Seamands addresses these kinds of deadly thoughts: "While there are varying degrees of performance concentration, the syndrome itself is a kind of disease, a malignant virus at the heart of every human being. It is the ultimate lie behind myriads of ordinary lies, persuading us that every relationship in life is based on performance, that is, on what we do. This lie insists that everything depends on how well we perform – our relationship with God, with ourselves and with others…Performance-oriented Christians represent a wide range of despairing humanity. There are the very young in the Christian life, who are struggling to believe in a grace which just seems too good to be true. There are those who, like the Galatians, started out living by grace but now are mixing law (performance) and grace (gift). There are the perfectionists who feel sure nothing they do is ever good enough for God, others, or themselves." [36]

What a relief it is to recognize the lie that we have to perform to please God. When we receive, embrace and apply the truth that salvation is a gift, we experience freedom to walk in the Spirit.

> *You are not saved by how you behave;*
> *you are saved by how you believe.*

Something to consider: *You are not saved by how you behave; you are saved by how you believe.* Salvation is based on what you believe and confess. (Romans 10:10) Behaving rightly will not get you saved (nor sanctified). I might tell myself, "I am keeping all the commandments so I must be okay." Even the Apostle Paul thought that and it wasn't enough for him either. (Philippians 3) Only believing in God will save you.

While godly thinking and behaving doesn't save you, developing godly thought patterns after you have been made a new creation is part of the process of being sanctified or changed into the likeness of Jesus. Having the same mind as Christ affects your emotions and your behavior. The Fruit of the Spirit grows when you adopt and live out godly thought patterns. When you think like Jesus you will behave like Jesus.

False doctrines and teachings lead you to live your life based on ungodly thought patterns. There is a way out of these patterns as you recognize the father of lies as the source, repent for living in disagreement with God, and then embrace His thoughts.

> *The natural man with an unsanctified mind will make worldly*
> *conclusions that are ungodly thought patterns.*

The unsanctified mind tries to figure out life's traumas that lead us to erroneous habit patterns of thought.

A mind submitted to the mind of Christ will *PAL*: *"Lord Jesus, I want to agree with you so would you tell me what are you thinking about this person/ situation?"*

You might *PAL* to assess the source of your thought: *"This thought sounds just like _____,"* or *"Right now I am acting just like _____. Is this thought or behavior like Jesus (walking in the Spirit) or according to the 'old me' (walking in the flesh)"?*

Ungodly thought patterns give legal grounds to demons to harass and influence us. Once the *Generational Patterns and Curses* are recognized and repented for, *Ungodly Thought Patterns* recognized and renewed and *Life's Hurts* healed by Jesus, the Enemy has no place to live and they can be dismissed.

Ungodly thought patterns take away the abundant life Jesus died to give us. They continually replace a faith in God's power and faithfulness to faith in the Enemy. That's what we are doing when we agree with the Enemy in our thoughts – we have more faith in him than in God. Many times ungodly thought patterns are a product of fear. They cause us to be double-minded (James 1). We put limitations on the destiny God has designed for us when we agree with the Enemy.

Change your thoughts and you will change your life!

MINISTRY TO UNGODLY THOUGHT PATTERNS

As we begin ministry to ungodly thought patterns let's think about some foundational truths and guidelines.

Who gets to choose what we think? Each person has *The Power to Choose* thoughts, feelings, and actions. Attitudes and thoughts don't just happen. They are a product of our own choices. If you don't like how you are feeling, *PAL*: *"What thought is producing this emotion?"* If you don't like how you are behaving, *PAL*: *"What thought and feeling produces this kind of behavior?"*

Merriam-Webster Dictionary defines the word attitude as "a system of thoughts, the mental posture, the mindset, or the way of thinking with which a person approaches life". [37]

A system of thought is either godly or ungodly. What are you choosing?

PAL: *"Holy Spirit, what is the most important thought affecting me in a negative way that you want me to change?"*

"Holy Spirit, what is the biggest emotional challenge I face when life gets tough? What thought is producing that emotion?"

"Holy Spirit, is this thought robbing, killing and destroying me? (John 10:10) Is this thought producing life and freedom?"

As you are working on renewing your mind, let's agree on some ground rules:

1. *Don't quit* when the going gets tough. There will be a challenge! Learn the strategies of the Enemy. Don't be ignorant of his schemes. He prowls around like a lion, looking for someone to destroy. Resolve it will not be you! Be ready! Resist the Enemy by standing firm in your faith. (1 Peter 5:8-9, 2 Corinthians 2:11)

   Dr. Caroline Leaf presents supporting scientific and scriptural evidence that when our thoughts become toxic our brains cannot function the way God designed us to function. [38] Do you know what your weak, vulnerable spots are? Be assured your Enemy knows them and will use them against you.

2. *Take hope* – this won't last forever. There will be a breakthrough. "Don't get tired of doing what is good. At just the right time you will reap a harvest of blessing if you don't give up." (Galatians 6:9)

3. *Stay in touch* with the source of your strength to do all things – JESUS! (Philippians 4:13) Pray in the Spirit and build yourself up in Him – not the Devil! (Jude 1:20) If you are continually thinking negative, ungodly thoughts you are building yourself up in the Devil. That's *not* what you want!!

4. *Ask for God's perspective.* PAL: *"God is there another way for me to look at this circumstance/person?"*

Remember that your perception is your reality, but what you you *need* is His perception, His thoughts. The patterns of thought in which you have habituated yourself become truth in your mind, and you "feel" and "behave" based on those thoughts. (Romans 14:14)

5. *Don't make major decisions* in the midst of fiery trials. Until you are agreeing with God's thoughts you are likely to make a decision that won't turn out for your well being. And God's plans for you are always for your well being. (Jeremiah 29:11)

Let's get our brains and our thoughts working for and with us instead of against us. It will be a challenge, but it is doable because God has commanded it in His Word. "Be transformed by the renewing of the mind." (Romans 12:2) Deuteronomy 30:11-14 tells us what God commands us to do is *not too hard*! Why? Because the Word is very near to us. In fact it is in our mouth and in our heart so that we *can* observe it.

Here is something to think about: If you have learned an ungodly thought pattern, you can unlearn it by learning a godly thought pattern. You don't have to be stuck in old, ungodly patterns of thought and patterns of behavior. You will never move or grow beyond what you think and believe. You are being changed into His image from glory to glory. (2 Corinthians 3:18)

You will never move or grow beyond what you think and believe.

If you are used to thinking and/or saying Murphy's law:

"Nothing is as easy as it looks; everything takes longer than you expect; if anything can go wrong it will – at the worst possible moment."

Let's change it to:

164

*"If anything can go right, it will; nothing is as difficult as
it appears; everything is more rewarding than it appears;
if anything good can happen to anybody, it will happen to
me."*

Ungodly thought patterns produce a negative life - a life lived walking according to the flesh. Thinking God's way produces a godly life – the life of a New Creation, a life lived walking according to the Spirit. (Romans 8:5-7)

In the prayer session to minister to ungodly thought patterns, our goal is to legally break our agreement with the ungodly thought pattern and identify and agree with God's thought. We want to be able to join in His plans for our future that are for our well-being and to experience hope.

"5 R's" ACTIVATION

We pray through a "*5 R's*" model to activate a new thought process:

Recognize

Repent

Renew through

Repetition

Rehearsal

The first step is to identify a thought, belief or expectation that is not in agreement with God. We want to *Recognize* the lie we have believed and lived our life based on.

If this seems to be difficult, take a look at the emotions that are being negatively displayed – fears, worries, anger, resentments, hurts, unbelief, doubts, bitterness, blaming. Think about recent occurrences of the emotions being negatively displayed.

Complete this statement: I feel (or felt) _____ because I was thinking _____.

When you *Recognize* an ungodly thought pattern, see if you can find one that goes even deeper so you can identify the ungodly root allowing the thought. *PAL: "Holy Spirit, is there more? Would you help me identify how I am thinking that is at odds with you?"*

Another key question to *PAL* in recognizing ungodly thought patterns is *"Are my thoughts, beliefs, and perceptions stealing, killing or robbing me of an abundant life, or bringing me into an abundant life?"* (John 10:10)

When the Holy Spirit ministers in the Healing Life's Hurts session you are likely to discover more ungodly thought patterns associated with the unhealed hurts and wounds. Remember that the Enemy likes to take advantage of you when you are most vulnerable so he plants many seeds of deception and doubt in your thoughts during traumatic events.

As you *Recognize* the ungodly thought pattern, write it down. Somehow seeing something in black and white makes it harder for us to ignore it. We begin to take responsibility for it. Write the ungodly thought pattern as a statement, making it as blunt and clear as you possibly can. Don't ramble. Be concise. Be as honest as you can possibly be. This helps emphasize the reality of the belief and how it is in opposition to God's Thoughts.

Repent for embracing, believing and living your life based on the ungodly lie. Remove and break the power of the ungodly thought pattern.

Then *PAL: ("Holy Spirit what do you want me to think instead of this ungodly thought?")* This new thought will agree with God's Word. Express this new truth as a declarative statement. Again, be concise and clear. You want it to be easily memorable.

Declare and receive your new godly thought pattern.

THOUGHTS TO KEEP IN MIND WHILE CRAFTING A GODLY THOUGHT PATTERN

A godly thought pattern is usually the opposite of the ungodly thought pattern and expresses the godly way of looking at the same concept or principle or thought that is revealed by the ungodly thought pattern. I encourage you – don't write out Scripture to begin with. Our religious training and culture has conditioned us to quote Scripture without knowing how to apply it or having no experience of it. We are caught in a pattern of a having a form of godliness but denying its power. (2 Timothy 3:5) Many of us can quote a lot of Scripture but have not experienced transformation. It has not become real in our hearts. We have not received it as truth, otherwise we would be free. When we "know" the truth, which includes experiencing it, we become free.

The goal of writing a godly thought to replace the ungodly thought pattern is to write one we can embrace, receive and apply with the help of the Holy Spirit. Ask the Holy Spirit what He wants to say to you, write it down, *then* go to the Scripture to make sure it agrees with and doesn't contradict the Word of God. If in listening to the Holy Spirit you hear a Scripture, write it down then *PAL: "Holy Spirit, what does this mean for me, right now, as it relates to this ungodly thought pattern I am giving up? How will you help me apply this Word this afternoon? Tomorrow? In the coming week? As I habituate myself in a new thought pattern? How will this help me change the way I think, feel, act and talk?"*

If the new godly thought pattern seems too big a step to make from the ungodly thought pattern, choose an intermediate thought you could believe and embrace and apply. ("I can never remember names" to "I always remember names" is a BIG jump and seems daunting. Unless God does a sovereign work – which He sometimes does – it probably won't happen that way.) In order to diminish the pressure to change all at once, write a godly thought pattern that will change as you grow. Use phrases like "As I am healed, as God is healing me, I will be able to…". You can also include phrases like "Because of the power of God's grace I will be able to…", "God is with me as I…" or "As God is empowering me to habituate my mind with godly thought patterns, He is transforming me. I am growing and changing."

God loves process.

God loves process…and He loves walking through it *with* us!

Make sure the godly thought pattern addresses all of the real issues revealed in the ungodly thought pattern. It should counteract the essence of the ungodly thought pattern.

Use your own words. We are not looking for a nice, clean antiseptic religious statement that sounds like "it should". You want a statement that agrees with God and speaks to your heart.

Use Scripture to support and verify the truth of the godly thought pattern. Write down supporting scriptures, memorize them, meditate on them, and craft prayers from them.

Review the new thought and *PAL: "Holy Spirit is there anything You want to change or clarify?"*

You are now ready to renew your mind. Your mind is *Renewed* through *Repetition* and *Rehearsal* (practice). For the next 21 - 30 days think about and habituate your mind in and speak out your godly thought pattern seven to twelve times a day. Caroline Leaf says, "You can expect definite "brain change" within 21 days – *if* you work consciously and intensively at least seven to twelve times a day. Change will happen in your brain as soon as you start the process (of renewing your thought pattern). Within four days you will feel the effects of changed thinking; within 21 days you will have built a whole new thought pattern, literally, a new circuit in your brain.

Though change begins immediately, the entire process takes time to complete. Because it is a process and you are working on renewing your mind, breaking toxic thinking is ongoing. The first four days will be the most difficult. The fifth through the twenty-first days will become easier as you progress. Even though you'll feel a significant change after 21 days, you will need to still be mindful of practicing your new thought pattern." [39] *Repetition is crucial!!*

The part of the brain that supported the old thought process actually dries up and falls away because of disuse. God's creation is amazing! Dr. Leaf calls ungodly thought patterns Toxic Thinking and shares some facts that are a wake up call. She says, "75% to 95% of the illnesses that plague us today are a direct result of our thought life. What we think about affects us physically and emotionally. The average person has over 30,000 thoughts a day. When we don't exercise self-control in our thought life, we create the conditions for illness. Research shows that fear triggers more than 1,400 known physical and chemical responses and activates more than 30 different hormones. There are intellectual and medical reasons as well as spiritual reasons to forgive." [40]

The exercise and discipline of renewing your mind is not just a positive confession, but a way to change your heart. Proverbs 23:7 says, "As a man thinks in his heart, so is he." (AMP) I call this exercise *Intentional Thinking*:

> *Set your mind and keep it set.*
> > Decide you are going for total victory! (Colossians 3:2, Hebrews 6:11)
>
> *Renew your mind.*
> > At conversion, our spirit is regenerated but our mind needs to be renewed. (Romans 12:2)
>
> *Gird up your mind.*
> > To gird means to get your minds off everything that would cause you to stumble as you run the race God has set before you. (1 Peter 1:13)

Is there demonic interference? Tell them there is no room for them – renounce them. Say something like this, "I am full of faith…there is no room for you doubt, unbelief, wavering, etc. I am full of hope…there is no room for you depression, discouragement, etc."

This is the principle of *Renouncing* in action. It means to say "I recognize this thought, feeling, and/or behavior as ungodly and I don't have any space for you in me anymore. You have to stay away from me. I will not entertain you anymore." It means to *disown* and to *forbid the approach* of the things disowned. You give it up and speak it out that it has to stay away from you.

Use your mental energy to think God's thoughts, not negative, ungodly thoughts. Think and say this seven to twelve times a day to combat fear: *I will not be afraid; I will not let fear control me; I know it will come from time to time, but even if I have to do something of which I'm afraid, I am going to do it with God's help! Whenever I am afraid I will put my trust in you. You are my safe refuge and whenever I am afraid I will run to You!*

As you are repeating your new thought, include *Rehearsal* – practice it. PAL: *"Holy Spirit how do you want me to apply this new truth to my thoughts, feelings, actions and conversations?"* This is called transformation.

It is important to note we are not casting out a demon here. We are changing a habit. An ungodly thought pattern is expressed as a habit of the flesh – a habit of our mind, will and emotion. A demon can use this habit against us, but as we change the habit to a godly one, the demon has no place to stay and harass or influence us. We are pulling down strongholds and casting down imaginations and every thing that puts itself against the knowledge of God. (2 Corinthians 10:4-5)

PRAYER FOR UNGODLY THOUGHT PATTERN

1. I now **recognize** I have believed a lie. I agree with you and I **confess** my sin of believing the lie that _____.

2. I **forgive** those who have contributed to my forming this lie (*PAL: "Lord, who has contributed to my forming this belief, this way of thinking?"*) Be specific.

3. I ask You, Lord, to **forgive me** and I **repent** for receiving this lie, for living my life based on it, and for any way I have judged others because of it. (*PAL: "Lord who have I judged?"*)

   I **receive** your forgiveness, Lord.

4. Because you have forgiven me, Lord, I choose to **forgive myself** for believing this lie.

5. I **repent** for believing this lie. I am ready to change my mind and receive your truth.

6. I **renounce** and **break** my agreement with this lie. I cancel my agreement with the kingdom of darkness. I break all agreements I have made with demons.

7. I choose to **accept**, **believe**, and **receive** what You say is true Lord so my mind can be **renewed**. (*PAL: "What do you say is true Lord?"* _____) (See notes on crafting a new Godly Thought Pattern.)

8. With the help of the Holy Spirit I will begin to **Renew** my mind by **Repeating** and **Rehearsing** this new way of thinking. Instead of behaving like I used to (how was that?_____), I will (*PAL: "Holy Spirit what do you want me to do instead?"* _____). My **warning** system will be old ways of thinking, feeling and behaving. My **weapon** will be this new thought that will produce new behavior. Thank you for helping me change, Father.

CHAPTER 17

HEALING LIFE'S HURTS

"I pray that in all respects you may prosper and be in good health,
just as your soul prospers."
3 John 1:2

"O Lord, be gracious to me; Heal my soul, for I have sinned against You."
Psalm 41:4

"He has sent me to bind up the broken hearted…"
Isaiah 61:1

YOU MAY HAVE HEARD IT SAID THAT YOUR PAST does not get to define who you are. That is true! It is also true that your past does not get to define your future. Hurts and wounds from people in our past do not get to define us, either. The problem is, however, that many of us have experienced hurts and wounds that have not yet been touched by Jesus. The perceptions we formed about life and God from those experiences are hindering us in the present. They keep us from walking in the Spirit. One of the mission points for Jesus we read about in Isaiah 61 and Luke 4 is that He came to heal the broken-hearted and bruised. He came to heal the inner person.

We certainly are a society of broken-hearted people. The gift of salvation Jesus accomplished on the Cross includes healing broken hearts. Jesus understands all our hurts, pains and griefs. He was "…despised and forsaken of men, a man of sorrows and acquainted with grief." (Isaiah 53:3)

HEALING LIFE'S HURTS DEFINED

Life's Hurts are those wounds to our soul, places inside of us, that can't be seen but affect how we present ourselves to our world of influence. Their presence is known by how they are expressed through our thoughts, feelings and behavior.

God wants to heal our "inner" person as well as the visible, physical body that carries our spirit and soul. This is the dynamic we call Healing Life's Hurts – God touching and making whole the places inside of us that affect our thought and feeling development.

While I will not address in this book the issue of the differentiation between "soul" and "spirit" as used in Scripture, I encourage you to read Chester and Betsy Kylstra's book, "*Restoring The Foundations.*" They have done an excellent word study on these terms and list scriptures and definitions on pages 409 and 411.

In "*The Power of Forgiveness*" we explored how unforgiveness keeps our hearts from being healed and free from pain. We also learned that during traumatic events the Enemy plants seeds of doubt and ungodly patterns of thinking about God and others that hinder us from wholeness.

In the sanctification process (our mind, will and emotions being transformed to look like Jesus) we discover and progressively experience what an exchanged life looks like. The truth of Galatians 2:20 rocks us as we discover the BIG EXCHANGE God offers us in Jesus Christ. "I have been crucified with Christ; and it is no longer I who live, but Christ lives in me; and the life which I now live in the flesh I live by faith in the Son of God, who loved me and gave Himself up for me."

Wow! To really be able to walk in this truth in the midst of challenging, hurtful life situations is an incredible gift. I give Him my life and He gives me His. He lives in and through me as I continue to say *"Yes, Lord. You can live through me. You can be love, joy, peace, patience, goodness, kindness, gentleness, faithfulness and self-control through me. I yield to you living in and through me. I give you my hurts, my broken heart and receive your healing. I give you my fears and receive your peace. I give you my thoughts and receive instead your thoughts."*

We are learning to *PAL*: *"Holy Spirit what fruit of the Spirit are you wanting to be in me and for me? How do you want to express this fruit through me right now?"* This enables us to walk in the Spirit as we learn to yield to His life being lived in and through us instead of reacting in the flesh according to our old nature.

In my workbook "Growing Kingdom Fruit" I explore the connection between emotional health and the growth of the Fruit of the Spirit. I came to the conclusion that "how I respond to life emotionally is directly related to allowing God to grow the Fruit of the Spirit in my life." [41] Now I would expand that conclusion to include the importance of renewing the mind.

The BIG EXCHANGE…yes we all have hurts and wounds from our past that still affect our thinking, emotions and behavior. If we are experiencing ungodly behavior patterns that we seem to be stuck in, we might *PAL*: *"Holy Spirit, is there an unhealed hurt in my life that is affecting how I think, feel and behave today?"* He wants us to bring those hurts to Him and let Him heal them.

Here is the truth: God is our healer!

Here is the truth: God is our healer! (Exodus 15:26)

In the Bible the psalmist David models for us how to express our deepest thoughts, hurts and feelings to the Lord. He "poured out" his inner most thoughts to the Lord and looked to Him for understanding and healing. (Psalm 142) David knew he could be honest with the Lord. He could count on God's faithfulness to be his place of safety, strength and healing. Psalm 142 is a wonderful prayer to personalize and pray. It not only helps you recognize and express your thoughts and feelings, it reminds you of God's sovereignty and power and faithfulness.

Healing Life's Hurts ministry requires honesty with the Lord about what you are thinking and feeling. Perhaps you have been told like I was in my childhood, "If you have bad feelings and thoughts and dare to share them, then you are a 'bad' Christian." You desperately want to be a "good" Christian, so you learn to stuff your real thoughts and feelings and become a guilt-ridden, fearful person. As a follower of Jesus Christ you walk by faith, not feelings. You need to know that feelings are affected by what you think. If you are thinking thoughts that don't agree with God, you will produce behavior that does not look like Jesus. The heart of the Father is for you to look like His Son, Jesus Christ.

In Psalm 41:4 David asks the Lord to be gracious to him and heal his soul. He acknowledges he has sinned against God, taking responsibility for his actions. He is asking God to heal him from the anguish he is experiencing in his inner most being, the hidden places of his heart.

Psalm 147:3 says that God heals the broken-hearted and binds up their wounds. That's good news. Rehearsing God's character in Psalm 23, David acknowledges that it is God who restores his soul.

We can't leave a discussion on life's hurts without talking about Isaiah 53:3-5. This passage describes Jesus and we get a glimpse into His inner thoughts and emotions. He was despised, forsaken, acquainted with grief, carried our sorrows. He was stricken, afflicted, wounded, and crushed. He was chastised for our well-being and was scourged for our healing.

We have only a glimpse of what He thought and felt in the Garden of Gethsemane. He said, "Father if it be possible, could this cup pass from me? Nevertheless, not my will but yours be done." (Matthew 26:39) Can you sense the mental, emotional and physical pain of Jesus? He knows what it is like to be betrayed, wounded, rejected, abandoned, and abused. Knowing all of that, He chose to come from heaven to earth, making a way for us to experience healing in our own story with Him.

He chose to come from heaven to earth, making a way for us to experience healing in our own story with Him.

Some people don't like to talk about their negative feelings because they think it is making a negative confession, or that they "shouldn't" be feeling that way. Feelings are a warning to us that something needs attention. There is a thought connected to the feeling that needs to be identified and discerned. Dr. Caroline Leaf says, "We can actually feel our thoughts through our emotions." [42] When working with negatively expressed feelings you must *PAL: "Is this thought godly or ungodly?"*

Feelings are a warning to us that something needs attention.

It is okay to talk about your negatively expressed feelings when you are seeking help for transformation. There are many examples in Scripture of people expressing their emotions and thoughts to the Lord. I love how David expresses himself freely and always comes back to the truth of how God is his refuge and strength and strong tower. Reading through the Psalms is helpful to learn this healing skill.

Whenever you catch yourself coupling your thoughts or feelings with words like "should," "shouldn't," or "ought" I get suspicious that a religious spirit is interfering with someone's belief system. "Shoulds" and "oughts" keep you boxed into a set of rules you will never be able to keep. You are to live in a relationship with Jesus Christ and your expressions of life are a "get to" not a "should" or "ought". Reevaluate thought patterns and eliminate the "should" and "oughts" with "I get to… " The Holy Spirit knows when the Enemy is putting false guilt on you and sets you free from that mentality.

PAL: *"Holy Spirit, I'm caught in a "should" or "ought to" trap. Will you help me see the truth and set me free? What is the "get to" in this situation?"*

You need to learn how to be genuine about your thoughts and feelings without agreeing with the Enemy and indulging in a pity party. Pity parties can lead to doubt, depression, deception, and death to intimacy with God. Learning to identify feelings and thoughts before they become a habit empowers you to reject the lies of the Enemy and to discern, receive and apply God's truth.

> ## Learning to identify feelings and thoughts before they become a habit empowers you to reject the lies of the Enemy and to discern, receive and apply God's truth.

You can evaluate your feelings to determine the godliness of your thoughts. Fill in the blanks in this exercise to help you: *I feel _____ because I think _____. When I think and feel this way, I usually behave _____. This behavior is _____ (godly or ungodly). When I behave this way I am walking _____ (in the Spirit or according to the flesh).*

If you have difficulty identifying your feelings you can process this exercise like this: *When I think _____ I then feel _____. Then I behave like this _____. This behavior is _____ (godly or ungodly).*

Use this exercise along with this *PAL: "Holy Spirit, is there an unhealed hurt currently affecting my thoughts, feelings and behavior?"* This will help you partner with the Holy Spirit as He heals your heart.

You must be willing to recognize that unhealed pain from the past can control you in the present. Once you recognize that reality, you can choose to do something about it and ask God for healing. You might need to pray a prayer like this: *"Father, I will lay down my control so you can be in control. You are God…I'm not. I don't want to behave in this ungodly manner anymore. Would you help me discern what thoughts I am having that are leading me to behave this way?"* Another important realization might come as you have the person pray: *"Holy Spirit, I'm really tired of having this pain. I am deciding today to let go of it and give it to you. Will you take it?"*

Sometimes you use pain to protect you from reality. It is difficult to face what really happened in some circumstances so you allow pain to stay in place. The familiar pain will demand your attention. It will keep you from asking God to reveal the truth He wants you to know so your heart can be healed. *Fear of facing pain can paralyze you and keeps you stuck.*

> *Fear of facing pain can paralyze you and keeps you stuck.*

Pain can also be a way to get attention from people in order to feel loved. If you stop doing what you do to avoid pain (defense mechanisms) when things go wrong, you will expose the wound. Then healing can begin. You have probably heard the saying "It's going to get worse before it gets better." Sometimes it seems that way, but when you face the pain of the situation and hear God's perspective you truly can begin to put the past in the past and not allow it to affect you in the present and future. Only God's truth and His healing presence make this possible.

When people ask me what I do I love answering something like this: "One of my passions is to help people get *"unstuck"* from the hurts and pains from the past, help them learn to live in the present moment and get them ready to move into their future with God." There's nothing more satisfying than to see someone engaged with the Holy Spirit, experiencing healing from past experiences that have been hindering them from seeing God bring transformation and hope. We serve an amazing God!

Only the Holy Spirit knows those wounds and hurts that are affecting us today. If there is bad fruit (ungodly behavior), there is a bad root. We don't go probing around to find something; we simply *PAL*: *"Holy Spirit, is there a hurt or wound that resulted in a perception I adopted that is contributing to my current challenge?" "Holy Spirit, where is the bad root? When was the bad seed planted?" "What do I need to know to be healed?"*

SOURCES OF LIFE'S HURTS AND WOUNDS

Life's hurts and wounds come from many sources. We don't have to look far in our society to see broken-hearted, wounded people. Families are ripped apart, murders and robberies increase every day, and sexual assaults are constantly in the news. Likely someone you know has been sexually assaulted in some way. No longer is it just someone on the news. Occult practices are becoming the norm in many areas of our country. Some people experience traumatic hurts when they lose a parent or loved one. All kinds of abuse happen: sexual, emotional, verbal, physical, mental, and spiritual. Memories of traumatic experiences such as murders or other acts of violence leave wounds of fear, anger, hate or terror that can affect emotional health, leaving a person vulnerable to similar incidents later on in life.

Some people experience hurt not by what was done to them, but by the things that were neglected or left out. For example, parents might not been physically abusive to their children, but if they were not capable of nurturing or being physically and emotionally available to their children, the hurt could be just as damaging.

Some people experience different levels of hurt as a result of similar situations. We may not understand this, but we need to realize and learn to recognize the hurt and the effect of the hurt that is living on the inside of another person. Those hurts affect their thoughts, feelings and behavior. We can help them get to Jesus to hear His voice speak truth and healing.

It is true that Jesus died to sin once for all (Roman 6:10) and it is finished business. We also know that our perception about hurtful events in the past have affected our thoughts, feelings and behavior in the present. The pain and ungodly perceptions need the healing touch of Jesus. We need God's viewpoint in order to experience freedom.

> *Our perception about hurtful events in the past have affected our thoughts, feelings and behavior in the present.*

We have learned that sin patterns can be passed down in a family from generation to generation. With those sins, such as alcoholism or abuse, similar hurts can continue from generation to generation. Looking at family history in regards to similar types of wounding is invaluable.

When an unhealed life hurt is revealed, sometimes we see a connection to a generational pattern. Since hurting people hurt people, similar wounds to the soul continue until there is repentance, forgiveness and healing.

Listening carefully during the healing prayer for life's hurts will almost always reveal an ungodly thought pattern. Many of those perceptions were adopted during times of trauma. An unhealed hurt reinforces the ungodly thought pattern and keeps it in place. The hurt plus the negative thought pattern work together to form a stronghold.

Chester and Betsy Kylstra say it so well, "If the heart says, "I'm hurting", and the mind that is being renewed says, "I'm healed," which one will win out? That's right, the heart! The unhealed hurt causes the heart to cry out, "The new godly belief is a lie! I can't receive it!" Why? Because the pain is still present. The hurt must be healed before God's truth can fully settle into the heart." [43]

Have you ever noticed that demons don't play by a fair set of rules? They like to take advantage of you when your defenses are down in moments of tragedy. That is the time they come operating in lies and planting those seeds of doubt that keep us in bondage. They tend to exaggerate the hurt in your thoughts to keep you discouraged and make you doubt the goodness of God.

It is usually best to wait until the hurt is healed, the ungodly thought pattern has been exposed and any generational pattern dealt with before commanding the demons to leave. When they have no legal ground to claim they can be dismissed.

If the demons are interfering with the healing prayer, bind them up until it is time for them to go. I pray something like this: "In the Name of Jesus I bind demonic spirits, in particular demons of doubt, unbelief, and confusion, from interfering in this person's life as he/she is receiving healing. Cease your activity now until Jesus says it is time for you to go." If possible have the person pray the prayer in agreement with you, declaring they belong to the Lord Jesus Christ and will be available only for Him.

HEALING LIFE'S HURTS MINISTRY

Healing Life's Hurts often includes feeling the painful emotions associated with the memory and remembering what thoughts were adopted at the time. Forgiveness for any involved in the event and a realization of the presence of Jesus and hearing what He wants to say to you in light of what happened is part of the healing process. When the pain of the situation is healed and God gives you a new way of thinking about what happened, you begin to walk in that new way of thinking. It will take time to apply the new godly thought to daily life. Scientific research has shown that repetition of a thought seven to twelve times a day for 30 days actually changes your brain and you develop a new habitual pattern of thought. [44] Patterns of thought affect your feelings and behavior. The pathway for the old way we used to think about the painful event actually dries up in our brain because of disuse and falls away. Repetition and rehearsal (practice) are key to developing a new way of thinking. This is what we call being transformed by the renewal of the mind. It is part of the process of sanctification – our souls learning to walk in the power of the Spirit.

We refer to this Holy Spirit-led prayer interaction as Listening Prayer. As we begin a session to pray for an unhealed hurt, we ask the person to pray a prayer of submission. We ask them to lay down any fear of what might happen and ask Jesus to come do what only He can do. We recognize that only Jesus knows the deep places in your heart and what needs to be healed. We ask Him to bring to mind only the thing(s) He wants to heal in this session and acknowledge His presence that will enable us all to see and hear Him as He does His work.

One thing I want to make clear is we **cannot change the memory** of what happened. We do not enter the memory and the pain of it in order to change the details. In fact it is helpful to have the person describe the memory as he is experiencing it both in physical and emotional detail. The important thing to think about is that God can change *how* you think about the memory to His viewpoint. That is where the healing happens. *Your problem or challenge is not what happened to you, but your perception about what happened.*

> *Your problem or challenge is not what happened to you, but your perception about what happened.*

Your thoughts (belief system) affect your feelings, which in turn affect your behavior. You will see that concept espoused throughout this book because it is a fundamental truth. You act according to what you believe to be true. (Proverbs 23:7) And the Lord instructs us, *after* we have become believers, to renew our minds so we can become like Jesus. (Romans 12:2) This is an ongoing *process* as He changes us into the image of His dear Son, Jesus, from glory to glory. This doesn't happen all at once, but in a process. We work out the reality of our salvation (total healing), walking daily in the Fruit of the Spirit. (2 Corinthians 3:18, Philippians 2:12-13, Galatians 5:25)

This ministry session to heal life's hurts relies heavily on the skill of hearing God's voice. I like to ask the question, *"How do you hear from or connect the best with God?"* There are a variety of ways to hear His voice: you can hear in your head, see pictures or words, or sense or feel something. I have even heard testimony that some people taste or smell what God is trying to say to them. He engages us with all of our senses.

Review the principles presented in the section *"The Power of Hearing God Speak."* Knowing how the person best connects with God will help you frame appropriate, helpful questions as you facilitate ministry. (i.e. If the person connects best with God through "seeing" pictures or visions, frame questions with "seeing" language: *"What are you seeing? What is God showing you?"* If the person connects best through hearing, frame questions with "hearing" language: *"What are you hearing? What is God saying to you?"*)

As we pray, we are directing the attention of the person that is receiving ministry to the Lord, not to the facilitator or ministry leader. Our desire is that the person will connect with Jesus and hear His voice so that deep healing can occur. Your skill as a facilitator in participating but not being the focus is crucial at this point. The ministry needs to be seen as from the Holy Spirit and not the ministry team. Talk in 1st person to keep the person engaged with God. As you are leading them in prayer you are praying as if you were in their place.

Here are some of the questions we encourage the one seeking healing to ask during Healing Life's Hurts.

PAL: "Holy Spirit would you reveal to me what event or memory is connected to the behavior I am currently seeking to change? What do you want to bring up so it can be healed?"

If there is a lot of fear and anxiety we might have them pray, *"Holy Spirit I'm really afraid right now. I don't know what is going to happen. Will you be with me as I go through this healing? (Pause and Listen.) I choose to give you my fear and anxiety – will you take it? (Pause and Listen.) I will give it to you and receive your peace instead."*)

Any time you ask the Lord a question, take time to Pause and Listen for Him to respond.

Sometimes people have a belief that God won't or doesn't want to help them. We pause and have them *PAL: "Father will you help me _____?"* Or, *"I have been thinking you don't want to help me. Is that true?"* Pause and Listen. Encourage people that when they journal and have asked the Lord a question, they need to Pause and Listen for what He might say to them. Let's not be rude to the Holy Spirit!

183

As the Lord reveals the memory or hurt, have the person describe what they are seeing and feeling and what they were thinking when it happened. Instruct them to describe their feelings and thoughts to the Lord – not to you. Ask them to share this out loud, as it helps you follow the process and listen to the Holy Spirit for nudges about going deeper with questions or direction. As the ministry leader, *PAL: "Holy Spirit, what do you want to heal? How will you heal this hurt? What questions can I lead this person in that will bring them closer to you and deeper into healing?"*

Some people think this is cruel as the person relives the pain in this moment. I would rather have someone revisit and experience the pain in a moment, with some loving guidance and oversight, rather than carry it around with them for years, reliving it every time an incident triggers that memory and feeling. *That* is cruel. If we know taking someone to Jesus and having them hear Him speak words that will bring healing and change how they think about what happened to them, that's what we should do. Our tendency might be to try to comfort them out of their pain, but we need to let them experience this moment with the Lord and let it happen. I don't encourage any touching or sympathizing during this session. The Lord is quite capable of caring for the person and knows exactly what they need to experience and let go of in order to embrace His healing presence. Let it happen on His terms.

It usually doesn't take long for a memory to come when you ask the Holy Spirit what He wants to reveal and heal. Sometimes the person is hesitant to share what they thought of because (1) it doesn't make any sense how it could be connected to their current issue, (2) it may be embarrassing or (3) it may seem so very small and insignificant.

Encourage them to share the first thought they have since we know the Holy Spirit is present to help us. Even though we don't understand, He is leading this prayer time. He will tell us what we need to know as we follow His leading. If they are embarrassed I usually remind them that absolutely nothing they could ever share will cause me to love them any less and I know it won't cause Jesus to love them less. I also remind them that what they share is confidential and will not be shared outside the room (unless there are legal issues involved). If they think it is too small and shouldn't have mattered, remind them that something is affecting them in the present that is still in place from the past and Jesus is present to bring healing today. Nothing is insignificant to Jesus!

It is important for them to stay in the memory and allow the Holy Spirit to work. We are working with "yesterday's feelings" that are affecting today. Feelings we see expressed in the moment can be indicative of the wound. If the person wanders, gently redirect them to the memory God revealed and ask them to share just what they are seeing, hearing and feeling as it is happening in their memory.

If other memories pop up, write them down. *PAL: "Holy Spirit is this connected and do you want to deal with it later in this session?"*

God works in this session to bring healing to the thoughts that provoked the feelings and behavior for which He wants to bring new insight.

If the person doesn't understand something they are seeing or hearing have them *PAL* (even if you think you understand it): *"Holy Spirit I heard you say, I saw _____. I don't understand that. What do you want me to know about that? What does that mean for me right now?"*

As a ministry facilitator your goal is to connect the person to Jesus and keep their attention turned towards Him until you sense a release that the Holy Spirit is done.

Often during a Healing Life's Hurt session we visit *forgiveness, ungodly thought patterns, generational patterns, and at times demonic interference.* Sometimes *soul ties, word curses, vows and judgments* are revealed. Listen especially for ungodly thought patterns as those are what sustain the hurt. Be listening and take notes. *PAL: "Holy Spirit, when do you want to take care of that?"* Deal with the issues as the Holy Spirit directs, forgiving when necessary and shifting from ungodly to godly thought patterns. This is all in the context of Listening Prayer while the person is engaged in conversation with the Lord.

If the person seems to be stuck, *PAL: "Holy Spirit, is there any person I need to forgive in order to receive healing from this memory?"* Or *"I seem to be stuck. What now Lord?"*

Another hindrance might be demonic interference that needs to be bound so the Holy Spirit can work healing in the memory. When the house of lies that the Enemy constructed is recognized, torn down, and replaced with God's way of thinking, the demons living there will have no home. They have been served their eviction notice. In the mean time, bind them up in Jesus' Name and declare they will not be able to operate until Jesus says it is time for them to go. If you try to cast demons out before the legal ground is taken back, you will struggle to get them to leave. Don't mess with them. Do the work of taking back the ground they have invaded and then dismiss them based on the finished work of Jesus on the Cross.

While the person is still in the memory, after describing what they are seeing, feeling and hearing, have them *PAL*: *"Dear Jesus, while I am remembering* _____ *are you here with me? What would you like to say to me? What are you doing right now? Would you heal my heart? It really hurts right now."* Pause and Listen!

We have had many beautiful scenarios described at this point of how Jesus wants to interact with the person and how a soothing, calming healing comes to the heart. Jesus' presence is really what we need!

When you sense the healing is complete or done for the current session, ask how they are doing. You might ask, *"What is your level of discomfort or pain as you now think about this memory?" "On a scale of 0-10 what emotion arises and how strong is it when you think about the memory?"* Compare it to how intense it was when you began the session. The goal is to reach "0", but remember this is a process and the Holy Spirit knows timing in this process. Have the person say something like, *"Thank you Lord for the healing you brought to me today. I know you will finish what you have started. Thank you for being with me."*

You want the person's participation at every level. If they can ask the questions or pray the prayers, lead them to say them aloud. They are taking ownership for their life; you are not doing it for them.

If you are not sure the Holy Spirit is done, *PAL*: *"Holy Spirit, are you done for today?"* If you sense the Lord wants to do more, have the person *PAL*: *"Holy Spirit, is there forgiveness you want me to extend to someone?"* Or, *"Holy Spirit what is this connected to?"* Or, *"Holy Spirit, what do you want to say to me about this right now? I am still experiencing some emotional pain."*

Make sure the person is back in the present with you and they are at peace in their thinking and emotions. They will most likely be tired, as they have just experienced a "spiritual surgery". It would be good to instruct them to go home and rest if possible and spend some time soaking in worship and letting Jesus hold them close to Him.

Have them *PAL*: *"Holy Spirit, now that you have taken my pain and healed my heart, what would you like to say to me or give to me that will help me walk in newness of life as I leave here?"* *"What will be my warning that I am trying to default to my old pattern of thinking?"* *"What is my weapon to embrace and use to continue to put off the old and put on the new way of thinking?"*

Record what the Lord has said and done for them during this session. Give it to them as they leave, instructing them to meditate on it. They will need to remember so they can begin walking in the Spirit and developing new ways of thinking through *repetition* and *rehearsal*.

This is an exciting prayer session, even though at times a painful one, because we don't know how the Holy Spirit is going to lead and heal. We know from experience that He does! The results are always tailor-made just for that specific person sitting in front of you! You are watching and participating in a spiritual healing and transformation right in front of your eyes. What an honor and privilege to partner with God to see captives set free and healed!

SUMMARY OF MINISTRY TO HEALING LIFE'S HURTS

1. *PAL*: *"Holy Spirit, if there is a memory you want to bring healing to, would you bring it to my mind? I want to experience freedom from _____ and if it is connected to a memory I am ready for you to help me."*

2. Ask the person to describe what they are seeing/hearing/feeling in the memory. Help them be present in the memory and become part of it, not just look at it from a distance.

3. Have the person talk to Jesus about what they are feeling. Help them ask Jesus questions. Keep the dialogue going between them and Jesus. As a facilitator stay out of the way, but direct as needed to keep the focus on Jesus.

4. Listen for ungodly thought patterns and forgiveness issues that come up during the prayer session. Ask the Holy Spirit to give you wisdom on when and how to deal with each one, leading in prayers of forgiveness and inviting truth to be revealed.

    As appropriate, refer to prayers for *Generational Patterns and Curses*, *Ungodly Thought Patterns*, and *Forgiveness*.

5. Do a heart check. How is the pain level? Does the Holy Spirit want to do more now, or wait?

CHAPTER 18

DEMONIC INTERFERENCE

"The Son of God appeared for this purpose, to
destroy the works of the devil."
1 John 3:8

THIS SECTION OF MINISTRY IS THE LAST STEP IN
the process of ministering to the whole person. The reason for this is that the
ministry has reclaimed legal ground that once was occupied by demons. At
this point in ministry the demons have no house left to survive in as their
legal rights (unforgiveness, ungodly thought patterns, unhealed hurts, bitter
root judgments, curses, soul ties and ungodly generational patterns) have
been demolished.

*Demonic Interference is the influence demons can insinuate into our lives
as a result of unfinished business.* Sins we have not confessed and repented of,
generational patterns, ungodly ways of thinking, and hurts not healed are just
a few areas that demons can take advantage of. They rob, kill and steal from us
an abundant, exchanged life.

In our experience casting out demons without addressing unfinished
business gives the demons a right to reinforce their power. They bring some
of their "friends" back to an unswept house. (Matthew 12:43-45) It becomes

difficult for the person to experience ongoing freedom. It leaves opportunity for disappointment, doubt and discouragement to take hold in the person's thoughts. Embracing, receiving and applying the provisions of the Cross crowds out demonic influence.

Some people have difficulty accepting the reality that Christians can be oppressed by demonic interference. While a Christian is "possessed" only by God, not demons, they *can* experience oppression. Interference from demonic activity affects areas of the soul that are still in the process of being transformed into the likeness of Jesus Christ.

1 John 3:8 says the Son of God appeared for this purpose: to destroy the works of the Devil. This verse is positioned in the middle of a section where the Apostle John is writing to believers. He encourages us that we have the power to *choose* to not sin because of His indwelling presence. The provision for forgiveness and cleansing is available to the believer for ongoing transformation because He knows the soul will need ongoing freedom from the work of the Enemy. He set us free, is setting us free and will continue to set us free. That is God at work in us, both to will and to work for His good pleasure. (Philippians 2:13)

Part of my story includes a season where I began to recognize demonic interference as a result of being sexually abused as a child. The event was so traumatic I repressed the memory until my mid-thirties, when I began to experience flashbacks. I was horrified and embarrassed and pained all at the same time as the memories came. This happened in a season of the church when helpful tools for healing were not available. There was no one for me to turn to for help except to God.

I could read about "inner healing" but it didn't include learning to recognize patterns of thinking that were ungodly and how they were attached to the pain of the abuse. I could read about deliverance but there was no inclusion about the importance of forgiveness and generational patterns of thought and behavior that allowed demonic interference to continue even after casting them out. I was told to "Just forgive and you will be okay." My heart was not healed. It wasn't okay. How could this be?

I began to understand some of my responses to life and attitudes about God, life and other people. In my life I experienced a continual underlying feeling of not being good enough, feeling betrayed and rejected and a sense of sadness that never went away. There was also anger that lay dormant until a situation would occur that triggered the emotions experienced as a result of the abuse. Then the anger would arise, seemingly out of proportion for what the current situation might warrant. The Enemy made sure I had experience after experience of rejection and betrayal without being equipped to engage with the Holy Spirit to gain God's perspective on each situation I faced.

I would try my best, over and over again, to get rid of the anger and overwhelming feelings of shame, rejection and betrayal. Surely repenting and trying to do the "Christian" thing would make it all better. Just do the right things, say the right things, learn applicable Scriptures and repeat them over and over. Isn't that the formula for being a victorious Christian?

I experienced what some would call "inner healing" from prayers similar to ones in this book, but there were pieces missing I couldn't explain. I just "knew" there was more to embrace and experience.

It wasn't until the connection was made for me that generational sins, ungodly thought patterns and unhealed wounds in my life (starting with sexual abuse) were all connected. For the fruit of freedom to be experienced they all needed to be considered as part of the prayer focus.

It has been a process, one that started with repenting for and forgiving ancestors' sins. Patterns of sexual sins in generation lines were recognized as an influence passed down. The Enemy was taking advantage of this sinful behavior. Forgiving the person who abused me was a painful but fruitful exercise. Recognizing the importance of perceptions I adopted about God, other people and myself as a result of the abuse was breakthrough point for me.

My emotions were healed as God spoke His truth to me to replace the lies I had believed. Some of those lies were: *God is not there for me. God is not just. No one will be there for me so I have to take care of myself. Don't ever trust anyone. People who are suppose to be there to protect you will let you down. People who say they love you will betray you in a moment. I'm not worth being protected.* These were just some of the lies I had subconsciously embraced and had been living life based on them.

Forgiveness for sins committed against me, as well as the consequences they caused me, brought a deep release and cleansing. A genuine spiritual house cleaning had begun.

I began to intentionally engage with the Holy Spirit, allowing Him to BE the Fruit He is in and through my life. As I embraced His work in growing the Fruit of the Spirit my emotional life began to get healthy. I embraced the truth expressed in Galatians 2:20: "I have been crucified with Christ: and it is no longer I who live, but Christ lives in me." This truth started to become a reality in my life.

It is an amazing thing to live life knowing He wants to live His life in, for and through me. It was a paradigm shift for me to think, "All the Fruit of the Spirit live in me. I can choose love, joy, peace, patience, kindness, goodness, faithfulness, gentleness and self-control because they are available all the time." I started assessing every thought and interaction by asking, "Is this response a Fruit of the Spirit?" I would fill in the blanks to these statements: *I am feeling _____ because I think _____. Holy Spirit is that what you want me to think? What fruit of the Spirit do you want to be for me and through me right now? My emotions are out of control right now. What thoughts are producing these feelings?*

In my workbook for pursuing emotional wholeness, "*Growing Kingdom Fruit*," I have presented activations for each Fruit of the Spirit that are helpful along these lines. [45]

This process revealed a lot of ungodly thinking. It taught me how to bring every thought captive to the obedience of Jesus Christ and embrace the exchange Jesus provided for me. He gave His life for mine. He gave His life in the Spirit for my life in the flesh. He gave His love for my hatred and anger. He gave His peace for my turmoil. Giving is the nature of our God. "For God so loved the world that He *gave*..." (John 3:16)

Giving is the nature of our God.

At first it freaked me out that I could have a "demon" interfering with my life and having a place of influence in me. The most helpful teaching about demonic interference I've learned is the reality that demons live in houses made of lies. When we tear down the lies (strongholds) the demons have nothing to sustain their life on and they have to leave. We have authority when we obey Jesus. We have the power to tell them to leave when their legal right to be there is gone. We don't have to be afraid of them because we have Someone living in us who is greater than they are. (1 John 4:4)

We cannot be possessed by a demon because we belong to Jesus Christ, but we have a residue from the old man's nature in our souls (our mind, will and emotions) that God is sanctifying. He continues to set us free from the old man nature as we learn to walk in the Spirit. Being changed from glory to glory into the likeness of Jesus is a process that continues after we are "born again." We are cleaning up the habit patterns of thinking, feeling and behaving that we acquired before salvation.

The reality is this: Demons do exist. Christians can and do experience demonic interference. Jesus has given us authority over them. (Acts 10:38, Mark 16:17, Luke 10:19)

I don't know what your perception of Satan and demons is but I grew up thinking they were imaginary beings. I had a picture in my mind of an ugly cartoon figure dressed up in a red suit with horns on his head and a pitch fork in his hand. My religious training did not address the issue of demons at all.

The apostle Paul instructs us: Don't be ignorant of Satan's schemes. Otherwise, he takes advantage of us. (2 Corinthians 2:10-11) This next section explores some Biblical truths that will help us be aware of the nature of our Enemy and how he operates.

WHO IS SATAN?

The first time Satan appears in the Bible is in Genesis 3:1-5. He appeared to Eve in disguise as a serpent and is described as crafty in nature. He spoke to Eve with intelligence so he has the ability to think and make choices like a person. His purpose was to deceive Eve by sowing seeds of doubt about God's character and motives. He directly challenged what God had said to Adam and Eve. Satan's purposes are no less for us. He is the great deceiver and continues to operate in doubt, fear and deception.

What are demons and where do they come from? Demons are spirit beings. They do not have physical bodies, but they are real. They willfully torment, deceive, harass and attack humans. They are invisible to us unless they choose to appear to us in ways that we can see and hear. In the book of Revelation they appear like locusts with the power of scorpions. (Revelation 9:2-3, 5-6; 16:13-14)

"God did not spare angels when they sinned, but sent them to hell, putting them in chains of darkness to be held for judgment." (2 Peter 2:4)

"Then war broke out in heaven. Michael and his angels fought against the dragon, and the dragon and his angels fought back. But he was not strong enough, and they lost their place in heaven. The great dragon was hurled down – that ancient serpent called the Devil, or Satan, who leads the whole world astray. He was hurled to the earth, and his angels with him." (Revelation 12:7-9)

These demons are present on earth to interfere in human affairs so they can work out their evil ways. Jesus calls Satan the "prince of this world." (John 12:31) The apostle Paul says the Devil is "the god of this age," (2 Corinthians 4:4) and the "ruler of the kingdom of the air, the spirit who is now at work in those who are disobedient." (Ephesians 2:2)

Demons are called spirits, evil spirits and impure spirits in Matthew and Acts. The apostle Paul also describes them as rulers, authorities, powers of this dark world, and spiritual forces of evil in the heavenly realms. (Ephesians 6:12) He also says they are deceiving spirits. (1 Timothy 4:1)

Satan is described as a roaring lion (1 Peter 5:8), a serpent (Genesis 3), an angel of light (2 Corinthians 11:14-15), and a dragon (Revelation 12).

Satan hates us and wants to destroy us. He wants to see us die and be separated from God's love forever. He hates God. This is what Jesus said about Satan and his demons: "You are of your father the devil, and you want to do the desires of your father. He was a murderer from the beginning, and does not stand in the truth because there is no truth in him. Whenever he speaks a lie, he speaks from his own nature, for he is a liar and the father of lies." (John 8:44)

SATAN'S NATURE

Satan's nature is the total opposite of God's. Since we are created in God's image, Satan hates us too. We are unique in this manner. Not even angels are said to be created in His image. In God's image we are to reflect who He is to a world He wants to save. We are privileged to partner with Him by being Kingdom of God ambassadors in our world. (Matthew 10:1; 28:18-20, Luke 10:19) We also have an assignment unique to us to have dominion over all the earth. Satan is jealous of this. He wants the power, control and attention focused on him.

Demons are powerful and evil. They want to destroy us. The good news is this: Jesus indwells us and empowers us to overcome and be victorious because of what He did on the Cross. He gave His life and destroyed the power of sin and death forever. (Romans 6:8-11, Galatians 2:20) God is greater than the Devil and his demons! (1 John 4:4)

We want to give more attention to God than we do to the Enemy, but we need to be aware of how our Enemy operates. (1 Peter 5:8)

Satan influences decisions we make. (Genesis 3:4-5, Matthew 16:22-23)

Satan blinds us to the truth. (2 Corinthians 4:3-4)

Satan tries to catch us in his traps. (2 Timothy 2:25-26)

Satan wants to possess us. This is the devastating goal Satan has for us. When someone is actually "possessed" they have no control over themselves. This is extreme. (Mark 5:2-5) Most of us are oppressed or influenced by the Enemy.

We learn to break out from under his influence in the process of sanctification as God transforms us through the renewal of our minds. We learn how to tear down the strongholds as we receive, embrace and apply His thoughts to every relationship and circumstance in our life. This is SoulCare at its best and why we believe it is necessary in our care for people.

Satan has the ability to influence our thoughts. At the Last Supper he influenced Judas's thoughts: "During supper, the devil having already put into the heart of Judas Iscariot, the son of Simon, to betray Him…" (John 13:2)

Satan also persuaded King David to do something he shouldn't have done. "Satan rose up against Israel and incited David to take a census of Israel." (1 Chronicles 21:1 NLT) Please note there is no clear evidence Satan can read our minds. Only God knows everything. But Satan does influence our thoughts. That is a powerful weapon he uses against us. The sins we commit have first been conceived in our thought life. That is why God is so emphatic that we carefully watch what we think and invites us to be transformed through renewing our minds. (Romans 12:2, Philippians 4:8-9)

The apostle Paul shows his concern writing to the Corinthians when he says in 2 Corinthians 11:3, "I am afraid that, as the serpent deceived Eve by his craftiness, your minds (*thoughts*) will be led astray from the simplicity and purity of devotion to Christ."

Satan has been around a long time and is an observer of human nature. We can be predictable creatures of habit. With God's help we can resist the Devil by standing firm in our position in Christ and declaring God's truth.

> With God's help we can resist the Devil by standing firm in our position in Christ and declaring God's truth.

Satan is relentless. Even though he has been defeated he continues to harass us and tries to deceive us through fear and doubt. The spiritual battle continues. We must learn to walk through this life as a journey with Jesus. It is a marathon, not a 100 yard dash. At times we experience a breakthrough or a miracle, but we live in between the already and the not-yet. (Hebrews 2:8) We learn to walk through all the trials and challenges of life with God's help. We have been saved, we are being saved and we will be saved. He has delivered us, is delivering us and will continue to deliver us. He has healed us, is healing us and will continue to heal us.

The Holy Spirit did a work of creating a new spirit within us when we made a decision and confession that Jesus is Lord. We are now walking out that reality as we learn how to be saints, taking off the old and putting on new ways of thinking, feeling and behaving.

Jesus will come again and Satan and his forces will be banished forever. (Matthew 25:41) Satan continues to fight because he wants to take as many people to hell with him as he possibly can. He knows there is a time for all the battles to end. (Matthew 8:29) Even demons will declare that Jesus Christ is Lord of all. (Philippians 2:9-11)

Demonic interference follows generational sins and curses. Sometimes a generation is passed over, but the open door for their presence remains until the sin and curses are recognized, confessed and repented for. Even after the power of the sin is broken through the shed blood of Jesus on the Cross we learn to walk a new way. We renounce the Enemy, disowning his thoughts and embracing God's thoughts. This takes repetition and rehearsal to change and be habituated in God's ways and thoughts.

Demons use circumstances to reinforce the "truth" of the ungodly perspective.

Another way demons interfere in our lives is to reinforce ungodly thought patterns we have adopted about God, others and ourselves. They use circumstances to reinforce the "truth" of the ungodly perspective. Because the pattern keeps repeating itself we convince ourselves we must be thinking correctly. The facts support the reality of the belief system. For example: People keep betraying me, so it must be true that I can't trust people because no matter what I do they will reject me and leave me.

If a person's belief system does not change to agree with God, even if a demon leaves, it will most likely be temporary as there is unbelief present, which is a sin against God. This question is a foundational one to ask if you are stuck in a particular behavior pattern and struggle to find lasting relief and change. *PAL: "Holy Spirit, this is what I have been thinking _____. Is that okay with you? If not, what do you want me to think about this?"*

Satan likes to keep offenses alive.

Demons do their work by using our thought patterns to keep reminding us of our hurts and how unjust God and other people are. Satan likes to keep offenses alive. He keeps our wounds infested with lies so they won't heal properly. Just when someone gets close to making progress, the Enemy makes sure another circumstance stirs up the old hurt and tempts the mind to think old thoughts that aren't true.

When God heals a wound that has caused damage to emotional health and has fostered ungodly behavioral patterns, demonic powers lose their strength. They also lose their right to continue to interfere in the person's life.

It takes God's power at work in me to work out my salvation. It takes His power at work for my character to be changed into the likeness of Jesus Christ. (Philippians 2:13) God does His part and I do mine from a place of rest and belief that He will finish what He starts. He will be with me all the way through the journey enabling me with His empowering Presence.

The Israelites were told the Promised Land belonged to them. Yet they still had to conquer the enemies that lived there. Likewise, we have an Enemy that doesn't want to leave his place of control and comfort in us. We must learn how to drive him out little by little and learn how to keep him out. (Exodus 23:20-33)

SoulCare's approach to ministry is an excellent strategy to drive the Enemy out of our lives and to establish a place for the Fruit of the Spirit to flourish and grow to maturity. We want to be a resting place for Jesus. (Isaiah 66:1) Jesus not only had a deliverance ministry (Acts 10:38), He also healed the broken-hearted and preached the message of the Kingdom of God everywhere He went. The gospel accounts are full of stories of deliverance, many times accompanied with physical healing. I challenge you to sit down and read the Gospels in one sitting, noting the healings, deliverances, conversations and messages of Jesus, the Son of God. You will fall in love with Him and want to be like Him and do what He did. This is what He wants for us! Sometimes we hinder our journey into wholeness because we want to do what Jesus does, miracles and signs and wonders without *being* like He is.

> ## Sometimes we hinder our journey into wholeness because we want to do what Jesus does, miracles and signs and wonders without *being* like He is.

There are other references in the New Testament that describe believers casting out demons. They give instructions to believers on what to do to stand against demons and the work they do to destroy us. (Acts 5:16, 8:7, 19:13-16; 2 Corinthians 2:10-11; Ephesians 1:19-23, 4:26-27, 6:10-17; James 4:7; 1 Peter 5:8-9.)

When I am asked if we have a deliverance ministry, I say no. We approach being set free from demonic interference as a part of ministering to the whole person – body, soul and spirit. John 8:32 presents the principle that we are set free by truth – not by a power encounter. It is the application of truth that heals. Jesus has given us authority and power. As amazing as that is, He says there is something greater to cause us to rejoice. Luke 10:19-20 says, "Behold, I have given you authority to tread on serpents and scorpions, and over all the power of the Enemy, and nothing will injure you. Nevertheless do not rejoice in this, that the spirits are subject to you, but rejoice that your names are recorded in heaven."

> ## It is the application of truth that heals.

Neil Anderson points out that "authority" is the "right" to rule and "power" is the "ability" to rule. [46] We are equipped to deal with the Enemy, but our freedom comes in a revelation and appropriation of truth. Jesus is The Truth! We might operate in "deliverance" all day and experience freedom for a period of time. We will not move forward on our journey to wholeness until we receive a revelation of who Jesus is and what He can do; we will not mature until we know who He says we are and what we can do with His help. We must apply biblical truth to daily life to walk in freedom and wholeness.

There are many thoughts associated with deliverance ministries that put the focus entirely on casting out the demons. Little consideration is given to how they gained access and what allows them to stay in a person's life. There are models that encourage throwing up, sneezing, burping and other manifestations in order to get rid of the demon.

I'm not into manifestations, but freedom. After a few people threw up on my living room floor as we were learning about demonic interference, I decided I could take authority over those manifestations and not let them do that. We have authority because of the shed blood of Jesus Christ and the work He finished on the Cross. Proclaiming His name in that authority is what we need - not a show of antics to entertain us and make us think we are doing something. And best of all, when the house they live in has been demolished through confession, forgiveness, repentance, renouncing, healing and renewal of the mind, there is little, if any struggle, in commanding them to leave.

If at this point in the ministry you experience a bit of resistance or struggle, *PAL: "Holy Spirit is there anyone else I need to forgive? Are there other consequences of what was done to me you want to make me aware of? Are there any other wounds in my heart you want to heal?)*

This is what it means to pull down strongholds and take thoughts captive to the obedience of Christ in a fruitful manner. (2 Corinthians 10:4-6)

Don't engage in conversations with the demons. They will lie to you and distract you from your main goal – to get rid of them. Identify them by their behavior and once the legal ground has been taken, command them to leave. Demons operate in legalism, so if there is any way for them to find a loophole to stay in place, they will. We are filled with the wisdom of God and He will help us discern what is taking place.

One time a guest minister was praying about some demonic interference in my life and he was calling me "Caroline" as he was addressing the demonic to leave. Something in my mind said, "You don't have to listen to him, that's not even your name." I knew enough to stop and tell the minister what was going on, because I wanted freedom. I didn't want the legalism of the Enemy to win the day. I said to him "My name is Carolyn, not Caroline so please address me as such because the Enemy doesn't want me to listen to you." The prayer time went on to a successful outcome. Pay attention to those Holy Spirit nudges as you are praying or being prayed for.

It is important for a person to take responsibility for themselves during a session where demons are being commanded to leave. While we can lead a person in a prayer, I find it very powerful for them to take the authority God has given them as a believer and begin to learn how to speak in confidence with boldness to the demonic interference to leave in the name of Jesus. Declarations of who they are in Christ and what He wants to be in and for them are a way to begin filling the mind with godly thoughts to get established in a new pattern. Any believer can engage in this ministry: it is not reserved for a special few. Knowing who Jesus is in you and who you are in Him helps your confidence. Operating in the gifts of the Holy Spirit empower the ministry. The only requirement is that you are a believer. (Mark 16:17)

One statement I have come to despise is, "My situation is not too bad. I can live with this. I've got it (anger, hatred, fear, anxiety, etc.) under control." Having ungodly thoughts, emotions and behavior "under control" is not the goal of Jesus for us. He came so we can be set FREE! Don't settle for "It's not too bad, or I've got it under control most of the time." There is more. The "more" includes an abundant life with His indwelling supernatural presence that empowers us to walk in newness of life. This is the gift of His grace to us as believers.

One doesn't need to shout or yell at demons. Being weird doesn't increase the anointing. Just be the supernatural person you are in a natural way, helping the person stay focused with you by maintaining eye contact.

Being sensitive without compromising ministry in pastoral care can be difficult. If someone is terrified of having a demon you might be tempted to back off and let it go. While you may need to address the issue another time, staying calm and doing some teaching or giving a quick testimony can help alleviate their fearful emotions. I usually have someone who is afraid pray something like this: *PAL: "Father, I'm really scared right now because I don't know what to expect. I am afraid I might lose control and embarrass myself. I'm afraid my minister might reject me after they see what is exposed in me. But I am really desperate to be free from _____. I am tired of being stuck and never getting around the corner with my problem. With your help I am going to step out and risk praying prayers for freedom from demonic interference. Will you be with me and help me?" Listen for and ask what the Spirit says to them.*

The person mainly needs to know they are in a safe environment and that you will not think less of them no matter what happens in the prayer time. Reassure them of your love for them and your commitment to them in their journey, no matter how unpleasant, embarrassing or fearful it might be for them.

Demons tend to cluster together in groups. Identify the main demonic activity as the root issue and put other associating demons with that group. When you minister through prayer you will usually deal with groups. Through their experience in ministry to demonic interference, Chester and Betsy Kylstra have compiled a list of common groupings they have identified. [47]

MINISTRY TO DEMONIC INTERFERENCE

The person who is receiving ministry may be apprehensive when you come to this session. Reassure them they are in a safe place, they don't have to "do" anything except make the decision they are going to be active with you in dismissing the demonic activity from their life. They are going to declare their position and authority IN Christ because of His shed blood on the Cross.

No doubt the person has heard weird or horror stories about deliverance sessions. Take them to a place of peace and safety in the presence of the

Lord and help them put their confidence in the Lord Jesus Christ who lives in them and is greater than the Enemy. (1 John 4:4)

You can have them pray a prayer of submission like this, yielding to what the Holy Spirit wants to do: *"Dear Jesus, I'm anxious about this session because I don't know what will happen. But I want to be free so I am giving my fears and anxiousness to You because you have invited me to. I am stepping into your Presence that is my peace. I receive You as my peace right now and I submit myself to you. Thank you for being here, living in me, and empowering me to resist the Enemy. I will take authority to kick him out of my life. Amen."*

As the facilitator for the session, you can pray a prayer to bind up any demons that want to block the ministry, hindering it with doubt, unbelief, fear or passivity.

As you have prayed and discerned root causes and supporting demonic activity, start ministering to each group of demons praying the following prayers. Do a heart check at the end of each grouping to determine they are gone. Two of the most common legal grounds that allow demons to remain are unforgiveness and ungodly thought patterns. If the person says something just doesn't seem right yet *PAL: "Holy Spirit is there anyone else you want me to forgive?" "Holy Spirit are there any ungodly thought patterns you want to talk to me about?"*

PRAYERS FOR DEMONIC INTERFERENCE

1. Make sure you have already prayed through Generational Patterns and Curses Prayers.

2. Lord Jesus, in your Name, I **renounce** and break all agreements I have made with the demonic stronghold of _____, including the associated demons of _____, _____, etc.

   PAL: "Lord, are there any other demons I need to include?"

3. I am taking **authority** over the demonic stronghold of _____ and I **command** this controlling demon and all demons associated with it to

leave me now based on the finished work of Jesus Christ on the Cross and the authority Jesus has given me as a believer.

4. Address each demon and tell them to go in Jesus' Name.

5. Do a heart check. Have the person pray: *"Jesus, is everything okay? Is there any other business to take care of regarding this issue?"*

6. *PAL: "Jesus, what would you like to give me today to replace this demonic activity?"* Write this down for them.

7. Pray a blessing over the person, asking the Holy Spirit to seal the work He has just done.

8. Rehearse their new godly thought patterns with them, making sure they are aware of **WARNING** signs they are about to entertain old ways of thinking, feeling or behaving. Some people will recognize old thought patterns, others will have a rise of negative feelings and others will notice their behavior falling into old habits. Help them identify what will warn them so they can renounce (disown) them and pick up the **WEAPON** God has just given them – their new godly thought pattern. Help them see how they can apply the new thought to situations they will face when they leave the ministry room.

"I'm a saint, I am loved
I'm anointed from above
I am chosen, I am blessed
God has given me His best
I am the righteousness of God
I am, Yes, I am.

I am known, I am healed
By Your Spirit I am sealed
I am blameless, baptized
I'm the apple of Your eye
Each promise I have in You
Is Amen, Amen

I'm redeemed, sanctified
I am raised up with Christ
I'm a warrior, I am free
Now I live in victory
I am more than a conqueror
I am, Yes, I am

I'm a ruler, I'm a priest
A disciple at Your feet
I'm ordained, justified
I'm co-heir with Christ
Each promise I have in You
Is Amen, Amen

I am a new man,
A new creation
I find myself in the presence of my God
Here I stand, in Jesus
A new creation in the presence of my God"

© Justin Clifton, Heartland Church, 2014
Free download for this song at
www.unitedadoration.com/here-i-stand-in-jesus

PART 3

APPLICATION

CHAPTER 19

WALKING IN NEWNESS OF LIFE (WIN)

A section designed to help you get UNSTUCK (and STAY UNSTUCK!) from unhealthy habit patterns of thoughts, feelings and behavior.

"I'M DEAD TO SIN,
ALIVE TO GOD
AND I'M WALKING IN NEWNESS OF LIFE!"
(Heartland's Rap by Pastor Ron Allen based on Romans 6)

INTRODUCTION

WELCOME TO WALKING IN NEWNESS OF LIFE
(WIN!) Perhaps you have discovered a lie you believed and based your life on. You want some practical tools to help you get established in a new way of thinking and living. You may have discovered your ungodly thought pattern(s) in sessions with a SoulCare prayer ministry team or in your prayer time with God. Either way you are tired of missing out on the abundant life Christ has provided for you. You have decided enough is enough, and you want help because you know there is something better for you.

I applaud you – you are on your way to developing a habit of walking as the new creation Jesus Christ says you are. During your time of ministry or times of prayer, with the help of the Holy Spirit, you identified generational patterns of thought, feeling and behavior that kept you "stuck" and not free to live in God's freedom. You identified lies that you based your life on that have kept you from God's truth, a truth from which you desire to live as a foundation for your life. You have perhaps been healed from some traumatic wound that has affected your perspective on life, God, others and yourself. In prayer you have closed the doors to demonic interference in this particular area of your life that has kept you vulnerable.

If you have not experienced a SoulCare prayer ministry team, this workbook section can still help you if you feel "stuck" in your life at some point and desire to get "unstuck". If you have tried everything you know to try, but find yourself in the same patterns of behavior, feelings or thoughts, some questions for you to *PAL* might be:

> *What is hurting the most in my life?*

> *What is broken?*

> *What emotion habitually expressed negatively is one I have tried to change, but it keeps overpowering my willpower to change?*

> *What thought pattern that affects my life negatively have I tried over and over again to change keeps its place in my mind? I just can't seem to think any other way.*

> *What behavior do I keep repeating that I don't want to do?*

> *What behavior do I keep repeating that hinders my freedom in Christ?*

> *What type of person or situation seems to stir up this emotion, thought pattern or behavior the most?*

> *Holy Spirit what are you desiring to work on in my life in this season?*
>
> *I would really like to respond to life in this area of my life in Your fruit…the Fruit of the Holy Spirit. Will you help me?*
>
> *Lord Jesus, what truth do you want me to hear about this issue?*
>
> *What do you want to say to me about this situation?*

What do you hear God saying to you in answer to these questions? As you listen for what He wants to say or show you, it will give you a place to start applying the principles and exercises suggested in this section.

You have a sense of who God wants to be for you and the particular habit pattern of thought, feeling or behavior He is transforming. Now you are ready to take hold of your new godly way of thinking and start a new habit. What must I do? How can I do this?

The purpose of this workbook is to help you take ahold of a new thought that has a godly, scriptural foundation and begin to make it a habitual response to life. The following principles will help you learn how to apply Truth to your daily activities and relationships. Scientific studies have shown that it takes from 21-30 days of reinforcement *seven to twelve times a day* to develop a habit to think a new way. Your brain is actually physically changed as a new pathway is burned according to a new thought on which you are focusing. It then takes another 30 days to develop a new habitual pattern of behavior as a fruit or end result of the thought. It takes **Repetition** and **Rehearsal** (practice) to embrace a new thought from which to live your life. We begin to focus on the new instead of the old. Our old nature is dead, our new nature is alive to Jesus Christ – let's focus on that and habituate ourselves in light of this Truth.

Please review *Ungodly Thought Patterns* in Part Two of this book. I present suggestions on how to recognize ungodly thought patterns and how to write a new godly thought pattern that will renew your mind and produce godly behavior.

Once you have recognized an ungodly thought pattern and have received a godly thought pattern from God, it will be helpful for you to do some journaling, filling in the following thoughts:

> The Ungodly Thought Pattern: _____
> The Godly Thought Pattern: _____
> This is how the Ungodly Thought Pattern controlled my life:
>> How did I think, feel and behave?
>> How did it affect my relationships?
>
> What behavior did this old thought pattern produce in my daily life?
>
> The people that were affected the most are _____.
>
> Be aware of what has triggered your trouble spot in the past and decide how you will respond in the present and in the future – write it down.
>> When this happens I will _____.

A declaration is the formal announcement of the beginning of a state or condition. Scripture tells us in Proverbs 18:21 that "Death and life are in the power of the tongue, and those who love it will eat its fruit." When you make a declaration concerning your new godly thought pattern you are proclaiming the state or condition God is saying He wants for you as you take the next step in renewing your mind. Declarations help us focus on where God is taking us, displacing the old ways of thinking with the new. Declarations have the power to draw us into the future, calling us to live the new life God has provided for us.

Jesus began His ministry with the declarations we read in Luke 4. He was agreeing with the Father about His identity and mission. Let's do the same as we make some declarations of intent about our identity and mission.

Make the following declarations:

> I am deciding to take responsibility for the revelation of my new Godly Thought Pattern. I will _____.

I am declaring today (and every day) that (New Godly Thought Pattern). Start a journal of your own declarations that agree with God and keep you positively focused.

I will demonstrate my new Godly Thought Pattern today/this week by _____ (*PAL: Holy Spirit what do you want me to do differently in my relationship with* _____ *in light of this Godly Thought Pattern?*)

I will, with the help of the Holy Spirit, take the following steps to continue learning how to walk as a Saint:

Worship – I will set aside regular times to focus on thanking God for who He is (do a study on the attributes of God – who He really is) and praise Him for all He has done and is doing. (I will listen to music, journal, paint, draw - express thankfulness in however God has gifted me creatively.)

Word – I will fill my heart and mind with the Word of God. (*PAL: Holy Spirit, what portion of Scripture would you like for me to read and meditate on through the next 60 days?*)

Works – I will be other-oriented and give away what God has given to me. This week I will (*PAL: Holy Spirit what would you like for me to do this week to demonstrate your love to others?* i.e. serve in Food Pantry, do something for your family, neighbors or co-workers, find an outreach in the community that needs help, etc.)

Walk Forward – I will press on and look ahead to what You will direct me to do today, Holy Spirit. I will have an expectant anticipation of what is going to happen today and tomorrow instead of being pulled back into the past.

If you have a physical condition and a medical practitioner has prescribed a medicine for you to take at certain times every day because your life depends on it, you most likely set a timer or have a way of making sure you take your medicine as many times a day as required for your health.

I suggest to you that your spiritual well being is at stake if you have been stuck in a cycle of negative, ungodly thoughts, feelings and behaviors. You need a transformation in the way you think. It is proven you can change your life if you change the way you think. That is a scriptural principle and a part of the sanctification process God takes us through to transform us into the

character and conduct of Jesus Christ. Romans 12:2 instructs us to be transformed by the renewing of our mind.

> The responsibility for walking
> in newness of life and staying
> free belongs to each believer.

The responsibility for walking in newness of life and staying free belongs to each believer. The epistles are full of instructions for how to live the Christian life. In a helping role, ministers and counselors can provide instruction and wisdom on how to apply truth, but ultimately the success is up to each person to appropriate biblical truth as directed by the Holy Spirit.

I am asking you to entertain and embrace this process for the next 60 days and see what God will do in and through you. Your new thought is waiting to be activated will need to be exercised at least seven to twelve times daily. That is your prescription. Set the timer on your phone or watch, and when the beeper goes off, rehearse your new thought. Speak it out loud, thinking about what you are saying as you do so. Think deeply about it. Assess how you have been doing through the day with putting it in to practice.

PAL: "Holy Spirit, would you give me the ability to allow this truth to become part of who I am? I desire to think, feel, behave and talk like you, so would you please help me?"

This section will lay out a plan for you to take the new thought God has given you and develop it into a mindset that will become part of who you are so that you will live it out naturally. Eventually you won't even have to think about it because it will become a part of your nature. It will become second nature to you, just like breathing, driving a car, playing an instrument – like many things we do every day without thinking about them. That's what a habit is - an acquired behavior pattern regularly followed until it has become almost involuntary. Since we live what we believe, we must take a look at habituated thoughts that have led to our becoming "stuck". Ungodly habituated thoughts lead to ungodly behavior. Godly habituated thoughts lead to godly behavior – Christ-likeness. That's our goal.

Most of us have developed negative habits that have developed ungodly fruit in our lives. We have some work to do, the working out of our salvation, to change those habits. We cannot do it alone – we have the help of the Holy Spirit enabling us with His supernatural indwelling presence to walk in newness of life. The work begins with changing the way we think.

As much as I would like to have had this section be one page of instruction for you to Walk In Newness of Life, I found that limiting the tools to one page would be a dis-service, especially for someone doing this work on their own. Some explanation and instruction are necessary for lasting benefit.

It may seem overwhelming if you think you have to do every exercise in this section on Walking In Newness. Some of you will respond to one activation over another.

Please use the tools that you connect with and will produce the fruit of repentance – changed thoughts and behaviors. The most crucial that *all* will need to engage with is the *5 R Activation*. The other journals and 3 D activation are included to help you in the process of maturing as a disciple of Jesus Christ, learning how to be the saint God says you are.

When you start to feel overwhelmed, *PAL*: *"Holy Spirit, I'm feeling overwhelmed with this process right now. What do you want to engage with me about in this moment so I can change? I give you my anxiousness and receive your peace as I choose to keep moving towards total freedom. Thank you for being with me."*

CHAPTER 20

EXERCISE ONE – The Five "R's" Activation

LET'S BEGIN WITH WHAT I CALL THE *FIVE "R'S"*
Activation. The Five "R's" are

Recognize

Repent

Renew

Repetition

Rehearsal

This activation may take your attention for the first few days of your journey. Take your time *Recognizing* your need and praying through the *Repentance* prayer.

We first began to *recognize* we needed help because we were stuck in an unhealthy pattern. We either recognized the behavior(s), the feeling(s) or the thought(s) that were destructive and the resulting fruit.

Although some teach that you have to identify your feelings or behavior before you can change, I have come to believe that while you can start with identifying those key elements in your life, you will need to go back to what you are believing to be true, what you are thinking, in order to have lasting change.

Repentance means to change the way you think so you can change the way you live. The fruit of repentance is changed behavior. Scripture says to be transformed by the way we think (Romans 12:2). It also says, "As a man thinks in his heart, that is the way he is." (Proverbs 27:3)

Here are some great questions to *PAL* as you are identifying a lie or ungodly belief: *"Lord, I have been living my life based on a belief that leads me to express emotions negatively and to act based on those negatively expressed emotions. The results are not good fruit. What have I been thinking to be true that leads to those negatively expressed emotions? I feel _____ (negatively expressed emotions) because I think _____. What would you like to say to me about this belief/thought? What would you like me to think instead of this? Where in scripture would you like me to read so I can think like you?"*

When we repent of living our life based on lies, we are agreeing with God that we have sinned against Him, and are asking for Him to forgive and cleanse us according to 1 John 1:9. The following prayer is a pattern I use to pray not only for myself but also with others as I help facilitate the Five "R" Activation.

PRAYER OF RECOGNITION AND REPENTANCE

I **confess** my sin of believing the lie that _____.

I **forgive** and **release** all who have contributed to my forming this lie. Lord, who has contributed to my forming this belief? Be specific.

Lord, what **consequences** are working in my life as a result of living my life based on this lie? I also forgive those who contributed to the formation of this lie for these consequences. They don't owe me anything. Their record is erased from their account.

Would you please **forgive me** Father for embracing this lie, living my life based on it and for any way I have judged others because of it? (Wait to listen to His response to you. Hearing Him tell you that you are forgiven will bring an impartation you don't want to miss as it deepens the reality of God's forgiveness.) Write down what you hear Him say or what He shows you.

Thank you for forgiving me, Father. I **receive** your forgiveness.

Because you have **forgiven me**, I choose to let myself off the hook for believing this lie and living my life based on it. I will not continue to beat myself up over the struggles I experience(d) as a result of this lie. I agree with you God that I am forgiven!

I **renounce** and break my agreement with this lie. I now **choose** to embrace a Kingdom of God perspective and forsake any tie to this lie.

I choose to **accept, believe and receive** what you say is true Lord. What do you want me to think/believe instead of this lie? What scripture would you lead me to so I can embrace the mind of Christ? (Listen and record what He says…these words are your new weapon to defeat the old way of thinking.) God might show you a picture or give you a phrase or scripture to meditate on.

Take your time working through this prayer. Let it soak into your inner being, becoming a reality in you as the Holy Spirit brings transformation.

We *RENEW* our mind through *Repetition* and *Rehearsal* of the truth God has spoken to us.

Renewal of the mind can begin once we have a new, godly thought to think instead of the lie. When we focus on a new thought pattern long enough it becomes a habit and the old way of thinking dries up and falls away from our brain (literally) because of disuse. We are embracing the principle of spiritual displacement (take this off, put this on). The indwelling, supernatural presence of the Holy Spirit enables us to walk in newness of life as we embrace the process of having our mind renewed. (Romans 12:2 Be transformed by the renewing of your mind.)

We are ready to begin *Repetition* of the new thought seven to twelve times a day. Say it out loud, thinking about what you are saying. As you are repeating the new thought, *PAL: "Holy Spirit, would you show me ways I can apply this new thought to my behavior and begin to Rehearse it – practice it? How will this new thought change my behavior?"* Think about the people and circumstances that you have had difficulty practicing this particular skill/behavior with and intentionally apply what you have learned in each opportunity presented.

Scripture reinforces this principle in many places but here are a few of my favorite verses that relate.

Joshua 1:8 "This book of the Law shall not depart from your mouth, but you shall meditate on it day and night, so that you may be careful to do according to all that is written in it. For then you will make your way prosperous, and then you will have good success."

Romans 10:8-10 "The word is near you, in your mouth and in your heart (that is, the word of faith that we proclaim); because, if you confess with your mouth that Jesus is Lord and believe in your heart that God raised him from the dead, you will be saved. For with the heart one believes and is justified, and with the mouth one confesses and is saved."

Deut. 30:11-14 "For this commandment that I command you today is **not too hard for you**, neither is it far off. It is not in heaven, that you should say, 'Who will ascend to heaven for us and bring it to us, that we may hear it and do it?' Neither is it beyond the sea, that you should say, 'Who will go over the sea for us and bring it to us, that we may hear it and do it?' But the word is very near you. It is in your mouth and in your heart, **so that you can do it**."

We think it is too hard to change, but God says it is possible, so it is. We have to have this mindset as we begin to develop new ways of thinking. It is possible…with God's help! Otherwise He wouldn't ask us to do it!

SUMMARY

1. Recognize the lie you have believed and based your life on.

2. Repent for believing the lie, (See Prayer of Recognition and Repentance) and ask the Holy Spirit to help you write a Godly belief.

3. Renew your mind according to this Word from God,

    Through:

4. Repetition

5. Rehearsal

CHAPTER 21

EXERCISE TWO – Warning and Weapon

ONE DAY AS I WAS PRAYING WITH SOMEONE TO help them in their journey of changing old habit patterns, the words **Warning** and **Weapon** dropped into my spirit. I heard the Lord say, "Ask them what their warning sign is when they are about to fall into an old way of thinking, feeling, or behaving. Ask them how they know when they are about to revert to an old default system."

As I have worked with this principle it has proved to be helpful to myself as well as many others. I *PAL:* "*What feelings begin to arise within that let me know I will need to choose a new way of thinking? Or, What negative thought pattern am I thinking that will lead me to act in a way I don't want to?*" Remember when the Apostle Paul said in Romans…Why do I "do the things I don't want to do?" I believe we can pay attention to **Warning Signals**, whether it is a particular thought (that doesn't agree with God) or an old familiar feeling we have been trying to change. Sometimes we behave in a way we don't want, and that is a warning that something needs to change. As I explained in Part One, we can change the way we feel and behave by changing the way we think.

A *Warning* is an opportunity for us to take a time out, *PAL*, to help us identify what we are thinking that is allowing a negative feeling and behavior to be expressed. "*Lord what am I thinking that is making me feel _____?*") Or

"When I think _____, I feel _____, then I _____(behav-ior). Or, "I feel _____because I think _____ and then I _____ (behavior)."

This is what I call my "Yellow Light Theology". Several years ago I was approaching a yellow light and didn't give it a second thought but to go through it. I didn't even think about stopping. As I was going through the yellow light I heard the Holy Sprit say to me, "Carolyn, is that how you are going to respond to me if I give you a caution about slowing or stopping when you are about to let your feelings dictate your behavior? When I am trying to teach you to stop and evaluate your perspective in order to change your responses? Are you going to keep right on moving?" I was taught in that moment that *I really do have a choice when it comes to my thoughts, feelings and behavior.* If I choose to go through the yellow lights (caution, warning) instead of taking a time out to evaluate I will "do the things I don't want to do" and end up back in the cycle of defeating behaviors from which I am working to be transformed.

> I really do have a choice when it comes to my thoughts, feelings and behavior.

What thought, feeling or behavior helps you be aware you are starting to respond in an old habit, that an old default system is about to be reactivated? We are vulnerable to these old habit patterns as we work towards developing new habits. We might recognize old feelings, thoughts or behaviors rising up. We can say to them, "I recognize you and I will stop right now and renounce you and use my new Weapon by speaking it and releasing it as my new reality in the Kingdom. I will no longer entertain these negative feelings, thoughts or behaviors. I will no longer entertain this lie. I disown you. This is how I think now."

Renounce is a very powerful word that is used only a few times in the Bible, depending on the translation you read. One place in the New Testament it is used is in 2 Corinthians 4:2 where it talks about disowning the "hidden things of shame."⁴⁸ For most of us, the habit patterns we are trying to change have come from shameful things in our past that have and still continue to affect our lives today, holding us in patterns (the Bible calls these strongholds) that keep us from experiencing the freedom Christ has given to us as His children…keeping us STUCK!

To "renounce" is to say to a thought, feeling or behavior, "I recognize you and I am telling you to stay out there away from me because you no longer have influence over me. I disown you. I recognize your tactics and I refuse to allow you to continue." We have a short period of time between the time we start thinking a thought and deciding whether to meditate on it and let it into our memory bank long term. If we decide we don't want the thought and we reject it, it does not enter into the place in our brain that facilitates long-term memory. Once that occurs we have a stronghold to tear down and that takes more energy and work than if we decide immediately, "This thought is not in agreement with Christ and will lead me to negatively expressed emotions and behaviors. Therefore, I renounce you and tell you that you are not welcome." Immediately refocus on the thought you want to be your new default system or your new habitual way of thinking.

A familiar emotion for me is fear and anxiety when I think about provision for the future. I experience warning signs in my feelings and thoughts and behavior. My body tenses up, I feel stressed and start thinking up different scenarios that could happen. I might recognize thoughts I am having like "You won't have enough. God won't come through. You better figure this out or you will be in big trouble. Why didn't you…you sure were stupid…you should have…"

If I don't stop and realize I am in a warning phase, I will allow my mind to think all kinds of thoughts (make up stories in my head) that will produce negative feelings and I will spend several days even weeks sometimes, in a grumpy, fearful, stressed out attitude. This makes me miserable and most likely those around me will be affected. Learning to recognize the warnings signs that take me to old habit patterns of thought, feeling and behavior is crucial to walking in newness of life.

When I am intentionally working on changing a habit pattern now, one of the first things after I have determined a new thought that agrees with God is to *PAL: "Lord what weapon do you want to give me to offensively establish this new thought so it becomes a new habit for me?"*

This becomes our offensive *Weapon* – the specific Word that God has spoken to us to replace the lie. 2 Corinthians 10:4 – "For the weapons of our warfare are not of the flesh but have divine power to destroy strongholds. :5 We destroy arguments and every lofty opinion raised against the knowledge of God, and take every thought captive to obey Christ."

Our weapon might be a Bible verse, a picture God showed us, a thought or phrase or an action He has inspired in order to put us on the offensive when we are tempted to live out of an old habit structure. The weapon needs to be something simple and concise so we can easily take hold of it and use it. We need it accessible to be ready when attacks come. 1 Peter 1:13 encourages us to prepare our minds for action. We are not to be conformed to former ways of living, but to the ways of Jesus Christ. What weapon has He given you so you are prepared for any situation you will face?

I have learned to stop and say to fear "I recognize you and your tactics and you have no place in me. I renounce you and stand here with Jesus. Because He is right here at my right hand, I will not be shaken!" The Lord spoke that verse from Psalm 16:8 to me to calm my fears, and now it is one of my life verses. It immediately brings peace to my mind and emotions. Unexpected circumstances that happen to us in our lives do not have to shake us and take us off the foundation of the Life of Christ within. But we have to know our *Warning* signals in order to take the offensive and stay in a place of agreement with God, using our *Weapons*.

I now say "I have given up fear and anxiousness for the future. I forbid you to even approach me. I will not entertain you in my thoughts." When I catch the warning sign at this stage, the feelings of fear and anxiousness aren't allowed because a new godly thought (i.e. "Jesus is right here at my right hand and I will not be shaken,") is in place and feelings of security follow.

When we learn to renounce ungodly thoughts, and repeat and rehearse godly thoughts as soon as we have a *Warning* signal we change the direction of our feelings and behavior. **We get to choose our feelings and behaviors.** Changing our mind so we can change our feelings and behavior - that is what scripture calls repentance. Renounce also means to "take leave of" or forsake. We must learn to forbid old habit patterns to influence us when we have a new way to think given to us in Jesus Christ. We are now new creations and have the mind of Christ and His supernatural indwelling presence to enable us to walk in newness of life. (1 Corinthians. 2:16, Philippians 2:13, 2 Corinthians. 5:17)

For every new thought we are developing as a habit, we must be aware of our Warning and our Weapon and be ready to use them at a moment's notice. Don't rush past the warning signals or you will find yourself in trouble. My husband had to teach me about the warning lights on the dash of our car. Don't ignore them, he said, or you may find yourself on the side of the road, stuck, and have to call for emergency help. Thankfully I have not had to learn that lesson the hard way. But I will say that I have run past my emotional warning signals and found myself repeating behaviors so that I say along with the Apostle Paul out of frustration…why do I keep doing the things I don't want to do? (Romans 7:15)

We truly have a new nature living in us that is empowered by the Holy Spirit. Let's learn to live from that place as a habit (walking in the Spirit), knowing that we have the DNA of God living in us. (2 Peter 1:4) We ARE dead to sin and ALIVE to God in Christ Jesus and have the grace to walk in newness of life! (Romans 6:11)

What is your **Warning**? What is your **Weapon** of choice when the warning system goes off?

SUMMARY

Know your **Warning** (what thought, feeling, behavior are you about to reactivate that pulls you back into your old nature?)

Know your **Weapon** (what has God given you to go on the offense against this specific lie?)

CHAPTER 22

EXERCISE THREE – Emotional Growth Journal

EXERCISE THREE IS TAKEN FROM MY BOOK "Growing Kingdom Fruit…a Workbook for Pursuing Emotional Wholeness."

As part of your journey in establishing new patterns of walking in the Spirit, it can be helpful to be aware of your emotional responses to people and situations. When you are able to identify the emotions, you can more readily identify the areas of thought/beliefs that are hindering the freedom in Christ you so desire. Following are some instructions on how to use an Emotional Growth Journal and an exercise to practice to gain spiritual health.

HOW TO USE YOUR EMOTIONAL GROWTH JOURNAL

It is helpful to think of an emotion as being compiled of the following components:

An EVENT that triggers an emotion

Your BELIEF (thought) about that event

The responding FEELING to that event and thought

What you do (ACTION) in response/reaction to the event

What FRUIT is displayed?

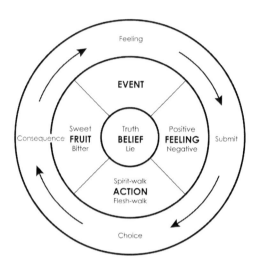

It may appear that we instinctively react/respond to an event with an emotion. We *can* train ourselves to stop and think before we respond/react. I encourage you to look beyond the emotion and see what you *perceive* to be true about the situation. It may be that you believe a lie, and your emotive response is following the reasoning of the lie. Perhaps your *thought* needs to be *renewed* in order to line up with God's perspective about the situation. We believe either the *truth* or a *lie* about every event in our life.

Once you have identified what you think about the event and have written it down, ask yourself…is this *thought* the *truth* or a *lie*? What does God's Word have to say? Does my thought need to be renewed to line up with God's Word?

As you work through your belief system, you will realize that you have a choice about the *feeling* you will have. If behavior follows belief, then it is imperative we believe the truth. As a Christian we want to *submit* to the Holy

Spirit. Is your feeling *positive* or *negative*? Either way, realize you will have a choice about how you are going to *act*. Work through issues in your heart that cause you to want to make your own choice instead of submitting to the work of the Holy Spirit.

Identify the *action* you took in response to the event. What did you choose to do? Did you make a wise *choice*? Was it according to the *Spirit* or the *flesh*? Be honest…that is the only way you will change and mature.

What was the *consequence* to your *choice* of *action*? What fruit was displayed in your action? What fruit was the Holy Spirit working on? Was good fruit grown? Was it *sweet* or *bitter*? What could you have done differently so you would have advanced in godly character being developed in your life?

How did you feel about the fruit that was displayed? Was it fruitful or fruitless? Don't give up if once again you find yourself in the position of having displayed bitter fruit. Choose anew to submit to the Spirit's working and you'll be on another cycle that will allow you to have your mind renewed so you can make good choices.

You can choose any place to start recording in your emotional cycle from the circle diagram, but you will always find yourself in a position of asking "Am I willing to submit to the work of the Spirit, or do I want my own way?" Sometimes our feelings and actions need to be identified before we can discern what we really believe to be true. We can even say we believe one way, when in reality our feelings, actions and resulting fruit say otherwise.

Sometimes we have blind spots that keep us from discerning lies we believe. We need each other's help to see these blind spots. If we keep getting results we don't like, we might suspect that we have a blind spot, a wrong belief that is causing us to feel and act in ungodly ways. That's when we need to do something to change.

I discovered I had one of those blind spots with the help of a counselor friend. He stayed in our home when he came to do ministry at Heartland, so he had ample opportunity to observe our home life. He is gifted in counsel and wisdom, so he observed interchanges between Ron and myself that spoke beyond the spoken. He could see and feel what was unspoken. Can anyone relate?

Our friend observed one of these interchanges between Ron and myself. Ron and I had invited him into our lives on a level of vulnerability and accountability. We knew we needed a peer to speak truth into our lives. We wanted to grow and change, so when he came to our home, we usually set time aside for each of us to talk for counsel. These conversations usually led to some "robust" dialogue!

I don't even remember "the issue" that prompted a conversation with me, but he noticed I was angry about something Ron said and did, but I stuffed it and carried around an attitude about it. He wanted to know where the emotion was coming from.

Something like this came out of my mouth, "I was angry because I thought if Ron would only change his behavior and tone of voice, then I could be something different myself. I could do and be all that God wants to me." Wow. I said it. The earth didn't tremble and I wasn't struck dead.

Almost immediately my friend said, "Have you ever considered that thoughts like that are what a victim thinks?" I was taken aback. No one had ever said that to me. I had no realization that was my mindset. He talked to me a while about that and then said, "Are you aware you are assigning a motive to Ron's character when you think that? Have you ever told him what you think and feel in these kinds of conversations?"

No, I hadn't. I was fearful of conflict and didn't want to hurt his feelings. But hiding truth and stuffing feelings was not producing good fruit. The initial "event" that evoked an angry, resentful response from me was used to provoke myself to a healthier way of thinking, feeling and behaving. In my anger and resentment I carried a grudge and unspoken words left tension in the air that even our guest could see and feel.

That was definitely not the Fruit of the Spirit I desired in my life. As I worked through the conversation with my counselor friend, I realized in order to allow the Holy Spirit to grow His fruit, I needed to change. I had a choice. The next time something triggered the victim mentality and feelings of anger and resentment in me, I could be ready with a new thought so I could feel differently and behave differently.

My new thought? The Holy Spirit said this to me, "Carolyn it is time to take responsibility for your own thoughts and feelings and behaviors." He wanted me to learn to challenge my thought system so I would not live life from a victim mentality. He wanted me to be open with Ron (and others) and be brave to say, "When that just happened I thought _____ and I felt _____. Is that what you wanted to convey to me?"

I began to realize my reactions to Ron's behavior, tone of voice and words that day had more to do with *my* thoughts and perceptions than *his* actions. This insight has helped me in all my relationships. It has helped me to be slow to judge others intentions and perceptions.

With the Holy Spirit's help, we can change!

God wanted me to quit assigning motives to other's motives without asking them their intentions. I had to consider the truth that others do not get to define who I am. Only God gets to do that. It was time to take the responsibility that God gave to me for my own choices. A hard lesson to learn when one has habituated herself in the way a victim thinks for all her life. With the Holy Spirit's help, we can change! I first had to recognize the lie I believed and choose to change. I needed help to start that process.

Don't be embarrassed or hesitant to ask for help. James tells us to confess our sins to one another so we can pray for each other and be healed (James 5:16). We have a true friend when someone can help us see our sins and walks with us toward wholeness.

EMOTIONAL GROWTH JOURNAL

DURING THE DAY AND/OR AT THE END OF EACH DAY, ANSWER THE FOLLOWING QUESTIONS:

When this event happened:

I felt:

Because I thought/believed:

I responded by (what did you do or say? what action did you take?):

My response was:

a. according to the Spirit

b. according to the flesh

The consequential fruit was:

a. sweet…(how?)

b. bitter…(how?)

If I responded in the flesh, the next time this happens, with the help of the Holy Spirit I will:

God was/is working on the fruit of in my life.

If you need to ask forgiveness of God and/or another because of your ungodly action/words, do so immediately so you are ready to go forward!

FEELING WORDS

Some of us have difficulty identifying our feelings. I include this list for your use, not only to recognize your own feelings, but also to use as an inventory to help you identify negatively displayed emotions and what they might be replaced with.

POSITIVE		NEGATIVE	
affectionate	kind	awkward	guarded
appreciative	loving	anxious	horrified
awed	lifted up	angry	haughty
aware	light	incompetent	alone
blissful	loved	abandoned	insensitive
bold	moved	alarmed	jealous
boisterous	nice	apprehensive	jittery
bright	positive	annoyed	locked-in
bubbly	peaceful	apathetic	lukewarm
beautiful	pretty	burdened	mournful
calm	protected	bad	naughty
carefree	reassured	betrayed	nervous
cared for	refreshed	overwhelmed	bitter
comforted	relieved	controlled	pressured
complete	reverent	controlling	proud
composed	rewarded	confused	provoked
confident	relaxed	cold	panicked
contented	satisfied	cut-off	restless
cozy	settled	condemned	shy
daring	strong	cowardly	sulky
elated	sure	defeated	sensitive
eager	tender	disturbed	sad
ecstatic	touched	drained	selfish
energetic	trusted	dumb	shameful
expectant	vital	disappointed	scared

free	warm	defensive	tired
glad	good	envious	tense
high	honored	exhausted	timid
intimate	impressed	exposed	touchy
		feeble	used
		fearful	vulnerable
		grouchy	worried

CHAPTER 23

EXERCISE FOUR – New Godly Thought Journal

You can also use the model for the Emotional Growth Journal and design questions for a New Godly Thought Journal. It would look something like this:

The Godly Thought Pattern the Holy Spirit is focusing on in my life right now is: _____.

When this happened today _____, I thought _____. This thought was (in agreement, not in agreement) with the Godly Thought Pattern I am embracing and learning to apply in my life.

When I had this thought _____, I felt _____.

I responded by _____. This behavior was (ungodly, Godly).

If it was ungodly, declare this: This is not who I really am. I am a saint learning how to be a saint and the next time something like this happens, with the help of the Holy Spirit, I will be aware of my **Warning** signals (they are _____), and be ready with my **Weapons** (they are _____).

I will continue to *Repeat* and *Rehearse* my Godly Thought for the next 30 days because I want to be like Jesus. I will not give up. This is not too hard for me because Jesus Christ indwells me and empowers me to walk in newness of life! I receive, embrace and desire to apply _____ (this thought) in my relationships. *PAL: "Holy Spirit how will this new thought change my behavior in situations/relationships in which I have struggled?"*

PAL: "Holy Spirit what are some scriptures I can meditate on as I am establishing this new Godly Thought Pattern and will help me stay engaged so I will finish this process?"

CHAPTER 24

EXERCISE FIVE – Three "D's" Activation
Decide | Declare | Demonstrate

"As for me, it is good to be near God. I have made the Sovereign
LORD my refuge; I will tell of all your deeds."
Psalm 73:28

THIS ACTIVATION IS EASY TO REMEMBER AND can help you train your mind to focus on the very thoughts and activities in which the Lord wants you to participate. Every day you have many opportunities to make choices about emotional responses in your relationship with God and others. As you think about each of the Fruit of the Spirit that God is establishing in you, use this activation to help you move from "hearing only" to "doing" (James 1:22-25).

DECIDE

I have decided (in this situation, with this person) to agree with God, and have the fruit of (_____) grown in my life. Father, I ask you to help me get free from the lies I believe (about this situation, about this person). As I renew my mind with your Word, I ask you to set me free.

"We are to work out our salvation with fear and trembling."
Philippians 2:12

"Once you have made a decision, don't turn back."
Luke 9:62

DECLARE

I am declaring that I will do what God's Word says to do concerning (this situation, this person). God, you said you are my strength and I can do all things through you (Philippians 4:13). Thank you in advance for the strength to follow through.

"We are to believe in our heart and confess with our mouth."
Romans 10:9

It is important for our soul to hear and be brought under the rule of the Holy Spirit (Psalm 42). Speaking intentions in the hearing of a friend helps bring accountability.

DEMONSTRATE

I will demonstrate this decision and declaration this week by (ask the Holy Spirit to show you a practical way to show the fruit of _____ in your particular situation with a specific person.)

Tell a friend or prayer partner... this week I am going to _____.

"Faith without works is dead. Be a doer as well as a hearer."
James 1:22-25, 2:26

OTHER DECLARATIONS

I do not have to be a victim to my old patterns of thought and emotional responses to life.

I am not held captive to my thought life and emotional state at any given moment, in any situation.

I can choose my thoughts, feelings and behavior, any time, all the time, any place.

"I am to be under the rule of the Holy Spirit...a slave only to God" (Romans 6:15-23)

"God is the source of the Holy Spirit's fruit in my life. I will abide in Him" (John 15)

Add some of your own declarations, including the new thought God has given you to repeat and rehearse it seven to twelve times a day.

CHAPTER 25

EXERCISE SIX – Heart Check Assessment

ON A SCALE OF 1-10, HOW STRONG IS THE EMO-
tional response when I think of (person/situation/organization)? What is the
feeling? I am feeling _____ because I think _____. When I
think _____ and feel _____ I _____ (behavior).

PAL: "*Holy Spirit, what do you want to say to me about my thoughts, feelings and behavior?*" Ask of yourself: Is my behavior changing? Are my feelings
changing? Are my thoughts changing? Where is the Holy Spirit still working
in my life in regards to the issue I am overcoming and becoming more like
Christ? Is the end result of my thought(s) good, sweet fruit, or bitter? If there
is still some bitter fruit, PAL: "*Holy Spirit, it seems I am still stuck just a bit here.
What would you like for me to know in regards to this (person/situation)? What
is unfinished?*"

Sometimes it is a matter of continuing to **REPEAT** and **REHEARSE**
the godly thought you have been given until it moves naturally to your behavior. The *Power of Choice* is incredible, but it is just that…we get to choose.
So continue to make good choices and practice, practice, practice! Rehearse,
rehearse, rehearse!

Assess your progress in regards to the "stuck" issue in which you are
learning to walk as a saint. How much of the Fruit of the Spirit is evident in

239

your thoughts, your feelings, and your behavior? Are you learning to walk in the Spirit? Are you still working on it? Can you see the progress that is being made? Ask the Holy Spirit to help you as you do your heart check, like David did in Psalm 139:23-24. "Search me, O God, and know my heart; Try me and know my anxious thoughts; And see if there be any hurtful way in me, And lead me in the everlasting way."

THOUGHTS AND QUESTIONS TO HELP YOU ON YOUR
JOURNEY INTO WHOLENESS

Remember when you *PAL* to the Lord Jesus, posture yourself for an answer. Believe that He will speak to you. Have your journal ready to write down what He says, what you see or sense. It would be rude to ask someone a question and walk off without waiting for his/her response. Let's learn to wait and listen and look for what the Lord wants to communicate to us. Have a dialogue with Him. Take this opportunity to develop your relationship with your Creator.

PAL:

"Lord Jesus, who do you want to be for me right now, in this situation?"

"Lord Jesus, what Fruit of the Spirit do you want to be for me, in me, right now in this moment?"

"Lord Jesus, what Fruit of the Spirit do you want to express through me for the benefit of the person involved in this situation with me?"

"Lord Jesus, I am thinking _____ about this (person/situation), is there another way for me to be thinking about this (person/situation)? What are you thinking about this (person/situation)? What would you like for me to know about this (person/situation)?"

"Lord Jesus, is what I am experiencing in this 'stuck' place connected to unforgiveness in any way? Is there anyone I need to forgive? Are there any consequences affecting me in my daily life as a result of the actions or words of another? Even someone I have already forgiven?"

SUMMARY

Perhaps the most important thing I can say to you is this is not too hard to accomplish! You have the indwelling, supernatural empowering presence of the Holy Spirit to teach you, remind you, help you and *be* what you need at any given moment. He dwells *in* you, is *for* you and wants to live *through* you to express His fruit to the world so they can know of the Father's love. This is the Exchanged Life in action – stepping into His provisions and living them as an expression of His fruit - a powerful offensive weapon (along with His Word) that advances the Kingdom of God here on earth.

Remember one of Pastor Ron's declarations:

"God is at work in my present circumstances to remove the wrong and impart the right, indwelling and empowering me so I can choose a willing heart towards Him as He forms the character and conduct of Jesus in me, so that the world may know the Father's love."

Don't give up…persevere and you will reap a sweet, godly harvest – every day you will look more and more like Jesus! C'mon, let's take this *Journey Into Wholeness* together!

APPENDIX A

"HOW TO HEAR GOD'S VOICE" DR. MARK VIRKLER

She had done it again! Instead of coming straight home from school like she was supposed to, she had gone to her friend's house. Without permission. Without our knowledge. Without doing her chores.

With a ministering household that included remnants of three struggling families plus our own toddler and newborn, my wife simply couldn't handle all the work on her own. Everyone had to pull their own weight. Everyone had age-appropriate tasks they were expected to complete. At fourteen, Rachel and her younger brother were living with us while her parents tried to overcome lifestyle patterns that had resulted in the children running away to escape the dysfunction. I felt sorry for Rachel, but, honestly my wife was my greatest concern.

Now Rachel had ditched her chores to spend time with her friends. It wasn't the first time, but if I had anything to say about it, it would be the last. I intended to lay down the law when she got home and make it very clear that if she was going to live under my roof, she would obey my rules.

But…she wasn't home yet. And I had recently been learning to hear God's voice more clearly. Maybe I should try to see if I could hear anything from Him about the situation. Maybe He could give me a way to get her to do what she was supposed to (i.e. what I wanted her to do). So I went to my office and reviewed what the Lord had been teaching me from Habakkuk 2:1,2: "I will stand on my guard post and station myself on the rampart; And I will keep watch to see what He will speak to me…Then the Lord answered me and said, 'Record the vision….'"

Habakkuk said, "I will stand on my guard post..." (Habakkuk 2:1). **The first key to hearing God's voice is to go to a quiet place and still our own thoughts and emotions.** Psalm 46:10 encourages us to be still, let go, cease striving, and know that He is God. In Psalm 37:7 we are called to "be still before the Lord and wait patiently for Him." There is a deep inner knowing in our spirits that each of us can experience when we quiet our flesh and our minds. Practicing the art of biblical meditation helps silence the outer noise and distractions clamoring for our attention.

I didn't have a guard post but I did have an office, so I went there to quiet my temper and my mind. Loving God through a quiet worship song is one very effective way to become still. In 2 Kings 3, Elisha needed a word from the Lord so he said, "Bring me a minstrel," and as the minstrel played, the Lord spoke. I have found that playing a worship song on my autoharp is the quickest way for me to come to stillness. I need to choose my song carefully; boisterous songs of praise do not bring me to stillness, but rather gentle songs that express my love and worship. And it isn't enough just to sing the song into the cosmos – I come into the Lord's presence most quickly and easily when I use my godly imagination to see the truth that He is right here with me and I sing my songs to Him, personally.

"I will keep watch to see," said the prophet. To receive the pure word of God, it is very important that my heart be properly focused as I become still, because my focus is the source of the intuitive flow. If I fix my eyes upon Jesus (Hebrews 12:2), the intuitive flow comes from Jesus. But if I fix my gaze upon some desire of my heart, the intuitive flow comes out of that desire. To have a pure flow I must become still and carefully fix my eyes upon Jesus. Quietly worshiping the King and receiving out of the stillness that follows quite easily accomplishes this.

So I used **the second key to hearing God's voice: As you pray, fix the eyes of your heart upon Jesus, seeing in the Spirit the dreams and visions of Almighty God.** Habakkuk was actually looking for vision as he prayed. He opened the eyes of his heart, and looked into the spirit world to see what God wanted to show him.

God has always spoken through dreams and visions, and He specifically said that they would come to those upon whom the Holy Spirit is poured out (Acts 2:1-4, 17).

Being a logical, rational person, observable facts that could be verified by my physical senses were the foundations of my life, including my spiritual life. I had never thought of opening the eyes of my heart and looking for vision. However, I have come to believe that this is exactly what God wants me to do. He gave me eyes in my heart to see in the spirit the vision and movement of Almighty God. There is an active spirit world all around us, full of angels, demons, the Holy Spirit, the omnipresent Father, and His omnipresent Son, Jesus. The only reasons for me not to see this reality are unbelief or lack of knowledge.

In his sermon in Acts 2:25, Peter refers to King David's statement: "I saw the Lord always in my presence; for He is at my right hand, so that I will not be shaken." The original psalm makes it clear that this was a decision of David's, not a constant supernatural visitation: "I have set (literally, I have placed) the Lord continually before me; because He is at my right hand, I will not be shaken" (Psalm 16:8). Because David knew that the Lord was always with him, he determined in his spirit to *see* that truth with the eyes of his heart as he went through life, knowing that this would keep his faith strong.

In order to see, we must look. Daniel saw a vision in his mind and said, "I was looking...I kept looking...I kept looking" (Daniel 7:2, 9, 13). As I pray, I look for Jesus, and I watch as He speaks to me, doing and saying the things that are on His heart. Many Christians will find that if they will only look, they will see. Jesus is Emmanuel, God with us (Matthew 1:23). It is as simple as that. You can see Christ present with you because Christ *is* present with you. In fact, the vision may come so easily that you will be tempted to reject it, thinking that it is just you. But if you persist in recording these visions, your doubt will soon be overcome by faith as you recognize that the content of them could only be birthed in Almighty God.

Jesus demonstrated the ability of living out of constant contact with God, declaring that He did nothing on His own initiative, but only what He saw the Father doing, and heard the Father saying (John 5:19,20,30). What an incredible way to live!

Is it possible for us to live out of divine initiative as Jesus did? Yes! We must simply fix our eyes upon Jesus. The veil has been torn, giving access into the immediate presence of God, and He calls us to draw near (Luke 23:45; Hebrews 10:19-22). "I pray that the eyes of your heart will be enlightened…."

When I had quieted my heart enough that I was able to picture Jesus without the distractions of my own ideas and plans, I was able to "keep watch to see what He will speak to me." I wrote down my question: "Lord, what should I do about Rachel?"

Immediately the thought came to me, "She is insecure." Well, that certainly wasn't my thought! Her behavior looked like rebellion to me, not insecurity.

But like Habakkuk, I was coming to know the sound of God speaking to me (Habakkuk 2:2). Elijah described it as a still, small voice (I Kings 19:12). I had previously listened for an inner audible voice, and God does speak that way at times. However, I have found that usually, God's voice comes as spontaneous thoughts, visions, feelings, or impressions.

For example, haven't you been driving down the road and had a thought come to you to pray for a certain person? Didn't you believe it was God telling you to pray? What did God's voice sound like? Was it an audible voice, or was it a spontaneous thought that lit upon your mind?

Experience indicates that we perceive spirit-level communication as spontaneous thoughts, impressions and visions, and Scripture confirms this in many ways. For example, one definition of *paga*, a Hebrew word for intercession, is "a chance encounter or an accidental intersecting." When God lays people on our hearts, He does it through *paga*, a chance-encounter thought "accidentally" intersecting our minds.

So **the third key to hearing God's voice is recognizing that God's voice in your heart often sounds like a flow of spontaneous thoughts.** Therefore, when I want to hear from God, I tune to chance-encounter or spontaneous thoughts.

Finally, God told Habakkuk to record the vision (Habakkuk 2:2). This was not an isolated command. The Scriptures record many examples of individual's prayers and God's replies, such as the Psalms, many of the prophets, and Revelation. I have found that obeying this final principle amplified my confidence in my ability to hear God's voice so that I could finally make living out of His initiatives a way of life. The **fourth key, two-way journaling or the writing out of your prayers and God's answers, brings great freedom in hearing God's voice.**

I have found two-way journaling to be a fabulous catalyst for clearly discerning God's inner, spontaneous flow, because as I journal I am able to write in faith for long periods of time, simply believing it is God. I know that what I believe I have received from God must be tested. However, testing involves doubt and doubt blocks divine communication, so I do not want to test while I am trying to receive. (See James 1:5-8.) With journaling, I can receive in faith, knowing that when the flow has ended I can test and examine it carefully.

So I wrote down what I believed He had said: "She is insecure."

But the Lord wasn't done. I continued to write the spontaneous thoughts that came to me: "Love her unconditionally. She is flesh of your flesh and bone of your bone."

My mind immediately objected: She is not flesh of my flesh. She is not related to me at all – she is a foster child, just living in my home temporarily. It was definitely time to test this "word from the Lord"!

There are three possible sources of thoughts in our minds: ourselves, satan and the Holy Spirit. It was obvious that the words in my journal did not come from my own mind – I certainly didn't see her as insecure *or* flesh of my flesh. And I sincerely doubted that satan would encourage me to love anyone unconditionally!

Okay, it was starting to look like I might have actually received counsel from the Lord. It was consistent with the names and character of God as revealed in the Scripture, and totally contrary to the names and character of the Enemy. So that meant that I was hearing from the Lord, and He wanted me to see the situation in a different light. Rachel was my daughter – part of my family not by blood but by the hand of God Himself. The chaos of her birth home had created deep insecurity about her worthiness to be loved by anyone, including me and including God. Only the unconditional love of the Lord expressed through an imperfect human would reach her heart.

But there was still one more test I needed to perform before I would have absolute confidence that this was truly God's word to me: I needed confirmation from someone else whose spiritual discernment I trusted. So I went to my wife and shared what I had received. I knew if I could get her validation, especially since she was the one most wronged in the situation, then I could say, at least to myself, "Thus sayeth the Lord."

Needless to say, Patti immediately and without question confirmed that the Lord had spoken to me. My entire planned lecture was forgotten. I returned to my office anxious to hear more. As the Lord planted a new, supernatural love for Rachel within me, He showed me what to say and how to say it to not only address the current issue of household responsibility, but the deeper issues of love and acceptance and worthiness.

Rachel and her brother remained as part of our family for another two years, giving us many opportunities to demonstrate and teach about the Father's love, planting spiritual seeds in thirsty soil. We weren't perfect and we didn't solve all of her issues, but because I had learned to listen to the Lord, we were able to avoid creating more brokenness and separation.

The four simple keys that the Lord showed me from Habakkuk have been used by people of all ages, from four to a hundred and four, from every continent, culture and denomination, to break through into intimate two-way conversations with their loving Father and dearest Friend. Omitting any one of the keys will prevent you from receiving all He wants to say to you. The order of the keys is not important, just that you *use them all*. Embracing all four, by faith, can change your life. Simply quiet yourself down, tune to spontaneity, look for vision, and journal. He is waiting to meet you there.

You will be amazed when you journal! Doubt may hinder you at first, but throw it off, reminding yourself that it is a biblical concept, and that God is present, speaking to His children. Relax. When we cease our labors and enter His rest, God is free to flow (Hebrews 4:10).

Why not try it for yourself, right now? Sit back comfortably, take out your pen and paper, and smile. Turn your attention toward the Lord in praise and worship, seeking His face. Many people have found the music and visionary prayer called "A Stroll Along the Sea of Galilee" helpful in getting them started. You can listen to it and download it free at www.CWGMinistries.org/Galilee.

After you write your question to Him, become still, fixing your gaze on Jesus. You will suddenly have a very good thought. Don't doubt it; simply write it down. Later, as you read your journaling, you, too, will be blessed to discover that you are indeed dialoguing with God. If you wonder if it is really the Lord speaking to you, share it with your spouse or a friend. Their input will encourage your faith and strengthen your commitment to spend time getting to know the Lover of your soul more intimately than you ever dreamed possible.

Is It **Really** God?

Five ways to be sure what you're hearing is from Him:

1. Test the Origin (1 John 4:1)

    Thoughts from our own minds are progressive, with one thought leading to the next, however tangentially. Thoughts from the spirit world are spontaneous. The Hebrew word for true prophecy is *naba,* which literally means to bubble up, whereas false prophecy is *ziyd* meaning to boil up. True words from the Lord will bubble up from our innermost being; we don't need to cook them up ourselves.

2. Compare It to Biblical Principles

    God will never say something to you personally which is contrary to His universal revelation as expressed in the Scriptures. If the Bible clearly states that something is a sin, no amount of journaling can make it right. Much of what you journal about will not be specifically addressed in the Bible, however, so an understanding of biblical principles is also needed.

3. Compare It to the Names and Character of God as Revealed in the Bible

    Anything God says to you will be in harmony with His essential nature. Journaling will help you get to *know* God personally, but knowing what the Bible says *about* Him will help you discern what words are from Him.

Make sure the tenor of your journaling lines up with the character of God as described in the names of the Father, Son and Holy Spirit.

4. Test the Fruit (Matthew 7:15-20)

 What effect does what you are hearing have on your soul and your spirit? Words from the Lord will quicken your faith and increase your love, peace and joy. They will stimulate a sense of humility within you as you become more aware of Who God is and who you are. On the other hand, any words you receive which cause you to fear or doubt, which bring you into confusion or anxiety, or which stroke your ego (especially if you hear something that is "just for you alone – no one else is worthy") must be immediately rebuked and rejected as lies of the Enemy.

5. Share It with Your Spiritual Counselors (Proverbs 11:14)

 We are members of a Body! A cord of three strands is not easily broken and God's intention has always been for us to grow together. Nothing will increase your faith in your ability to hear from God like having it confirmed by two or three other people! Share it with your spouse, your parents, your friends, your elder, your group leader, even your grown children can be your sounding board. They don't need to be perfect or super-spiritual; they just need to love you, be committed to being available to you, have a solid biblical orientation, and most importantly, they must also willingly and easily receive counsel. Avoid the authoritarian who insists that because of their standing in the church or with God, they no longer need to listen to others. Find two or three people and let them confirm that you are hearing from God!

The book *4 Keys to Hearing God's Voice* is available at www.CWGMinistries.org.

APPENDIX B

CHARACTERISTICS OF A TRUSTWORTHY PERSON

Work through this exercise to evaluate your trustworthiness.

PAL: "Holy Spirit, what areas in my life do you want to bring to my attention? What do you want to say to me about being trustworthy? Am I able to keep a secret? Do I keep my word?"

Follow this line of questioning with the Holy Spirit until you have worked through each point. If helpful, use the Development Key as the Holy Spirit speaks to you.

This is also a helpful exercise as you evaluate relationships you are in or are considering investing in.

PAL: "Holy Spirit, what do you want me to know about this person? Are they able to keep a secret? Do they keep their word?"

Work through each point, asking the Holy Spirit what He wants you to know. This is not to grade or "judge" the other person. Being aware of a person's character is helpful as you development relationship. Learning to communicate can develop intimacy when we know each other's shortcomings and practice love in spite of them.

Development Key

    S =walking in Spirit

    F =walking in flesh

    N =needs improvement

    P =progress being made

___A trustworthy person keeps a secret. (Proverbs 11:13) (no gossip)

___A trustworthy person keeps their word. (2 Samuel 7:28) (loyal, faithful)

___A trustworthy person brings healing. (Proverbs 13:17) (deliverance, remedy, cure) a tactful, honest approach benefits both parties (truth in love), a deceitful tongue crushes the spirit

___A trustworthy person brings refreshment. (Proverbs 25:13)

___A trustworthy person fears God. (Exodus 18:21)

___A trustworthy person hates dishonest gain. (Exodus 18:21)

___A trustworthy person tells the truth. (Exodus 18:21)

___A trustworthy person hates covetousness. (Exodus 18:21)

___A trustworthy person is responsible. (Nehemiah 13:13)

___A trustworthy person is faithful. (Nehemiah 13:13) (builds up, supports, fosters as a parent, is permanent, true, of long continuance, steadfast)

___A trustworthy person has no corruption. (Daniel 6:4)

___A trustworthy person is not negligent. (Daniel 6:4)

___A trustworthy person has nothing amiss. (Daniel 6:4) (no errors)

___A trustworthy person gets more when he is faithful in little. (Luke 19:17)

APPENDIX C

PARAPHRASING AND MEDITATION

Paraphrasing Scripture is one way to help you meditate on and habituate your thoughts. When you paraphrase you can look up key words in the dictionary or in Strong's Concordance to give a fresh personal meaning to the Word.

Spend some of your devotional time with God to let the truth of these Scriptures sink into your heart. Lectio Divina (Latin for "Divine Reading") is an ancient way of reading the Bible. It allows for and trains the participant in a quiet and contemplative way of approaching God's Word. This method of engaging with the Holy Spirit with Scripture will lead you deep into intimacy through your devotional time.

The key elements in Lectio Divina are:

1. Choose a passage of scripture.

2. Find a place of stillness before God.

3. Read the passage two times, slowly. Let the words sink into your heart. Meditate on what you have heard. Write down what stands out to you. If a word or phrase stands out to you, write it down.

4. Read the passage again two times.

   What are you hearing?
   What are you feeling?

Write it down.

Does this passage bring to mind any particular memories or experiences? Write these down.

PAL: *"Holy Spirit what do you want to say to me about these experiences?*

5. Read the passage a final two times.

Meditate on it. Be still and let the words minister to you.

PAL: *"God is there something you want me to do in response to this passage?"*

Write it down.

PAL: *"God what do you want me to think about in light of this passage and what you have been saying to me?"*

Write down His thoughts and your conversation with Him.

You can use these guidelines for Appendices D, E and F.

APPENDIX D

SCRIPTURES ON FORGIVENESS

Living a lifestyle of forgiveness is learning how to be like Jesus in character and conduct. To live this God-kind of life will require your thoughts to be filled with truth about forgiveness. Paraphrasing scripture is one way to help you meditate on and habituate your thoughts.

These Scriptures will lead you to think about forgiveness. Paraphrasing and/or meditating on these verses will deepen your understanding of the biblical principle of forgiveness.

Deuteronomy 30:11-14	Luke 23:34
Psalm 32:1	Romans 2:1-2
Proverbs 20:22	Romans 12:17-21
Zechariah 4:6	2 Corinthians 2:11
Matthew 5:23-24	Ephesians 1:7-8
Matthew 6:12	Ephesians 4:30-32
Matthew 7:1-5	Philippians 4:13
Matthew 18:21-22	Colossians 3:13
Mark 11:25	Hebrews 12:14-15
Luke 6:37	James 2:12-13
Luke 7:47	James 4:6
Luke 11:4	1 Peter 3:8-9
Luke 17:4	1 John 1:8

APPENDIX E

CHRIST IN ME IS...

The Creator of all things. (Colossians 1:16)

Holding All Things Together (Colossians 1:17)

The Head of the Church (Colossians 1:18)

The Alpha and Omega (Revelation 1:8, 22:13)

The Reconciler of all things in heaven and on earth (Colossians 1:20)

My Peace (Ephesians 2:14)

My Strength (Philippians 4:13)

My Portion (Psalm 119:57)

My Deliverer (Romans 11:26)

My Provider (1 Timothy 6:17)

My Healer (Luke 4:23)

The Great I AM (John 8:58)

The Bread of Life (John 6:35)

The Source of all Life (John 11:25, 14:6)

My Life (Colossians 3:4)

The Light of the World (John 1:1-9, 8:12, 9:5)

My Redeemer (Job 19:25, Isaiah 59:20, 1 Corinthians 1:30)

The Lifter of My Head (Psalm 3:3)

The Word (John 1:1, 14; Revelation 19:13)

The source of all the treasures of wisdom and knowledge (Colossians 2:3)

The Embodiment of the Fullness of the Godhead (Colossians 1:19)

The Author and Perfecter of my Faith (Hebrews 12:1)

ALL and IN ALL (Colossians 3:11)

My Advocate (1 John 2:1)

The Almighty (Revelation 1:8)

The Anointed One (Psalm 2:2, Daniel 9:25, Acts 4:25)

The High Priest (Hebrews 3:1)

My Banner (Isaiah 11:10, 12)

My Salvation (Luke 2:29-32)

The Bridegroom (Matthew 9:15, 25:1-13; John 3:29)

The Cornerstone (Matthew 21:42, 1 Peter 2:7)

The Good Shepherd (1 Peter 5:4, John 10:11)

The Chosen One (Isaiah 42:1, Luke 23:35)

The Christ (Matthew 1:16, 16:20, Mark 14:16, Luke 2:11, John 1:41, Acts 5:42)

The Lord (Luke 6:46, Acts 2:36, Romans 10:13)

The Great Physician (Luke 4:23, Matthew 9:12)

Eternal Life (1 John 5:20)

Everlasting Father (Isaiah 9:6)

Wonderful Counselor (Isaiah 9:6)

Prince of Peace (Isaiah 9:6)

The Exact Representation of God (Hebrews 1:3)

Faithful and True (Revelation 19:11)

Faithful Witness (Revelation 1:5)

My Foundation (1 Corinthians 3:11)

Friend of Sinners (Matthew 11:19)

Gift of God (John 4:10, 2 Corinthians 9:15)

Glory of the Lord (Isaiah 40:5)

The Heir of All Things (Hebrews 1:2)

The Holy One of God (Psalm 16:10, Mark 1:24, John 6:69, Acts 2:27)

Wisdom of God (1 Corinthians 1:23)

Our Righteousness (1 Corinthians 1:30)

Our Holiness (1 Corinthians 1:30)

Our Hope (1 Timothy 1:1)

Our Hope of Glory (Colossians 1:27)

Immanuel (Isaiah 7:14, Matthew 1:23)

The King of Kings (Revelation 17:14, 19:16; 1 Timothy 6:15)

The King over All the Earth (Zechariah 14:9)

The Lamb of God (John 1:29, 1:36; Revelation 5:6-13, 6:1, 17:14, 21:22, 22:1)

The Living One (Revelation 1:18)

The Living Stone (1 Peter 2:4)

The Lord of All (Acts 10:36, Romans 12:12)

The Lord of Glory (1 Corinthians 2:8)

The Lord of lords (Revelation 17:14, 19:16; 1 Timothy 6:15)

The Lord of the Sabbath (Matthew 12:8)

Son of Man (John 12:34)

Man of Sorrows (Isaiah 53:3)

The Master (Matthew 23:8)

Our Mediator (1 Timothy 2:5, Hebrews 8:6, 9:15, 12:24)

Our Intercessor (Romans 8:34, Hebrews 7:25)

The Bright and Morning Star (Revelation 22:16)

The Messiah (John 1:41, 4:25)

The One Who Is, Was and Is to Come (Revelation 1:4, 8)

The One Who baptizes us with the Holy Spirit (Mark 1:7-8)

The Only Begotten Son of the Father (John 1:14, 3:16; 1 John 4:9)

The Radiance of God's Glory (Hebrews 1:3)

A Ransom for us all (1 Timothy 2:5-6)

Our Refiner (Malachi 3:3)

The Resurrection (John 11:25)

The Righteous Judge (Acts 10:42, 2 Timothy 4:8)

The Righteous One (Acts 3:14, 7:52, 22:14; 1 John 2:1)

The Rock (1 Corinthians 10:4, 1 Peter 2:8)

The Ruler of God's Creation (Revelation 3:14)

Our Savior (Luke 2:11, John 4:42, Acts 5:31, 13:23; 2 Timothy 1:10, Titus 2:13, 2 Peter 1:11)

The Teacher (Matthew 19:16, 23:10, John 11:28, 13:13)

The Truth (John 14:6)

The Vine (John 15:1)

The Way (John 14:6)

APPENDIX F

IN CHRIST I AM…

I am His possession. (Deuteronomy t 4:20, 7:6, 26:18; Exodus 19:5,
     1 Peter 2:9)

I am a royal priesthood. (Exodus 19:6, 1 Peter 2:9)

I am alive to God. (Romans 6:11)

All grace abounds towards me. (2 Corinthians 9:8)

All sufficiency is in me through Him. (2 Corinthians 3:5, Philippians 4:19,
     Colossians 1:15-20)

I am anointed. (1 John 2:20, 27, 2 Corinthians 1:21)

I am the apple of God's eye. (Zechariah 2:8, Psalm 17:8)

As He is, so are we on this earth. (1 John 4:17)

I am baptized into one Spirit. (1 Corinthians 12:13)

I am baptized into Christ and His death. (Romans 6:1-4)

I am being protected. (John 10:28-30, 2 Thessalonians 3:3,
     Deuteronomy 31:6, Psalm 46:1)

I am loved. (Romans 1:7, 5:8, 8:37-39, Ephesians 2:4-5, 1 Thessalonians 1:4,
     Zephaniah 3:17)

I am blameless in His sight. (Colossians 1:22, Ephesians 1:4, 5:27)

I am blessed with all spiritual blessings. (Ephesians 1:3)

I have comfort and bold access to the throne of God.
     (Hebrews 4:16, 10:19)

I am born again of God. (John 3:3, 1 John 5:18, 1 Peter 1:23)

I am bold as a lion. (Proverbs 28:1)

I am part of the Bride of Christ. (Ephesians 5:27, 2 Corinthians 11:2, John 3:29)

I was buried with Christ in His death. (Romans 6:4, Colossians 2:12)

I can do all things in Christ. (Philippians 4:13)

I am chosen. (Colossians 3:12, Ephesians 1:4)

I am part of a chosen generation. (1 Peter 2:9)

Christ indwells me with all his fullness. (Colossians 1:19, 2:9; Ephesians 3:17)

I am a co-heir with Christ. (Galatians 4:7, Romans 8:17)

I was created for good works. (Ephesians 2:10)

I am curse-free. (Galatians 3:13, Romans 8:2)

I am dead to sin. (Romans 6:6-11, Colossians 3:3, 2 Timothy 2:11)

I have died with Christ. (Colossians 2:20)

I am raised with Christ. (Colossians 3:1, Ephesians 2:6-7, Romans 6:4)

I am declared holy. (Colossians 1:22, 1 Corinthians 6:11, 1 Peter 1:16)

I am a disciple of Jesus. (Matthew 28:19, Luke 14:27, Acts 26:28)

I am enriched (in all knowledge). (1 Corinthians 1:5, 2 Corinthians 9:11)

I belong to God. (Philippians 3:12)

I am faithful. (1 Timothy 1:12, Revelation 2:10, Galatians 5:22-23)

I am a fellow-citizen. (Ephesians 2:19)

I am free. (John 8:36, Galatians 5:1, Acts 13:38-39, Luke 4:18)

I am free from sin. (Romans 6:22, 8:1-4)

He has freely given me all things. (Romans 8:32, 1 Corinthians 2:12, 2 Peter 1:3)

I am a friend of Christ. (John 15:13, 15)

I am fruitful. (John 15:5)

I am gifted. (1 Corinthians 7:7)

I am a habitation of God. (Ephesians 2:22)

I have the mind of Christ. (1 Corinthians 2:16, Philippians 2:5)

God is at work in me. (Philippians 1:6, 2:13)

He is for me, not against me. (Romans 8:31, Psalm 118:6)

I am healed. (1 Peter 2:24, Isaiah 53:4, Psalm 103:1-5)

I am hidden in Christ. (Colossians 3:3)

I am highly favored. (Ephesians 1:3, 3 John 1:2, Proverbs 10:22)

We are His body. (1 Corinthians 12:27, Romans 12:5)

I am His workmanship. (Ephesians 2:10)

We are a holy nation. (1 Peter 2:9)

I am increasing in the knowledge of God. (Colossians 1:10, 2 Peter 3:18)

I am inseparable from the love of God. (Romans 8:35-39)

I am justified. (Romans 5:1, Galatians 2:16)

The Kingdom of God is within me. (Luke 17:20-21)

I am known by Him. (1 Corinthians 8:3, 13:12)

I am lacking in nothing. (Psalm 23:1, James 1:4)

I am the light of the world. (Matthew 5:14-16)

I am living and walking by faith. (2 Corinthians 5:7, Galatians 2:20,
    Hebrews 11:6)

I live by God's Word. (Psalm 86:11, Matthew 4:4, John 8:31-32,
    Ephesians 6:17)

I am a living stone. (1 Peter 2:5)

I am made in His image. (Genesis 1:27)

I am made rich in everything. (2 Corinthians 9:11, 6:10)

I am more than a conqueror. (Romans 8:37, 1 Corinthians 15:57,
    1 John 5:4)

I am a new creation. (2 Corinthians 5:17)

I have a sound mind. (2 Timothy 1:7)

I am ordained. (John 15:16, Ephesians 2:10)

I am a different person. (1 Peter 2:9, Colossians 3:10,
    2 Corinthians 3:18)

I am purified. (1 John 3:3, Hebrews 10:22, Ephesians 2:1-22)

I am filled with resurrection life. (Philippians 3:10, Colossians 1:29,
    Galatians 2:20, Ephesians 3:17)

I am redeemed. (Colossians 1:14, Isaiah 43:1, Ephesians 1:7, Romans 3:24-26)

I am the righteousness of God in Christ. (2 Corinthians 5:21,
    Romans 3:21-31)

I am a saint. (Ephesians 1:18, 2 Peter 1:4)

I am the salt of the earth. (Matthew 5:13)

I am sanctified. (1 Thessalonians 5:23-24, 2 Thessalonians 2:13,
    1 Corinthians 1:30, 6:11; Hebrews 10:10)

I am saved. (Acts 16:31, Romans 10:9-10, John 3:16, 10:28-30;
    Ephesians 2:8, Hebrews 7:25)

I am seated with Him in heavenly places. (Ephesians 2:6-7)

I am a servant of God. (John 12:26, 13:12-15; Philippians 2:5-8,
    1 Corinthians 4:1)

I share His authority. (Matthew 16:19, Mark 11:23, Luke 10:19, John 14:12,
    Acts 1:8, 1 John 4:4)

I am a sheep of His pasture. (Psalm 95:7, 100:3; Ezekiel 34:31)

I am a shining star. (Philippians 2:15)

I am a son of God. (Galatians 3:26, 4:6-7; John 1:12, Romans 8:14-16,
    2 Corinthians 6:18, 1 John 3:1-2)

I am a son of light. (1 Thessalonians 5:5, Ephesians 5:8, John 12:36)

I am a steward of the mysteries. (1 Corinthians 4:1)

I am strengthened by Him. (Philippians 4:13, Ephesians 3:16,
    Colossians 1:11, 2 Corinthians 12:9-10, Isaiah 40:29, 31)

I am the fullness of life and godliness. (2 Peter 1:3, Colossians 2:9,
    John 1:16, Romans 15:29, Ephesians 1:23, 3:19)

I am the temple of God. (1 Corinthians 3:16-17, 6:19)

I am a vessel of glory. (2 Corinthians 3:18, Romans 9:23)

I am a vessel of honor. (Romans 9:21, 2 Timothy 2:21)

I am a citizen of heaven. (Philippians 3:20)

I am a slave of righteousness. (Romans 6:18)

I walk in newness of life. (Romans 6:4)

I am a warrior. (Psalm 18:39, 44:5; Ephesians 6:10-18)

I am wise. (Psalm 37:30, 1 Corinthians 1:30, James 1:5)

I am a witness. (Matthew 5:16, Acts 1:8, 4:20, 22:15; Romans 1:16,
    1 Peter 3:15)

I am an ambassador for Christ. (2 Corinthians 5:20)

I am forgiven. (Matthew 6:14-15, Ephesians 1:7, Colossians 1:14, 3:13)

RECOMMENDED READING

Adams, Marilee, Ph.D., <u>Change Your Questions, Change Your Life</u>, (San Francisco, CA: Berrett-Koehler Pub. Inc., 2009).

Allen, Carolyn Ruth, <u>Growing Kingdom Fruit ... a Workbook for Pursuing Emotional Wholeness</u>, (Fort Wayne, IN: Kindling Ministries, Inc., 2012).

Arnott, John, <u>The Importance of Forgiveness</u>, (Kent, England: Sovereign World Ltd, 1997).

Boyd, Gregory A., <u>Seeing Is Believing</u>, (Grand Rapids, MI: Baker Books, 2004).

Frangipane, Francis, <u>Spiritual Discernment and The Mind of Christ</u>, (Cedar Rapids, IA: Arrow Publications, Inc., 2013).

Frangipane, Francis, <u>The Three Battlegrounds</u>, (Cedar Rapids, IA: Arrow Publications, Inc., 1989).

Frost, Jack, <u>School of Ministry Tapes</u>, (Toronto, CAN, 2003)

Frost, Jack, <u>Experiencing the Father's Embrace</u>, (Lake Mary, FL:

Charisma House Strang Communications Company, 2002).

Goldberg, Marilee C., Ph.D., <u>The Art of the Question</u>, (NY: John Wiley & Sons, Inc., 1998).

Jennings, Timothy R., M.D., <u>Could It Be This Simple? A Biblical Model For Healing The Mind</u>, (Chattanooga, TN: Lennox Publishing Association, 2012).

Kendall, R.T., Total Forgiveness, (Lake Mary FL: Charisma House Strang Communications Company, 2002).

Kylstra, Chester & Betsy, Restoring The Foundations, (Hendersonville, NC: Restoring The Foundations Publications, 2003).

Kylstra, Chester & Betsy, An Integrated Approach to Biblical Healing, (Kent, England: Sovereign World Ltd, 2003).

Leaf, Dr. Caroline, Who Switched Off My Brain, (Southlake, TX: Thomas Nelson Pub, 2009).

Meyer, Joyce, Battlefield of the Mind, (NY, NY: FaithWords, Hachette Book Group, 1995).

Nee, Watchman, The Spiritual Man, (New York, NY: Christian Fellowship Publishers, Inc., 1968).

Ortberg, John, Soul Keeping, (Grand Rapids, MI: Zondervan, 2014).

Prince, Derek, Blessings and Curses, (Grand Rapids, MI: Chosen Books, a Division of Baker Book House Company, 1994, 2003).

Sandford, John & Paula, The Transformation of the Inner Man, (Plainfield, NJ: Bridge Publishing Inc., 1982).

Seamands, David A., Healing Grace, (Wheaton, IL: Victor Books, 1988).

Seamands, David A., Healing of Memories, (Wheaton, IL: Victor Books, 1985).

Seamands, David A., Healing for Damaged Emotions, (Wheaton, IL: Victor Books, 1981).

Seamands, David. A., Freedom From the Performance Trap, (Wheaton, IL: Victor Books, 1988).

Virkler, Mark and Patti, 4 Keys to Hearing God's Voice, (Shippensburg, PA: Destiny Image Publishers, Inc., 2010).

Willard, Dallas, <u>Renovation of the Heart</u>, (Colorado Springs, CO: NavPress, 2002).

Willard, Dallas, <u>The Divine Conspiracy</u>, (NY: HarperCollins Publishers, 1998).

*"Now may the God of peace Himself sanctify you entirely;
and may your spirit and soul and body be preserved complete,
without blame at the coming of our Lord Jesus Christ.
Faithful is He who calls you and He will bring it to pass."*
1 Thessalonians 5:23-24

ENDNOTES

CHAPTER 1: Pastoral Care Foundations

[1] James L. Nicholson/William G. Fischer, *Lord Jesus I Long To Be Perfectly Whole*, 1872.

[2] Dallas Willard, *Renovation of the Heart*, (Colorado Springs, CO: NavPress, 2002), 199.

[3] John Ortberg, *Soul Keeping*, (Grand Rapids, MI: Zondervan. 2014), 23.

[4] Jack Frost, *Jack Frost Quotes*, www.goodreads.com.

[5] John Wimber, *Discipleship Leadership Seminar*, (Anaheim, CA: Vineyard Resources, 1996).

CHAPTER 2: The Power of God Speaking

[6] *Strong's Greek Lexicon*, G3874 - paraklēsis - (KJV). Retrieved from https://www.blueletterbible.org//lang/lexicon/lexicon.cfm?Strongs=G3874&t=KJV

[7] *Strong's Greek Lexicon*, G3875 - paraklētos - (KJV). Retrieved from https://www.blueletterbible.org//lang/lexicon/lexicon.cfm?Strongs=G3875&t=KJV

[8] *Strong's Greek Lexicon*, G3889 - paramythia - (KJV). Retrieved from https://www.blueletterbible.org//lang/lexicon/lexicon.cfm?Strongs=G3889&t=KJV

CHAPTER 3: The Power of Hearing God Speak

[9] Dr. Mark Virkler, *How to Hear God's Voice*, www.CWGMinistries.org.

CHAPTER 4: The Power of Forgiveness

[10] John Arnott, *The Importance of Forgiveness*, (Kent, England: Sovereign World Ltd., 1997).

[11] *Strong's Greek Lexicon*, G863 - aphiēmi - (KJV). Retrieved from https://www.blueletterbible.org//lang/lexicon/lexicon.cfm?Strongs=G863&t=KJV

[12] Ibid.

[13] *Strong's Greek Lexicon*, G5483 - charizomai - (KJV). Retrieved from https://www.blueletterbible.org//lang/lexicon/lexicon.cfm?Strongs=G5483&t=KJV

[14] Forgive, (n.d.). Retrieved January 23, 2017, https://www.merriam-webster.com/dictionary/forgive

[15] R. T. Kendall, *Total Forgiveness*, (Lake Mary FL: Charisma House Strang Communications Company, 2002). Kendall expounds on the principles he gives on *What Forgiveness Is* and *What Forgiveness Is Not*.

[16] Ibid.

[17] Appropriate. (n.d.). Retrieved January 23, 2017. https://www.merriam-webster.com/dictionary/appropriate

[18] Dr. Mark Virkler: paraphrase of a Dennis & Matt Linn quote.

CHAPTER 6: The Power of Perspective

[19] F. L. Cross &, E. A Livingstone, ed., *The Oxford Dictionary of the Christian Church*, 2nd Edition, (NY: NY: Oxford University Press, 1974).

[20] Joseph H Thayer, *Thayer's Greek-English Lexicon of the New Testament*, (Peabody, MA: Hendrickson Publishers, 1996).

[21] Spiros Zodhiates, ed., *The Complete Word Study New Testament*, 2nd Edition, (Chattanooga, TN: AMG Publishers, 1992).

[22] C. S. Lewis, *C. S. Lewis Quotes*, www.goodreads.com/quotes

CHAPTER 9: SoulCare

[23] *Strong's Greek Lexicon*, G2390 - iaomai - (NASB). Retrieved from https://www.blueletterbible.org//lang/lexicon/lexicon.cfm?Strongs=G2390&t=NASB

[24] *Strong's Greek Lexicon*, G4982 - sōzō - (KJV). Retrieved from https://www.blueletterbible.org//lang/lexicon/lexicon.cfm?Strongs=G4982&t=KJV

[25] Spiros Zodhiates, ed., *The Complete Word Study New Testament*, 2nd Edition, (Chattanooga, TN: AMG Publishers, 1992).

[26] Chester & Betsy Kylstra, *Restoring The Foundations*, (Hendersonville, NC: Restoring The Foundations Publications, 2003).

CHAPTER 10: Generational Patterns and Curses

[27] *Strong's Hebrew Lexicon*, H5771 - `avon - (KJV). Retrieved from https://www.blueletterbible.org//lang/lexicon/lexicon.cfm?Strongs=H5771&t=KJV

CHAPTER 11: Word Curses

[28] Curse. (n.d.). Retrieved January 23, 2017, https://www.merriam-webster.com/dictionary/curse

[29] Derek Prince, *Blessings and Curses*, (Derek Prince Ministries, 1984).

CHAPTER 13: Bitter Root Judgments

[30] Jack Frost, *Bitter Root Judgment Tape Series*, (https://www.shilohplacemin-istries.org, 2003).

[31] John & Paula Sandford, *The Transformation of the Inner Man*, (Plainfield, NJ: Bridge Publishing Inc., 1982).

CHAPTER 16: Ungodly Thought Patterns

[32] Jack & Trisha Frost, *Unbound*, (Shippensburg, PA: Destiny Image Publishers, Inc., 2012), 51.

[33] David A. Seamands, *Healing Grace*, (Wheaton, IL: Victor Books, 1988), 67.

[34] David A. Seamands, *David A. Seamands Quotes*, www.goodreads.com.

[35] Jack Frost, *Freedom Encounter Conference*, (Fort Wayne, IN, 2005).

[36] David A. Seamands, *Freedom From the Performance Trap*, (Wheaton, IL: Victor Books, 1988), 13.

[37] Attitude. (n.d.). Retrieved January 23, 2017, https://www.merriamwebster.com/dictionary/attitude

[38] Dr. Caroline Leaf, *Who Switched Off My Brain*, (Southlake, TX: Thomas Nelson Pub, 2009), Chapters 1 and 2.

[39] Ibid. 80-81.

[40] Dr. Caroline Leaf, *Switch On Your Brain: The Key to Peak Happiness, Thinking, and Health*, http://isbnarchives.com/pub/file.php?id=0801018390

CHAPTER 17: Healing Life's Hurts

[41] Carolyn Ruth Allen, *Growing Kingdom Fruit...a Workbook for Pursuing Emotional Wholeness*, (Fort Wayne, IN: Kindling Ministries, Inc., 2012), 14.

[42] Dr. Caroline Leaf, *Who Switched Off My Brain*, (Southlake, TX: Thomas Nelson Pub, 2009), 21.

[43] Chester & Betsy Kylstra, *Restoring The Foundations*, (Hendersonville, NC: Restoring The Foundations Publications, 2003), 203.

[44] Dr. Caroline Leaf, *Who Switched Off My Brain*, (Southlake, TX: Thomas Nelson Pub, 2009), 80-81.

CHAPTER 18: Demonic Interference

[45] Carolyn Ruth Allen, *Growing Kingdom Fruit…a Workbook for Pursuing Emotional Wholeness*, (Fort Wayne, IN: Kindling Ministries, Inc., 2012).

[46] Neil T. Anderson, *The Bondage Breaker*, (Eugene, OR: Harvest House Publishers, 1993), 59-60.

[47] Chester & Betsy Kylstra, *Restoring The Foundations*, (Hendersonville, NC: Restoring The Foundations Publications, 2003), 397-400.

CHAPTER 21: Exercise Two – Warning & Weapon

[48] *Strong's Greek Lexicon*, G550 - apeipon - (KJV). Retrieved from https://www.blueletterbible.org//lang/lexicon/lexicon.cfm?Strongs=G550&t=KJV